MznLnx

Missing Links Exam Preps

Exam Prep for

Calculus: Early Transcendentals

Anton & Bivens & Davis, 7th Edition

The MznLnx Exam Prep is your link from the texbook and lecture to your exams.
The MznLnx Exam Preps are unauthorized and comprehensive reviews of your textbooks.

All material provided by MznLnx and Rico Publications (c) 2010
Textbook publishers and textbook authors do not particpate in or contribute to these reviews.

MznLnx

Rico
Publications

Exam Prep for Calculus: Early Transcendentals
7th Edition
Anton & Bivens & Davis

Publisher: Raymond Houge
Assistant Editor: Michael Rouger
Text and Cover Designer: Lisa Buckner
Marketing Manager: Sara Swagger
Project Manager, Editorial Production: Jerry Emerson
Art Director: Vernon Lowerui

Product Manager: Dave Mason
Editorial Assitant: Rachel Guzmanji
Pedagogy: Debra Long
Cover Image: Jim Reed/Getty Images
Text and Cover Printer: City Printing, Inc.
Compositor: Media Mix, Inc.

(c) 2010 Rico Publications
ALL RIGHTS RESERVED. No part of this work
covered by the copyright may be reproduced or
used in any form or by an means--graphic, electronic,
or mechanical, including photocopying, recording,
taping, Web distribution, information storage, and
retrieval systems, or in any other manner--without the
written permission of the publisher.

For more information about our products, contact us at:
Dave.Mason@RicoPublications.com

For permission to use material from this text or
product, submit a request online to:
Dave.Mason@RicoPublications.com

Printed in the United States
ISBN:

Contents

CHAPTER 1
INTRODUCTION. CALCULUS: A NEW HORIZON FROM ANCIENT ROOTS — 1

CHAPTER 2
LIMITS AND CONTINUITY — 20

CHAPTER 3
THE DERIVATIVE — 28

CHAPTER 4
EXPONENTIAL, LOGARITHMIC, AND INVERSE TRIGONOMETRIC FUNCTIONS — 41

CHAPTER 5
THE DERIVATIVE IN GRAPHING AND APPLICATIONS — 48

CHAPTER 6
INTEGRATION — 57

CHAPTER 7
APPLICATIONS OF THE DEFINITE INTEGRAL IN GEOMETRY, SCIENCE, AND ENGINEERING — 72

CHAPTER 8
PRINCIPLES OF INTEGRAL EVALUATION — 84

CHAPTER 9
MATHEMATICAL MODELING WITH DIFFERENTIAL EQUATIONS — 93

CHAPTER 10
INFINITE SERIES — 102

CHAPTER 11
ANALYTIC GEOMETRY IN CALCULUS — 116

CHAPTER 12
THREE-DIMENSIONAL SPACE; VECTORS — 128

CHAPTER 13
VECTOR-VALUED FUNCTIONS — 141

CHAPTER 14
PARTIAL DERIVATIVES — 151

CHAPTER 15
MULTIPLE INTEGRALS — 165

CHAPTER 16
TOPICS IN VECTOR CALCULUS — 177

ANSWER KEY — 187

TO THE STUDENT

COMPREHENSIVE

The *MznLnx* Exam Prep series is designed to help you pass your exams. Editors at MznLnx review your textbooks and then prepare these practice exams to help you master the textbook material. Unlike study guides, workbooks, and practice tests provided by the texbook publisher and textbook authors, *MznLnx* gives you **all** of the material in each chapter in exam form, not just samples, so you can be sure to nail your exam.

MECHANICAL

The MznLnx Exam Prep series creates exams that will help you learn the subject matter as well as test you on your understanding. Each question is designed to help you master the concept. Just working through the exams, you gain an understanding of the subject--its a simple mechanical process that produces success.

INTEGRATED STUDY GUIDE AND REVIEW

MznLnx is not just a set of exams designed to test you, its also a comprehensive review of the subject content. Each exam question is also a review of the concept, making sure that you will get the answer correct without having to go to other sources of material. You learn as you go! Its the easiest way to pass an exam.

HUMOR

Studying can be tedious and dry. MznLnx's instructional design includes moderate humor within the exam questions on occassion, to break the tedium and revitalize the brain

Chapter 1. INTRODUCTION. CALCULUS: A NEW HORIZON FROM ANCIENT ROOTS

1. In mathematics, the _____ (or replacement set) of a given function is the set of 'input' values for which the function is defined. For instance, the _____ of cosine would be all real numbers, while the _____ of the square root would be only numbers greater than or equal to 0 (ignoring complex numbers in both cases.) In a representation of a function in a xy Cartesian coordinate system, the _____ is represented on the x axis (or abscissa.)
    a. BDDC
    b. BIBO stability
    c. Domain
    d. 15 theorem

2. Integration is an important concept in mathematics, specifically in the field of calculus and, more broadly, mathematical analysis. Given a function f of a real variable x and an interval [a, b] of the real line, the _____

$$\int_a^b f(x)\,dx,$$

is defined informally to be the net signed area of the region in the xy-plane bounded by the graph of f, the x-axis, and the vertical lines x = a and x = b.

The term '_____' may also refer to the notion of antiderivative, a function F whose derivative is the given function f.

   a. Integral test for convergence
   b. Indefinite integral
   c. Integrand
   d. Integral

3. In mathematics, a _____ is a definite integral taken over a surface (which may be a curved set in space); it can be thought of as the double integral analog of the line integral. Given a surface, one may integrate over it scalar fields (that is, functions which return numbers as values), and vector fields (that is, functions which return vectors as values.)

Surface integrals have applications in physics, particularly with the classical theory of electromagnetism.

   a. Symmetry of second derivatives
   b. Differential operator
   c. Contact
   d. Surface integral

4. In calculus, _____, was originally the use of expressions such as dx and dy and to represent 'infinitely small' (or infinitesimal) increments of quantities x and y, just as >Δx and >Δy represent finite increments of x and y respectively. So for y being a function of x, or

[×]>

the derivative of y with respect to x, which later came to be viewed as

[×]>

2   *Chapter 1. INTRODUCTION. CALCULUS: A NEW HORIZON FROM ANCIENT ROOTS*

was, according to Leibniz, the quotient of an infinitesimal increment of y by an infinitesimal increment of x, or

where the right hand side is Lagrange's notation for the derivative of f at x.

Similarly, although mathematicians usually now view an integral

as a limit

where >Δx is an interval containing x_i, Leibniz viewed it as the sum (the integral sign denoting summation) of infinitely many infinitesimal quantities f(x) dx.

    a. Smooth function   b. Time derivative
    c. Leibniz's notation   d. Stationary point

5. _____ typically refers to a state lacking order or predictability. In ancient Greece, it referred to the initial state of the universe, and, by extension, space, darkness, or an abyss. In modern English, it is used in classical studies with this original meaning; in mathematics and science to refer to a very specific kind of unpredictability; and informally to mean a state of confusion.
    a. Chaos   b. BDDC
    c. BIBO stability   d. 15 theorem

6. _____ generally conveys two primary meanings. The first is an imprecise sense of harmonious or aesthetically-pleasing proportionality and balance; such that it reflects beauty or perfection. The second meaning is a precise and well-defined concept of balance or 'patterned self-similarity' that can be demonstrated or proved according to the rules of a formal system: by geometry, through physics or otherwise.
    a. Symmetry   b. 15 theorem
    c. BIBO stability   d. BDDC

7. In mathematics, a (topological) _____ is defined as follows: let I be an interval of real numbers (i.e. a non-empty connected subset of $\mathbb{R}$); then a _____ γ is a continuous mapping $\gamma : I \to X$, where X is a topological space. The _____ γ is said to be simple if it is injective, i.e. if for all x, y in I, we have $\gamma(x) = \gamma(y) \implies x = y$. If I is a closed bounded interval $[a, b]$, we also allow the possibility $\gamma(a) = \gamma(b)$ (this convention makes it possible to talk about closed simple _____.)

a. Curve
b. Tractrix
c. Prolate cycloid
d. Closed curve

8. A _____ is a type of display using Cartesian coordinates to display values for two variables for a set of data. The data is displayed as a collection of points, each having the value of one variable determining the position on the horizontal axis and the value of the other variable determining the position on the vertical axis.

a. 15 theorem
b. BDDC
c. BIBO stability
d. Scatter plot

9. The _____ of an angle is the ratio of the length of the opposite side to the length of the hypotenuse. In our case

$$\sin A = \frac{\text{opposite}}{\text{hypotenuse}} = \frac{a}{h}.$$

Note that this ratio does not depend on size of the particular right triangle chosen, as long as it contains the angle A, since all such triangles are similar.

The cosine of an angle is the ratio of the length of the adjacent side to the length of the hypotenuse.

a. Sine
b. Trigonometric
c. Sine integral
d. Trigonometric functions

10. In mathematics, an _____ on a real vector space is a choice of which ordered bases are 'positively' oriented and which are 'negatively' oriented. In the three-dimensional Euclidean space, the two possible basis orientations are called right-handed and left-handed (or right-chiral and left-chiral), respectively. However, the choice of _____ is independent of the handedness or chirality of the bases (although right-handed bases are typically declared to be positively oriented, they may also be assigned a negative _____.)

a. Orientation
b. ACTRAN
c. Unit vector
d. ALGOR

11. In mathematics, a _____ is the graph of the system of parametric equations

$$x = A\sin(at + \delta), \quad y = B\sin(bt),$$

which describes complex harmonic motion. This family of curves was investigated by Nathaniel Bowditch in 1815, and later in more detail by Jules Antoine Lissajous in 1857.

The appearance of the figure is highly sensitive to the ratio a/b.

a. BDDC
b. 15 theorem
c. BIBO stability
d. Lissajous curve

12. _____ is finding a curve which has the best fit to a series of data points and possibly other constraints. This section is an introduction to both interpolation (where an exact fit to constraints is expected) and regression analysis. Both are sometimes used for extrapolation.

Chapter 1. INTRODUCTION. CALCULUS: A NEW HORIZON FROM ANCIENT ROOTS

a. Propagation of uncertainty
b. Well-posed problem
c. Curve fitting
d. Series acceleration

13. The terms '_____' and 'independent variable' are used in similar but subtly different ways in mathematics and statistics as part of the standard terminology in those subjects. They are used to distinguish between two types of quantities being considered, separating them into those available at the start of a process and those being created by it, where the latter (dependent variables) are dependent on the former (independent variables.)

In traditional calculus, a function is defined as a relation between two terms called variables because their values vary.

a. 15 theorem
b. BDDC
c. BIBO stability
d. Dependent variable

14. The terms 'dependent variable' and '_____' are used in similar but subtly different ways in mathematics and statistics as part of the standard terminology in those subjects. They are used to distinguish between two types of quantities being considered, separating them into those available at the start of a process and those being created by it, where the latter (dependent variables) are dependent on the former (independent variables.)

In traditional calculus, a function is defined as a relation between two terms called variables because their values vary.

a. ALGOR
b. AUSM
c. ACTRAN
d. Independent variable

15. In vector calculus, the _____ is an operator that measures the magnitude of a vector field's source or sink at a given point; the _____ of a vector field is a (signed) scalar. For example, consider air as it is heated or cooled. The relevant vector field for this example is the velocity of the moving air at a point.
a. Divergence
b. Green's theorem
c. Triple product
d. Gradient theorem

16. In vector calculus, the _____ Ostrogradskye;s theorem the _____ states that the outward flux of a vector field through a surface is equal to the triple integral of the divergence on the region inside the surface. Intuitively, it states that the sum of all sources minus the sum of all sinks gives the net flow out of a region.
a. Del
b. Divergence
c. Divergence Theorem
d. Green's theorem

17. In mathematics, the _____ of a function is the set of all 'output' values produced by that function. Sometimes it is called the image, or more precisely, the image of the domain of the function. If a function is a surjection then its _____ is equal to its codomain.
a. Constant function
b. Surjective
c. Piecewise-defined function
d. Range

Chapter 1. INTRODUCTION. CALCULUS: A NEW HORIZON FROM ANCIENT ROOTS

18. In computer science and information science, _____ could also be a method or an algorithm. Again, an example will illustrate: There are systems of counting, as with Roman numerals, and various systems for filing papers, or catalogues, and various library systems, of which the Dewey Decimal _____ is an example. This still fits with the definition of components which are connected together (in this case in order to facilitate the flow of information.)

   a. BDDC
   b. BIBO stability
   c. 15 theorem
   d. System

19. The _____ is a test to determine if a relation or its graph is a function or not. For a relation or graph to be a function, it can have at most a single y-value for each x-value. Thus, a vertical line drawn at any x-position on the graph of a function will intersect the graph at most once.

   a. Vertical line test
   b. BDDC
   c. BIBO stability
   d. 15 theorem

20. In calculus, _____ gives a sequence of approximations of a differentiable function around a given point by polynomials (the Taylor polynomials of that function) whose coefficients depend only on the derivatives of the function at that point. The theorem also gives precise estimates on the size of the error in the approximation. The theorem is named after the mathematician Brook Taylor, who stated it in 1712, though the result was first discovered 41 years earlier in 1671 by James Gregory.

   a. Local minimum
   b. Related rates
   c. Fresnel integrals
   d. Taylor's theorem

21. In mathematics, the _____ (or modulus) of a real number is its numerical value without regard to its sign. So, for example, 3 is the _____ of both 3 and −3.

   The _____ of a number a is denoted by $|a|$.

   a. Absolute value
   b. Exponential function
   c. ACTRAN
   d. Area hyperbolic functions

22. In mathematics, a _____ is a function whose definition is dependent on the value of the independent variable. Mathematically, a real-valued function f of a real variable x is a relationship whose definition is given differently on disjoint subsets of its domain

   The word piecewise is also used to describe any property of a _____ that holds for each piece but may not hold for the whole domain of the function.

   a. Surjective
   b. Range
   c. Piecewise-defined function
   d. Constant function

23. In mathematics and physics, a _____ associates a scalar value, which can be either mathematical in definition to every point in space. Scalar fields are often used in physics, for instance to indicate the temperature distribution throughout space or more specifically, differential geometry, the set of functions defined on a manifold define the commutative ring of functions.

   a. Symmetry of second derivatives
   b. Vector Laplacian
   c. Level curve
   d. Scalar field

24. If a function has an integral, it is said to be integrable. The function for which the integral is calculated is called the _____. The region over which a function is being integrated is called the domain of integration.
   a. Integrand
   b. Integration by parts
   c. Integral test for convergence
   d. Order of integration

25. The _____ of any solid, liquid, plasma, vacuum or theoretical object is how much three-dimensional space it occupies, often quantified numerically. One-dimensional figures (such as lines) and two-dimensional shapes (such as squares) are assigned zero _____ in the three-dimensional space. _____ is commonly presented in units such as mL or cm^3 (milliliters or cubic centimeters.)
   a. Volume
   b. Klein-Gordon equation
   c. Dirac equation
   d. Vector potential

26. A _____ is an expression which compares quantities relative to each other. The most common examples involve two quantities, but in theory any number of quantities can be compared. In mathematical terms, they are represented by separating each quantity with a colon, for example the _____ 2:3, which is read as the _____ 'two to three'.
   a. 15 theorem
   b. Ratio
   c. Y-intercept
   d. Sequence

27. In physics, and more specifically kinematics, _____ is the change in velocity over time. Because velocity is a vector, it can change in two ways: a change in magnitude and/or a change in direction. In one dimension, _____ is the rate at which something speeds up or slows down.
   a. ACTRAN
   b. Acceleration
   c. ALGOR
   d. AUSM

28. In mathematics, the _____ is a representation of a function as an infinite sum of terms calculated from the values of its derivatives at a single point. It may be regarded as the limit of the Taylor polynomials. If the series is centered at zero, the series is also called a Maclaurin series.
   a. BDDC
   b. 15 theorem
   c. BIBO stability
   d. Taylor series

29. In mathematics, even functions and odd functions are functions which satisfy particular symmetry relations, with respect to taking additive inverses. They are important in many areas of mathematical analysis, especially the theory of power series and Fourier series. They are named for the parity of the powers of the power functions which satisfy each condition: the function f(x) = x^n is an _____ if n is an even integer, and it is an odd function if n is an odd integer.
   a. Even function
   b. Infinite series
   c. Integral of secant cubed
   d. Operational calculus

30. In mathematics, even functions and odd functions are functions which satisfy particular symmetry relations, with respect to taking additive inverses. They are important in many areas of mathematical analysis, especially the theory of power series and Fourier series. They are named for the parity of the powers of the power functions which satisfy each condition: the function f(x) = x^n is an even function if n is an even integer, and it is an _____ if n is an odd integer.
   a. Even function
   b. Integration by substitution
   c. Integral of secant cubed
   d. Odd function

31. _____ is a type of motion in which the velocity of an object changes equal amounts in equal time periods. An example of an object having _____ would be a ball rolling down a ramp. The object picks up velocity as it goes down the ramp with equal changes in time.

    a. ACTRAN
    b. ALGOR
    c. AUSM
    d. Uniform Acceleration

32. In physics, _____ is movement that changes the position of an object, as opposed to rotation. For example, according to Whittaker:

A _____ is the operation changing the positions of all points (x, y, z) of an object according to the formula

$$(x, y, z) \rightarrow (x + \Delta x, y + \Delta y, z + \Delta z)$$

where $(\Delta x, \Delta y, \Delta z)$ is the same vector for each point of the object. The _____ vector $(\Delta x, \Delta y, \Delta z)$ common to all points of the object describes a particular type of displacement of the object, usually called a linear displacement to distinguish it from displacements involving rotation, called angular displacements.

    a. BDDC
    b. Translation
    c. 15 theorem
    d. BIBO stability

33. In elementary algebra, _____ is a technique for converting a quadratic polynomial of the form

$$ax^2 + bx + c$$

to the form

$$a(\cdots\cdots)^2 + \text{constant}.$$

The expression inside the parenthesis is of the form x − constant. Thus one converts $ax^2 + bx + c$ to

$$a(x - h)^2 + k$$

and one must find h and k.

_____ is used in

- solving quadratic equations,
- graphing quadratic functions,
- evaluating integrals in calculus,
- finding Laplace transforms.

In mathematics, _____ is considered a basic algebraic operation, and is often applied without remark in any computation involving quadratic polynomials.

There is a simple formula in elementary algebra for computing the square of a binomial:

$$(x+p)^2 = x^2 + 2px + p^2.$$

For example:

$$(x+3)^2 = x^2 + 6x + 9 \quad (p=3)$$
$$(x-5)^2 = x^2 - 10x + 25 \quad (p=-5).$$

In any perfect square, the number p is always half the coefficient of x, and then the constant term is equal to p^2.

a. Multinomial theorem
b. Closed-form expression
c. Hurwitz quaternion order
d. Completing the square

34. In mathematics and computer science, the floor and ceiling functions map a real number to the next smallest or next largest integer. More precisely, floor(x) is the largest integer not greater than x and ceiling(x) is the smallest integer not less than x.

The _____ is also called the greatest integer or entier function, and the floor of a nonnegative x may be called the integral part or integral value of x. Computer languages (other than APL) commonly use ENTIER(x) (Algol), floor(x), or int(x) (C and C++).

a. Multiplicative inverse
b. Floor function
c. Hyperbolic tangent
d. Hyperbolic functions

35. In geometry, a _____ is a special plane curve generated by the trace of a fixed point on a small circle that rolls within a larger circle. It is comparable to the cycloid but instead of the circle rolling along a line, it rolls within a circle. The red curve is a _____ traced as the smaller black circle rolls around inside the larger blue circle (parameters are R=3.0, r=1.0, and so k=3), giving a deltoid.

If the smaller circle has radius r, and the larger circle has radius R = kr, then the parametric equations for the curve can be given by either:

$$x(\theta) = (R-r)\cos\theta + r\cos\left(\frac{R-r}{r}\theta\right)$$
$$y(\theta) = (R-r)\sin\theta - r\sin\left(\frac{R-r}{r}\theta\right),$$

or:

$$x(\theta) = r(k-1)\cos\theta + r\cos((k-1)\theta)$$
$$y(\theta) = r(k-1)\sin\theta - r\sin((k-1)\theta).$$

If k is an integer, then the curve is closed, and has k cusps (i.e., sharp corners, where the curve is not differentiable.)

a. Kappa curve
b. Closed curve
c. Bullet-nose curve
d. Hypocycloid

36. A _____ is an algebraic equation in which each term is either a constant or the product of a constant and (the first power of) a single variable. Linear equations can have one, two, three or more variables. Linear equations occur with great regularity in applied mathematics.
a. Cubic function
b. Linear equation
c. Quartic function
d. Quadratic formula

37. In mathematics, a _____ is an ordered list of objects (or events). Like a set, it contains members (also called elements or terms), and the number of terms (possibly infinite) is called the length of the _____. Unlike a set, order matters, and the exact same elements can appear multiple times at different positions in the _____.
a. Slope
b. Y-intercept
c. 15 theorem
d. Sequence

38. In mathematics, the _____, named after German mathematician Bernhard Riemann, is a prominent function of great significance in number theory because of its relation to the distribution of prime numbers. It also has applications in other areas such as physics, probability theory, and applied statistics.

The Riemann hypothesis, a conjecture about the distribution of the zeros of the _____, is considered by many mathematicians to be the most important unsolved problem in pure mathematics.

a. 15 theorem
b. BIBO stability
c. Riemann zeta function
d. BDDC

39. _____ is used to describe the steepness, incline, gradient, or grade of a straight line. A higher _____ value indicates a steeper incline. The _____ is defined as the ratio of the 'rise' divided by the 'run' between two points on a line, or in other words, the ratio of the altitude change to the horizontal distance between any two points on the line.
a. 15 theorem
b. Slope
c. Y-intercept
d. Sequence

40. In coordinate geometry, the _____ is the y-value of the point where the graph of a function or relation intercepts the y-axis of the coordinate system.

In other words, the _____ of a function is the y-value of the point at which it intersects the line x=0 (the y-axis.) Thus, if the function is specified in form y = f(x), the _____ is easy to find by calculating f.

Chapter 1. INTRODUCTION. CALCULUS: A NEW HORIZON FROM ANCIENT ROOTS

a. Sequence
c. 15 theorem
b. Y-intercept
d. Slope

41. A _____ is a set of standard clothing worn by members of an organization while participating in that organization's activity. Modern uniforms are worn by armed forces and paramilitary organisations such as police, emergency services, security guards, in some workplaces and schools and by inmates in prisons. In some countries, some other officials also wear uniforms in their duties; such is the case of the Commissioned Corps of the United States Public Health Service or the French prefects.

a. ALGOR
c. AUSM
b. ACTRAN
d. Uniform

42. In physics, _____ is defined as the rate of change of position. it is vector physical quantity; both speed and direction are required to define it. In the SI (metric) system, it is measured in meters per second: (m/s) or ms^{-1}.

a. BDDC
c. Velocity
b. 15 theorem
d. BIBO stability

43. In mathematics, a _____ is a method for approximating the total area underneath a curve on a graph, otherwise known as an integral. It may also be used to define the integration operation.

Consider a function $f: D \rightarrowtail R$, where D is a subset of the real numbers R, and let $I = [a, b]$ be a closed interval contained in D. A finite set of points $\{x_0, x_1, x_2, ... x_n\}$ such that $a = x_0 < x_1 < x_2 ... < x_n = b$ creates a partition

$$P = \{[x_0, x_1), [x_1, x_2), ... [x_{n-1}, x_n]\}$$

of I.

a. Riemann sum
c. Risch algorithm
b. Solid of revolution
d. Signed measure

44. is called the proportionality constant or _____.

- If an object travels at a constant speed, then the distance traveled is proportional to the time spent travelling, with the speed being the _____.

- The circumference of a circle is proportional to its diameter, with the _____ equal to π.

- On a map drawn to scale, the distance between any two points on the map is proportional to the distance between the two locations that the points represent, with the _____ being the scale of the map.

- The force acting on a certain object due to gravity is proportional to the object's mass; the _____ between the the mass and the force is known as gravitational acceleration.

Since

$$y = kx$$

is equivalent to

$$x = \left(\frac{1}{k}\right)y,$$

it follows that if y is proportional to x, with (nonzero) proportionality constant k, then x is also proportional to y with proportionality constant 1/k.

If y is proportional to x, then the graph of y as a function of x will be a straight line passing through the origin with the slope of the line equal to the _____: it corresponds to linear growth.

    a. BDDC
    c. 15 theorem
    b. Reduction
    d. Constant of proportionality

45. In mathematics, a _____ is a function whose values do not vary and thus are constant. For example, if we have the function f(x) = 4, then f is constant since f maps any value to 4. More formally, a function f : A → B is a _____ if f(x) = f(y) for all x and y in A.
    a. Piecewise-defined function
    c. Surjective
    b. Range
    d. Constant function

46. In mathematics, the _____ of a function y = f(x) is a function that, in some fashion, 'undoes' the effect of f The _____ of f is denoted f⁻¹. The statements y=f(x) and x=f⁻¹(y) are equivalent.
    a. ACTRAN
    c. ALGOR
    b. AUSM
    d. Inverse

47. In economics, the _____ functional form of production functions is widely used to represent the relationship of an output to inputs. It was proposed by Knut Wicksell (1851-1926), and tested against statistical evidence by Charles Cobb and Paul Douglas in 1900-1928.

For production, the function is

    $Y = AL^{\alpha}K^{\beta}$,

where:

- Y = total production (the monetary value of all goods produced in a year)
- L = labor input
- K = capital input
- A = total factor productivity
- α and β are the output elasticities of labor and capital, respectively. These values are constants determined by available technology.

Output elasticity measures the responsiveness of output to a change in levels of either labor or capital used in production, ceteris paribus. For example if α = 0.15, a 1% increase in labor would lead to approximately a 0.15% increase in output.

a. Cobb-Douglas
b. BDDC
c. 15 theorem
d. BIBO stability

48. In mathematics, a _____ or quadratic is a polynomial of degree two. A _____ may involve a single variable x, or multiple variables such as x, y, and z.

Any single-variable _____ may be written as

$$ax^2 + bx + c,$$

where x is the variable, and a, b, and c represent the coefficients.

a. Characteristic equation
b. Difference polynomial
c. Binomial type
d. Quadratic polynomial

49. In mathematics, a _____ equation is a polynomial equation of degree five. It is of the form:

$$ax^5 + bx^4 + cx^3 + dx^2 + ex + f = 0,$$

where $a \neq 0$.

(if a = 0, then the equation becomes a quartic equation.)(if a and b = 0, then the equation becomes a cubic equation.)(if a, b and c = 0, then the equation becomes a quadratic equation.)(if a, b, c and d = 0, then the equation becomes a linear equation.)

a. BDDC
b. BIBO stability
c. 15 theorem
d. Quintic

50. In mathematics, a _____ is a polynomial equation of degree five. It is of the form:

Chapter 1. INTRODUCTION. CALCULUS: A NEW HORIZON FROM ANCIENT ROOTS

$$ax^5 + bx^4 + cx^3 + dx^2 + ex + f = 0,$$

where $a \neq 0$.

(if a = 0, then the equation becomes a quartic equation.)(if a and b = 0, then the equation becomes a cubic equation.)(if a, b and c = 0, then the equation becomes a quadratic equation.)(if a, b, c and d = 0, then the equation becomes a linear equation.)

a. 15 theorem
c. BIBO stability

b. Quintic equation
d. BDDC

51. In calculus, a branch of mathematics, the _____ is a measurement of how a function changes when its input changes. Loosely speaking, a _____ can be thought of as how much a quantity is changing at some given point. For example, the _____ of the position (or distance) of a vehicle with respect to time is the instantaneous velocity (respectively, instantaneous speed) at which the vehicle is traveling.

The process of finding a _____ is called differentiation. The fundamental theorem of calculus states that differentiation is the reverse process to integration.

a. Semi-differentiability
c. Stationary phase approximation

b. Derivative
d. Bounded function

52. In mathematics, a _____ of a function of several variables is its derivative with respect to one of those variables with the others held constant (as opposed to the total derivative, in which all variables are allowed to vary.) Partial derivatives are useful in vector calculus and differential geometry.

The _____ of a function f with respect to the variable x is written as f'$_x$, $\partial_x f$, or $\partial f/\partial x$.

a. Jacobian
c. Partial derivative

b. Level curve
d. Differentiation operator

53. In mathematics, a _____ is any function which can be written as the ratio of two polynomial functions.

$$y = \frac{x^2 - 3x - 2}{x^2 - 4}$$

In the case of one variable, x, a _____ is a function of the form

$$f(x) = \frac{P(x)}{Q(x)}$$

where P and Q are polynomial function in x and Q is not the zero polynomial. The domain of f is the set of all points x for which the denominator Q(x) is not zero.

Chapter 1. INTRODUCTION. CALCULUS: A NEW HORIZON FROM ANCIENT ROOTS

a. BIBO stability
c. 15 theorem
b. Rational function
d. BDDC

54. In mathematics, an _____ is informally a function which satisfies a polynomial equation whose coefficients are themselves polynomials. For example, an _____ in one variable x is a solution y for an equation

$$a_n(x)y^n + a_{n-1}(x)y^{n-1} + \cdots + a_0(x) = 0$$

where the coefficients $a_i(x)$ are polynomial functions of x. A function which is not algebraic is called a transcendental function.

a. Algebraic function
c. AUSM
b. ACTRAN
d. ALGOR

55. An _____ of a real-valued function y = f(x) is a curve which describes the behavior of f as either x or y tends to infinity.

In other words, as one moves along the graph of f(x) in some direction, the distance between it and the _____ eventually becomes smaller than any distance that one may specify.

a. Asymptote
c. ALGOR
b. ACTRAN
d. AUSM

56. Suppose f is a function. Then the line y = a is a _____ for f if

$$\lim_{x \to \infty} f(x) = a \text{ or } \lim_{x \to -\infty} f(x) = a.$$

Intuitively, this means that f(x) can be made as close as desired to a by making x big enough. How big is big enough depends on how close one wishes to make f(x) to a.

a. Third derivative
c. Second derivative
b. Mountain pass theorem
d. Horizontal asymptote

57. In mathematics, a _____ is a circle with a unit radius, i.e., a circle whose radius is 1. Frequently, especially in trigonometry, 'the' _____ is the circle of radius 1 centered at the origin (0, 0) in the Cartesian coordinate system in the Euclidean plane. The _____ is often denoted S^1; the generalization to higher dimensions is the unit sphere.

a. Unit circle
c. AUSM
b. ACTRAN
d. ALGOR

58. The line x = a is a _____ of a curve y=f(x) if at least one of the following statements is true:

1. $\lim_{x \to a} f(x) = \pm\infty$
2. $\lim_{x \to a^-} f(x) = \pm\infty$
3. $\lim_{x \to a^+} f(x) = \pm\infty$

Intuitively, if x = a is an asymptote of f, then, if we imagine x approaching a from one side, the value of f(x) grows without bound; i.e., f(x) becomes large (positively or negatively), and, in fact, becomes larger than any finite value.

Note that f(x) may or may not be defined at a: what the function is doing precisely at x = a does not affect the asymptote. For example, consider the function

$$f(x) = \begin{cases} \frac{1}{x} & \text{if } x > 0, \\ 5 & \text{if } x \leq 0 \end{cases}$$

As $\lim_{x \to 0^+} f(x) = \infty$, f(x) has a _____ at 0, even though f(0) = 5.

Another example is $f(x) = 1/(x-1)$ which has a _____ of x=1 as shown by the limit

$$\lim_{x \to 1^+} \frac{1}{x-1} = \infty$$

In the graph of $f(x) = x + \frac{1}{x}$, the y-axis (x = 0) and the line y = x are both asymptotes.

When a linear asymptote is not parallel to the x- or y-axis, it is called either an oblique asymptote or equivalently a slant asymptote.

a. Ramp function
c. Vertical asymptote
b. Monodromy
d. Third derivative

59. The _____ is a function in mathematics. The application of this function to a value x is written as exp(x). Equivalently, this can be written in the form e^x, where e is a mathematical constant, the base of the natural logarithm, which equals approximately 2.718281828, and is also known as Euler's number.

a. Area hyperbolic functions
c. Integral part
b. ACTRAN
d. Exponential function

60. The function $\log_b(x)$ depends on both b and x, but the term _____ in standard usage refers to a function of the form $\log_b(x)$ in which the base b is fixed and so the only argument is x. Thus there is one _____ for each value of the base b (which must be positive and must differ from 1.) Viewed in this way, the base-b _____ is the inverse function of the exponential function b^x.

a. BDDC
c. 15 theorem
b. BIBO stability
d. Logarithm function

61. _____ was a Greek philosopher, a student of Plato and teacher of Alexander the Great. He wrote on many subjects, including physics, metaphysics, poetry, theater, music, logic, rhetoric, politics, government, ethics, biology and zoology.

Together with Plato and Socrates (Plato's teacher), _____ is one of the most important founding figures in Western philosophy.

a. Augustin Louis Cauchy
c. Blue sky catastrophe
b. Augustin-Jean Fresnel
d. Aristotle

62. In mathematics, a _____ is a constant multiplicative factor of a certain object. For example, in the expression $9x^2$, the _____ of x^2 is 9.

The object can be such things as a variable, a vector, a function, etc.

a. Degree of the polynomial
c. Binomial type
b. Coefficient
d. Resultant

63. In probability theory and statistics, _____ indicates the strength and direction of a linear relationship between two random variables. That is in contrast with the usage of the term in colloquial speech, denoting any relationship, not necessarily linear. In general statistical usage, _____ or co-relation refers to the departure of two random variables from independence.

a. Geometric mean
c. Continuous random variable
b. Standard deviation
d. Correlation

64. The method of _____ or ordinary _____ is used to solve overdetermined systems. _____ is often applied in statistical contexts, particularly regression analysis.

_____ can be interpreted as a method of fitting data. The best fit in the _____ sense is that instance of the model for which the sum of squared residuals has its least value, a residual being the difference between an observed value and the value given by the model.

a. 15 theorem
c. Least squares
b. BIBO stability
d. BDDC

65. In statistics, _____ is a form of regression analysis in which the relationship between one or more independent variables and another variable, called dependent variable, is modeled by a least squares function, called _____ equation. This function is a linear combination of one or more model parameters, called regression coefficients. A _____ equation with one independent variable represents a straight line.

a. Standard deviation
c. Probability
b. Linear regression
d. Correlation

66. Trigonometry is a branch of mathematics that deals with triangles, particularly those plane triangles in which one angle has 90 degrees (right triangles.) Trigonometry deals with relationships between the sides and the angles of triangles and with the _____ functions, which describe those relationships.

Trigonometry has applications in both pure mathematics and in applied mathematics, where it is essential in many branches of science and technology.

   a. Trigonometric functions   b. Trigonometric
   c. Trigonometric integrals   d. Sine

67. In mathematics, the _____ are functions of an angle. They are important in the study of triangles and modeling periodic phenomena, among many other applications. _____ are commonly defined as ratios of two sides of a right triangle containing the angle, and can equivalently be defined as the lengths of various line segments from a unit circle.

   a. Trigonometric   b. Sine integral
   c. Trigonometric integrals   d. Trigonometric functions

68. In mathematics, _____ are a method of defining a curve. A simple kinematical example is when one uses a time parameter to determine the position, velocity, and other information about a body in motion.

Abstractly, a relation is given in the form of an equation, and it is shown also to be the image of functions from items such as R^n.

   a. Parametric equations   b. Shift theorem
   c. Partial derivative   d. Critical point

69. A _____ is the path a moving object follows through space. The object might be a projectile or a satellite, for example. It thus includes the meaning of orbit - the path of a planet, an asteroid or a comet as it travels around a central mass.

   a. BDDC   b. 15 theorem
   c. BIBO stability   d. Trajectory

70. In those hierarchically organised churches of Western Christianity which have an ecclesiastical law system, an _____ is an officer of the church who by reason of office has _____ power to execute the church's laws. The term comes from the Latin word ordinarius. In Eastern Christianity, a corresponding officer is called a hierarch, which comes from the Greek word á¼±ÎµÏÎ¬Ïχης meaning 'priestly ruler'.

   a. AUSM   b. ALGOR
   c. ACTRAN   d. Ordinary

71. A _____ is the curve defined by the path of a point on the edge of circular wheel as the wheel rolls along a straight line. It is an example of a roulette, a curve generated by a curve rolling on another curve.

The _____ is the solution to the brachistochrone problem (i.e. it is the curve of fastest descent under gravity) and the related tautochrone problem (i.e. the period of a ball rolling back and forth inside it does not depend on the ball's starting position.)

a. Prolate cycloid
b. Curtate cycloid
c. Tractrix
d. Cycloid

72. A _____ is the curve between two points that is covered in the least time by a body that starts at the first point with zero speed and is constrained to move along the curve to the second point, under the action of constant gravity and assuming no friction.

Given two points A and B, with A not lower than B, there is just one upside down cycloid that passes through A with infinite slope, passes also through B and does not have maximum points between A and B. This particular inverted cycloid is a _____. The curve does not depend on the body's mass or on the strength of the gravitational constant.

a. Prolate cycloid
b. Closed curve
c. Space curve
d. Brachistochrone curve

73. The _____ is a fractal named after the Polish mathematician Wacław Sierpiński who described it in 1915.

Originally constructed as a curve, this is one of the basic examples of self-similar sets, i.e. it is a mathematically generated pattern that can be reproducible at any magnification or reduction.

Comparing the _____ or the Sierpinski carpet to equivalent repetitive tiling arrangements, it is evident that similar structures can be built into any rep-tile arrangements.

a. 15 theorem
b. BDDC
c. BIBO stability
d. Sierpinski triangle

74. A _____ is a 2D geometric symbolic representation of information according to some visualization technique. Sometimes, the technique uses a 3D visualization which is then projected onto the 2D surface.

_____ has two meanings in common sense.

a. BIBO stability
b. 15 theorem
c. Diagram
d. BDDC

75. In mathematics, a _____ is an expression such as

$$x = a_0 + \cfrac{1}{a_1 + \cfrac{1}{a_2 + \cfrac{1}{a_3 + \cfrac{1}{\ddots}}}}$$

where a_0 is an integer and all the other numbers a_i ($i \neq 0$) are positive integers. Longer expressions are defined analogously. If the partial numerators and partial denominators are allowed to assume arbitrary values, which may in some contexts include functions, the resulting expression is a generalized _____.

a. Stern-Brocot tree
b. Restricted partial quotients
c. Continued fraction
d. Quadratic equation

77. In mathematics and the arts, two quantities are in the _____ if the ratio between the sum of those quantities and the larger one is the same as the ratio between the larger one and the smaller. The _____ is an irrational mathematical constant, approximately 1.6180339887.

At least since the Renaissance, many artists and architects have proportioned their works to approximate the _____ -- especially in the form of the golden rectangle, in which the ratio of the longer side to the shorter is the _____ --believing this proportion to be aesthetically pleasing.

a. BIBO stability
b. Golden ratio
c. 15 theorem
d. BDDC

77. _____ is the change in population over time, and can be quantified as the change in the number of individuals in a population using 'per unit time' for measurement. The term _____ can technically refer to any species, but almost always refers to humans, and it is often used informally for the more specific demographic term _____ rate , and is often used to refer specifically to the growth of the population of the world.

Simple models of _____ include the Malthusian Growth Model and the logistic model.

a. 15 theorem
b. Population growth
c. BDDC
d. BIBO stability

Chapter 2. LIMITS AND CONTINUITY

1. In mathematics, the concept of a '_____' is used to describe the behavior of a function as its argument or input either 'gets close' to some point, or as the argument becomes arbitrarily large; or the behavior of a sequence's elements as their index increases indefinitely. Limits are used in calculus and other branches of mathematical analysis to define derivatives and continuity.

In formulas, _____ is usually abbreviated as lim

   a. BDDC   b. Limit
   c. 15 theorem   d. BIBO stability

2. In mathematics, a (topological) _____ is defined as follows: let I be an interval of real numbers (i.e. a non-empty connected subset of $\mathbb{R}$); then a _____ γ is a continuous mapping $\gamma : I \to X$, where X is a topological space. The _____ γ is said to be simple if it is injective, i.e. if for all x, y in I, we have $\gamma(x) = \gamma(y) \implies x = y$. If I is a closed bounded interval $[a, b]$, we also allow the possibility $\gamma(a) = \gamma(b)$ (this convention makes it possible to talk about closed simple _____.)

   a. Closed curve   b. Tractrix
   c. Prolate cycloid   d. Curve

3. _____ is used to describe the steepness, incline, gradient, or grade of a straight line. A higher _____ value indicates a steeper incline. The _____ is defined as the ratio of the 'rise' divided by the 'run' between two points on a line, or in other words, the ratio of the altitude change to the horizontal distance between any two points on the line.

   a. Sequence   b. Y-intercept
   c. 15 theorem   d. Slope

4. In physics, _____ is defined as the rate of change of position. it is vector physical quantity; both speed and direction are required to define it. In the SI (metric) system, it is measured in meters per second: (m/s) or ms^{-1}.

   a. BIBO stability   b. Velocity
   c. 15 theorem   d. BDDC

5. Cantor defined two kinds of _____ numbers, the ordinal numbers and the cardinal numbers. Ordinal numbers may be identified with well-ordered sets, or counting carried on to any stopping point, including points after an _____ number have already been counted. Generalizing finite and the ordinary _____ sequences which are maps from the positive integers leads to mappings from ordinal numbers, and transfinite sequences.

   a. Infinite   b. ALGOR
   c. ACTRAN   d. AUSM

6. An _____ of a real-valued function y = f(x) is a curve which describes the behavior of f as either x or y tends to infinity.

In other words, as one moves along the graph of f(x) in some direction, the distance between it and the _____ eventually becomes smaller than any distance that one may specify.

   a. ALGOR   b. AUSM
   c. ACTRAN   d. Asymptote

7. The line x = a is a _____ of a curve y=f(x) if at least one of the following statements is true:

1. $\lim_{x \to a} f(x) = \pm\infty$
2. $\lim_{x \to a^-} f(x) = \pm\infty$
3. $\lim_{x \to a^+} f(x) = \pm\infty$

Intuitively, if x = a is an asymptote of f, then, if we imagine x approaching a from one side, the value of f(x) grows without bound; i.e., f(x) becomes large (positively or negatively), and, in fact, becomes larger than any finite value.

Note that f(x) may or may not be defined at a: what the function is doing precisely at x = a does not affect the asymptote. For example, consider the function

$$f(x) = \begin{cases} \frac{1}{x} & \text{if } x > 0, \\ 5 & \text{if } x \leq 0 \end{cases}$$

As $\lim_{x \to 0^+} f(x) = \infty$, f(x) has a _____ at 0, even though f(0) = 5.

Another example is $f(x) = 1/(x-1)$ which has a _____ of x=1 as shown by the limit

$$\lim_{x \to 1^+} \frac{1}{x-1} = \infty$$

In the graph of $f(x) = x + \frac{1}{x}$, the y-axis (x = 0) and the line y = x are both asymptotes.

When a linear asymptote is not parallel to the x- or y-axis, it is called either an oblique asymptote or equivalently a slant asymptote.

a. Third derivative
c. Ramp function
b. Vertical asymptote
d. Monodromy

8. Suppose f is a function. Then the line y = a is a _____ for f if

$$\lim_{x \to \infty} f(x) = a \text{ or } \lim_{x \to -\infty} f(x) = a.$$

Intuitively, this means that f(x) can be made as close as desired to a by making x big enough. How big is big enough depends on how close one wishes to make f(x) to a.

a. Horizontal asymptote
b. Third derivative
c. Mountain pass theorem
d. Second derivative

9. In mathematics, the _____ (or replacement set) of a given function is the set of 'input' values for which the function is defined. For instance, the _____ of cosine would be all real numbers, while the _____ of the square root would be only numbers greater than or equal to 0 (ignoring complex numbers in both cases.) In a representation of a function in a xy Cartesian coordinate system, the _____ is represented on the x axis (or abscissa.)
   a. 15 theorem
   b. BIBO stability
   c. Domain
   d. BDDC

10. In mathematics, in the field of ordinary differential equations, a non trivial solution to an ordinary differential equation

$$F(x, y, y', \ldots, y^{(n-1)}) = y^{(n)} \quad x \in [0, +\infty)$$

is called _____ if it has an infinite number of roots, otherwise it is called non-_____. The differential equation is called _____ if it has an _____ solution.

The differential equation

   y'' + y = 0

is _____ as sin(x) is a solution.

   a. Oscillating
   b. Exponential growth
   c. Integrating factor
   d. Inseparable differential equation

11. _____ is usually defined as the activity of using and developing computer technology, computer hardware and software. It is the computer-specific part of information technology. Computer science (or _____ science) is the study and the science of the theoretical foundations of information and computation and their implementation and application in computer systems.
   a. BIBO stability
   b. BDDC
   c. Computing
   d. 15 theorem

12. In calculus, a branch of mathematics, the _____ is a measurement of how a function changes when its input changes. Loosely speaking, a _____ can be thought of as how much a quantity is changing at some given point. For example, the _____ of the position (or distance) of a vehicle with respect to time is the instantaneous velocity (respectively, instantaneous speed) at which the vehicle is traveling.

The process of finding a _____ is called differentiation. The fundamental theorem of calculus states that differentiation is the reverse process to integration.

   a. Bounded function
   b. Stationary phase approximation
   c. Derivative
   d. Semi-differentiability

Chapter 2. LIMITS AND CONTINUITY

13. In mathematics, a _____ of a function of several variables is its derivative with respect to one of those variables with the others held constant (as opposed to the total derivative, in which all variables are allowed to vary.) Partial derivatives are useful in vector calculus and differential geometry.

The _____ of a function f with respect to the variable x is written as f'_x, $\partial_x f$, or $\partial f/\partial x$.

   a. Differentiation operator
   c. Level curve
   b. Jacobian
   d. Partial derivative

14. In mathematics, a _____ is any function which can be written as the ratio of two polynomial functions.

$$y = \frac{x^2 - 3x - 2}{x^2 - 4}$$

In the case of one variable, x, a _____ is a function of the form

$$f(x) = \frac{P(x)}{Q(x)}$$

where P and Q are polynomial function in x and Q is not the zero polynomial. The domain of f is the set of all points x for which the denominator Q(x) is not zero.

   a. BDDC
   c. 15 theorem
   b. Rational function
   d. BIBO stability

15. Integration is an important concept in mathematics, specifically in the field of calculus and, more broadly, mathematical analysis. Given a function f of a real variable x and an interval [a, b] of the real line, the _____

$$\int_a^b f(x)\, dx,$$

is defined informally to be the net signed area of the region in the xy-plane bounded by the graph of f, the x-axis, and the vertical lines x = a and x = b.

The term '_____' may also refer to the notion of antiderivative, a function F whose derivative is the given function f.

   a. Integral
   c. Integral test for convergence
   b. Indefinite integral
   d. Integrand

16. In mathematics, a _____ is a definite integral taken over a surface (which may be a curved set in space); it can be thought of as the double integral analog of the line integral. Given a surface, one may integrate over it scalar fields (that is, functions which return numbers as values), and vector fields (that is, functions which return vectors as values.)

Surface integrals have applications in physics, particularly with the classical theory of electromagnetism.

    a. Contact
    b. Surface integral
    c. Differential operator
    d. Symmetry of second derivatives

17. _____ is a type of motion in which the velocity of an object changes equal amounts in equal time periods. An example of an object having _____ would be a ball rolling down a ramp. The object picks up velocity as it goes down the ramp with equal changes in time.
    a. AUSM
    b. ALGOR
    c. ACTRAN
    d. Uniform Acceleration

18. In calculus and other branches of mathematical analysis, an _____ is an algebraic expression obtained in the context of limits. Limits involving algebraic operations are often performed by replacing subexpressions by their limits; if the expression obtained after this substitution does not give enough information to determine the original limit, it is known as an _____. The indeterminate forms include 0^0, $0/0$, 1^∞, $\infty - \infty$, ∞/∞, $0\times\infty$, and ∞^0.
    a. AUSM
    b. Indeterminate form
    c. ACTRAN
    d. ALGOR

19. In the various subfields of physics, there exist two common usages of the term _____, both with rigorous mathematical frameworks.

- In the study of transport phenomena (heat transfer, mass transfer and fluid dynamics), _____ is defined as the amount that flows through a unit area per unit time. _____ in this definition is a vector.
- In the field of electromagnetism and mathematics, _____ is usually the integral of a vector quantity over a finite surface. The result of this integration is a scalar quantity. The magnetic _____ is thus the integral of the magnetic vector field B over a surface, and the electric _____ is defined similarly. Using this definition, the _____ of the Poynting vector over a specified surface is the rate at which electromagnetic energy flows through that surface. Confusingly, the Poynting vector is sometimes called the power _____, which is an example of the first usage of _____, above. It has units of watts per square metre ($W \cdot m^{-2}$)

One could argue, based on the work of James Clerk Maxwell, that the transport definition precedes the more recent way the term is used in electromagnetism. The specific quote from Maxwell is 'In the case of fluxes, we have to take the integral, over a surface, of the _____ through every element of the surface. The result of this operation is called the surface integral of the _____.

    a. BIBO stability
    b. 15 theorem
    c. Flux
    d. BDDC

20. In mathematics, a _____ is an ordered list of objects (or events). Like a set, it contains members (also called elements or terms), and the number of terms (possibly infinite) is called the length of the _____. Unlike a set, order matters, and the exact same elements can appear multiple times at different positions in the _____.
    a. Slope
    b. Sequence
    c. 15 theorem
    d. Y-intercept

21. In vector calculus, the _____ is an operator that measures the magnitude of a vector field's source or sink at a given point; the _____ of a vector field is a (signed) scalar. For example, consider air as it is heated or cooled. The relevant vector field for this example is the velocity of the moving air at a point.
   a. Green's theorem
   b. Gradient theorem
   c. Triple product
   d. Divergence

22. In vector calculus, the _____ Ostrogradskye;s theorem the _____ states that the outward flux of a vector field through a surface is equal to the triple integral of the divergence on the region inside the surface. Intuitively, it states that the sum of all sources minus the sum of all sinks gives the net flow out of a region.
   a. Divergence Theorem
   b. Green's theorem
   c. Divergence
   d. Del

23. Continuous functions are of utmost importance in mathematics and applications. However, not all functions are continuous. If a function is not continuous at a point in its domain, one says that it has a _____ there. The set of all points of _____ of a function may be a discrete set, a dense set, or even the entire domain of the function.
   a. Vector
   b. 15 theorem
   c. BDDC
   d. Discontinuity

24. The _____ of an angle is the ratio of the length of the opposite side to the length of the hypotenuse. In our case

$$\sin A = \frac{\text{opposite}}{\text{hypotenuse}} = \frac{a}{h}.$$

Note that this ratio does not depend on size of the particular right triangle chosen, as long as it contains the angle A, since all such triangles are similar.

The cosine of an angle is the ratio of the length of the adjacent side to the length of the hypotenuse.

   a. Sine
   b. Trigonometric functions
   c. Sine integral
   d. Trigonometric

25. In mathematics and physics, a _____ associates a scalar value, which can be either mathematical in definition to every point in space. Scalar fields are often used in physics, for instance to indicate the temperature distribution throughout space or more specifically, differential geometry, the set of functions defined on a manifold define the commutative ring of functions.
   a. Symmetry of second derivatives
   b. Vector Laplacian
   c. Level curve
   d. Scalar field

26. In calculus, _____, was originally the use of expressions such as dx and dy and to represent 'infinitely small' (or infinitesimal) increments of quantities x and y, just as >Δx and >Δy represent finite increments of x and y respectively. So for y being a function of x, or

the derivative of y with respect to x, which later came to be viewed as

was, according to Leibniz, the quotient of an infinitesimal increment of y by an infinitesimal increment of x, or

where the right hand side is Lagrange's notation for the derivative of f at x.

Similarly, although mathematicians usually now view an integral

as a limit

where >Δx is an interval containing x_i, Leibniz viewed it as the sum (the integral sign denoting summation) of infinitely many infinitesimal quantities f(x) dx.

a. Stationary point
b. Leibniz's notation
c. Time derivative
d. Smooth function

27. In mathematics, a _____ is a method for approximating the total area underneath a curve on a graph, otherwise known as an integral. It may also be used to define the integration operation.

Consider a function f: D >→ **R**, where D is a subset of the real numbers **R**, and let I = [a, b] be a closed interval contained in D. A finite set of points {$x_0, x_1, x_2, ... x_n$} such that $a = x_0 < x_1 < x_2 ... < x_n = b$ creates a partition

$P = \{[x_0, x_1), [x_1, x_2), ... [x_{n-1}, x_n]\}$

of I.

a. Signed measure
b. Risch algorithm
c. Solid of revolution
d. Riemann sum

28. Trigonometry is a branch of mathematics that deals with triangles, particularly those plane triangles in which one angle has 90 degrees (right triangles.) Trigonometry deals with relationships between the sides and the angles of triangles and with the _____ functions, which describe those relationships.

Trigonometry has applications in both pure mathematics and in applied mathematics, where it is essential in many branches of science and technology.

   a. Sine
   b. Trigonometric functions
   c. Trigonometric integrals
   d. Trigonometric

29. In mathematics, the _____ are functions of an angle. They are important in the study of triangles and modeling periodic phenomena, among many other applications. _____ are commonly defined as ratios of two sides of a right triangle containing the angle, and can equivalently be defined as the lengths of various line segments from a unit circle.
   a. Sine integral
   b. Trigonometric
   c. Trigonometric integrals
   d. Trigonometric functions

30. In mathematics, the _____ is a representation of a function as an infinite sum of terms calculated from the values of its derivatives at a single point. It may be regarded as the limit of the Taylor polynomials. If the series is centered at zero, the series is also called a Maclaurin series.
   a. BDDC
   b. BIBO stability
   c. 15 theorem
   d. Taylor series

31. In physics, and more specifically kinematics, _____ is the change in velocity over time. Because velocity is a vector, it can change in two ways: a change in magnitude and/or a change in direction. In one dimension, _____ is the rate at which something speeds up or slows down.
   a. ACTRAN
   b. AUSM
   c. ALGOR
   d. Acceleration

Chapter 3. THE DERIVATIVE

1. A _____ of a curve is a line that (locally) intersects two points on the curve. The word secant comes from the Latin secare, for to cut.

It can be used to approximate the tangent to a curve, at some point P. If the secant to a curve is defined by two points, P and Q, with P fixed and Q variable, as Q approaches P along the curve, the direction of the secant approaches that of the tangent at P, assuming there is just one.

  a. Secant line
  b. Curve
  c. Witch of Agnesi
  d. Kappa curve

2. _____ is used to describe the steepness, incline, gradient, or grade of a straight line. A higher _____ value indicates a steeper incline. The _____ is defined as the ratio of the 'rise' divided by the 'run' between two points on a line, or in other words, the ratio of the altitude change to the horizontal distance between any two points on the line.

  a. Sequence
  b. Slope
  c. Y-intercept
  d. 15 theorem

3. In mathematics, a (topological) _____ is defined as follows: let I be an interval of real numbers (i.e. a non-empty connected subset of $\mathbb{R}$); then a _____ γ is a continuous mapping $\gamma : I \to X$, where X is a topological space. The _____ γ is said to be simple if it is injective, i.e. if for all x, y in I, we have $\gamma(x) = \gamma(y) \implies x = y$. If I is a closed bounded interval $[a, b]$, we also allow the possibility $\gamma(a) = \gamma(b)$ (this convention makes it possible to talk about closed simple _____.)

  a. Prolate cycloid
  b. Curve
  c. Tractrix
  d. Closed curve

4. The function difference divided by the point difference is known as the _____, it is also known as Newton's quotient):

$$\frac{\Delta F(P)}{\Delta P} = \frac{F(P + \Delta P) - F(P)}{\Delta P} = \frac{\nabla F(P + \Delta P)}{\Delta P}.$$

If ΔP is infinitesimal, then the _____ is a derivative, otherwise it is a divided difference:

$$\text{If } |\Delta P| = iota : \quad \frac{\Delta F(P)}{\Delta P} = \frac{dF(P)}{dP} = F'(P) = G(P);$$

$$\text{If } |\Delta P| > iota : \quad \frac{\Delta F(P)}{\Delta P} = \frac{DF(P)}{DP} = F[P, P + \Delta P].$$

Regardless if ΔP is infinitesimal or finite, there is (at least--in the case of the derivative--theoretically) a point range, where the boundaries are P ± (.5)ΔP (depending on the orientation--ΔF(P), δF(P) or ∇F(P)):

  LB = Lower Boundary; UB = Upper Boundary;

Chapter 3. THE DERIVATIVE

Anyone familiar with derivatives knows that they can be regarded as functions themselves, harboring their own derivatives. Thus each function is home to sequential degrees ('higher orders') of derivation, or differentiation. This property can be generalized to all difference quotients. As this sequencing requires a corresponding boundary splintering, it is practical to break up the point range into smaller, equi-sized sections, with each section being marked by an intermediary point ('P_i'), where LB = P_0 and UB = P_{A_n}, the nth point, equaling the degree/order:

LB = P_0 = P_0 + $0\Delta_1 P$ = P_{A_n} - $(Åf$-$0)\Delta_1 P$; P_1 = P_0 + $1\Delta_1 P$ = P_{A_n} - $(Åf$-$1)\Delta_1 P$; P_2 = P_0 + $2\Delta_1 P$ = P_{A_n} - $(Åf$-$2)\Delta_1 P$; P_3 = P_0 + $3\Delta_1 P$ = P_{A_n} - $(Åf$-$3)\Delta_1 P$; ↓↓↓↓ $P_{A_n\text{-}3}$ = P_0 + $(Åf$-$3)\Delta_1 P$ = P_{A_n} - $3\Delta_1 P$; $P_{A_n\text{-}2}$ = P_0 + $(Åf$-$2)\Delta_1 P$ = P_{A_n} - $2\Delta_1 P$; $P_{A_n\text{-}1}$ = P_0 + $(Åf$-$1)\Delta_1 P$ = P_{A_n} - $1\Delta_1 P$; UB = $P_{A_n\text{-}0}$ = P_0 + $(Åf$-$0)\Delta_1 P$ = P_{A_n} - $0\Delta_1 P$ = P_{A_n};

ΔP = $\Delta_1 P$ = P_1 - P_0 = P_2 - P_1 = P_3 - P_2 = ...

   a. Continuously differentiable   b. Directional derivative
   c. Notation for differentiation   d. Difference quotient

5. In geometry, the _____ (or simply the tangent) to a curve at a given point is the straight line that 'just touches' the curve at that point (in the sense explained more precisely below.) As it passes through the point of tangency, the _____ is 'going in the same direction' as the curve, and in this sense it is the best straight-line approximation to the curve at that point. The same definition applies to space curves and curves in n-dimensional Euclidean space.
   a. Lie derivative   b. Minimal surface
   c. North pole   d. Tangent line

6. In mathematics, especially in order theory, an _____ of a subset S of some partially ordered set (P, >≤) is an element of P which is greater than or equal to every element of S. The term lower bound is defined dually as an element of P which is lesser than or equal to every element of S. A set with an _____ is said to be bounded from above by that bound, a set with a lower bound is said to be bounded from below by that bound.

A subset S of a partially ordered set P may fail to have any bounds or may have many different upper and lower bounds. By transitivity, any element greater than or equal to an _____ of S is again an _____ of S, and any element lesser than or equal to any lower bound of S is again a lower bound of S. This leads to the consideration of least upper bounds: (or suprema) and greatest lower bounds (or infima.)

   a. Upper bound   b. AUSM
   c. ACTRAN   d. ALGOR

7. _____ is usually defined as the activity of using and developing computer technology, computer hardware and software. It is the computer-specific part of information technology. Computer science (or _____ science) is the study and the science of the theoretical foundations of information and computation and their implementation and application in computer systems.
   a. 15 theorem   b. BDDC
   c. BIBO stability   d. Computing

8. The _____ of an angle is the ratio of the length of the opposite side to the length of the hypotenuse. In our case

$$\sin A = \frac{\text{opposite}}{\text{hypotenuse}} = \frac{a}{h}.$$

Note that this ratio does not depend on size of the particular right triangle chosen, as long as it contains the angle A, since all such triangles are similar.

The cosine of an angle is the ratio of the length of the adjacent side to the length of the hypotenuse.

a. Trigonometric functions
b. Trigonometric
c. Sine integral
d. Sine

9. f'(x) is twice the absolute value function, and it does not have a derivative at zero. Similar examples show that a function can have k derivatives for any non-negative integer k but no (k + 1)-order derivative. A function that has k successive derivatives is called _____.

a. Differential calculus
b. Differential coefficient
c. Power series
d. K times differentiable

10. In calculus, a branch of mathematics, the _____ is a measurement of how a function changes when its input changes. Loosely speaking, a _____ can be thought of as how much a quantity is changing at some given point. For example, the _____ of the position (or distance) of a vehicle with respect to time is the instantaneous velocity (respectively, instantaneous speed) at which the vehicle is traveling.

The process of finding a _____ is called differentiation. The fundamental theorem of calculus states that differentiation is the reverse process to integration.

a. Semi-differentiability
b. Bounded function
c. Stationary phase approximation
d. Derivative

11. _____ is a type of motion in which the velocity of an object changes equal amounts in equal time periods. An example of an object having _____ would be a ball rolling down a ramp. The object picks up velocity as it goes down the ramp with equal changes in time.

a. ACTRAN
b. AUSM
c. ALGOR
d. Uniform Acceleration

12. In vector calculus, the _____ is an operator that measures the magnitude of a vector field's source or sink at a given point; the _____ of a vector field is a (signed) scalar. For example, consider air as it is heated or cooled. The relevant vector field for this example is the velocity of the moving air at a point.

a. Gradient theorem
b. Green's theorem
c. Triple product
d. Divergence

13. In vector calculus, the _____ Ostrogradskye;s theorem the _____ states that the outward flux of a vector field through a surface is equal to the triple integral of the divergence on the region inside the surface. Intuitively, it states that the sum of all sources minus the sum of all sinks gives the net flow out of a region.

Chapter 3. THE DERIVATIVE

a. Del
b. Green's theorem
c. Divergence
d. Divergence Theorem

14. In calculus, _____, was originally the use of expressions such as dx and dy and to represent 'infinitely small' (or infinitesimal) increments of quantities x and y, just as >Δx and >Δy represent finite increments of x and y respectively. So for y being a function of x, or

the derivative of y with respect to x, which later came to be viewed as

was, according to Leibniz, the quotient of an infinitesimal increment of y by an infinitesimal increment of x, or

where the right hand side is Lagrange's notation for the derivative of f at x.

Similarly, although mathematicians usually now view an integral

as a limit

where >Δx is an interval containing x_i, Leibniz viewed it as the sum (the integral sign denoting summation) of infinitely many infinitesimal quantities f(x) dx.

a. Smooth function
b. Stationary point
c. Time derivative
d. Leibniz's notation

15. In economics, the _____ functional form of production functions is widely used to represent the relationship of an output to inputs. It was proposed by Knut Wicksell (1851-1926), and tested against statistical evidence by Charles Cobb and Paul Douglas in 1900-1928.

Chapter 3. THE DERIVATIVE

For production, the function is

Y = AL^α K^β,

where:

- Y = total production (the monetary value of all goods produced in a year)
- L = labor input
- K = capital input
- A = total factor productivity
- α and β are the output elasticities of labor and capital, respectively. These values are constants determined by available technology.

Output elasticity measures the responsiveness of output to a change in levels of either labor or capital used in production, ceteris paribus. For example if α = 0.15, a 1% increase in labor would lead to approximately a 0.15% increase in output.

a. Cobb-Douglas
c. BIBO stability

b. 15 theorem
d. BDDC

16. In mathematics, a _____ is a constant multiplicative factor of a certain object. For example, in the expression 9x², the _____ of x² is 9.

The object can be such things as a variable, a vector, a function, etc.

a. Resultant
c. Degree of the polynomial

b. Binomial type
d. Coefficient

17. This article will state and prove the _____ for differentiation, and then use it to prove these two formulas.

The _____ for differentiation states that for every natural number n, the derivative of $f(x) = x^n$ is $f'(x) = nx^{n-1}$, that is,

$$(x^n)' = nx^{n-1}.$$

The _____ for integration

$$\int x^n \, dx = \frac{x^{n+1}}{n+1} + C$$

for natural n is then an easy consequence. One just needs to take the derivative of this equality and use the _____ and linearity of differentiation on the right-hand side.

Chapter 3. THE DERIVATIVE

a. Leibniz rule
b. Test for Divergence
c. Functional integration
d. Power rule

18. In calculus, the _____ is a formula used to find the derivatives of products of functions. It may be stated thus:

$$(f \cdot g)' = f' \cdot g + f \cdot g'$$

or in the Leibniz notation thus:

$$\frac{d}{dx}(u \cdot v) = u \cdot \frac{dv}{dx} + v \cdot \frac{du}{dx}.$$

Discovery of this rule is credited to Gottfried Leibniz, who demonstrated it using differentials. Here is Leibniz's argument: Let u and v be two differentiable functions of x.

a. Constant factor rule in differentiation
b. Quotient Rule
c. Differentiation rules
d. Product rule

19. In calculus, the _____ is a method of finding the derivative of a function that is the quotient of two other functions for which derivatives exist.

If the function one wishes to differentiate, f(x), can be written as

$$f(x) = \frac{g(x)}{h(x)}$$

and h(x) ≠ 0, then the rule states that the derivative of g(x) / h(x) is equal to:

$$\frac{d}{dx}f(x) = f'(x) = \frac{g'(x)h(x) - g(x)h'(x)}{[h(x)]^2}.$$

Or, more precisely, if all x in some open set containing the number a satisfy h(x) ≠ 0; and g'(a) and h'(a) both exist; then, f'(a) exists as well and:

$$f'(a) = \frac{g'(a)h(a) - g(a)h'(a)}{[h(a)]^2}.$$

The derivative of (4x − 2) / (x² + 1) is:

$$\frac{d}{dx}\left[\frac{(4x-2)}{x^2+1}\right] = \frac{(x^2+1)(4) - (4x-2)(2x)}{(x^2+1)^2}$$

$$= \frac{(4x^2+4) - (8x^2-4x)}{(x^2+1)^2} = \frac{-4x^2+4x+4}{(x^2+1)^2}$$

In the example above, the choices

g(x) = 4x − 2
h(x) = x² + 1

were made. Analogously, the derivative of sin(x) / x² (when x ≠ 0) is:

$$\frac{\cos(x)x^2 - \sin(x)2x}{x^4}$$

Another example is:

$$f(x) = \frac{2x^2}{x^3}$$

whereas g(x) = 2x² and h(x) = x³, and g'(x) = 4x and h'(x) = 3x².

a. Reciprocal Rule
b. Constant factor rule in differentiation
c. Quotient rule
d. Differentiation rules

20. Let f be a differentiable function, and let f'(x) be its derivative. The derivative of f'(x) (if it has one) is written f''(x) and is called the _____ of f. Similarly, the derivative of a _____, if it exists, is written f'''(x) and is called the third derivative of f.

a. Vertical asymptote
b. Slant asymptote
c. Stationary phase approximation
d. Second derivative

21. In mathematics, a _____ is an ordered list of objects (or events). Like a set, it contains members (also called elements or terms), and the number of terms (possibly infinite) is called the length of the _____. Unlike a set, order matters, and the exact same elements can appear multiple times at different positions in the _____.

a. Sequence
b. 15 theorem
c. Y-intercept
d. Slope

22. Let f be a differentiable function, and let f'(x) be its derivative. The derivative of f'(x) (if it has one) is written f''(x) and is called the second derivative of f. Similarly, the derivative of a second derivative, if it exists, is written f'''(x) and is called the _____ of f.

a. Differential coefficient
b. Mountain pass theorem
c. Derivative
d. Third derivative

23. Trigonometry is a branch of mathematics that deals with triangles, particularly those plane triangles in which one angle has 90 degrees (right triangles.) Trigonometry deals with relationships between the sides and the angles of triangles and with the _____ functions, which describe those relationships.

Trigonometry has applications in both pure mathematics and in applied mathematics, where it is essential in many branches of science and technology.

Chapter 3. THE DERIVATIVE

a. Sine
c. Trigonometric functions
b. Trigonometric integrals
d. Trigonometric

24. In mathematics, the _____ are functions of an angle. They are important in the study of triangles and modeling periodic phenomena, among many other applications. _____ are commonly defined as ratios of two sides of a right triangle containing the angle, and can equivalently be defined as the lengths of various line segments from a unit circle.
   a. Trigonometric functions
   c. Trigonometric integrals
   b. Trigonometric
   d. Sine integral

25. In a totally ordered set all elements are mutually comparable, so such a set can have at most one minimal element and at most one maximal element. Then, due to mutual comparability, the minimal element will also be the least element and the maximal element will also be the greatest element. Thus in a totally ordered set we can simply use the terms minimum and _____.
   a. Nth term
   c. Leibniz rule
   b. Racetrack principle
   d. Maximum

26. In calculus, the _____ is a formula for the derivative of the composite of two functions.

In intuitive terms, if a variable, y, depends on a second variable, u, which in turn depends on a third variable, x, then the rate of change of y with respect to x can be computed as the rate of change of y with respect to u multiplied by the rate of change of u with respect to x. Schematically,

$$\frac{dy}{dx} = \frac{dy}{du} \cdot \frac{du}{dx}.$$

   a. Reciprocal Rule
   c. Product rule
   b. Differentiation rules
   d. Chain rule

27. In computer science and information science, _____ could also be a method or an algorithm. Again, an example will illustrate: There are systems of counting, as with Roman numerals, and various systems for filing papers, or catalogues, and various library systems, of which the Dewey Decimal _____ is an example. This still fits with the definition of components which are connected together (in this case in order to facilitate the flow of information.)
   a. BIBO stability
   c. 15 theorem
   b. BDDC
   d. System

28. In physics (specifically mechanics and electrical engineering), _____ ω (also referred to by the terms angular speed, radial frequency, circular frequency, orbital frequency, and radian frequency) is a scalar measure of rotation rate. _____ is the magnitude of the vector quantity angular velocity. The term _____ vector $\vec{\omega}$ is sometimes used as a synonym for the vector quantity angular velocity .
   a. ACTRAN
   c. AUSM
   b. ALGOR
   d. Angular frequency

29. In acoustics and telecommunication, a _____ of a wave is a component frequency of the signal that is an integer multiple of the fundamental frequency. For example, if the fundamental frequency is f, the harmonics have frequencies f, 2f, 3f, 4f, etc. The harmonics have the property that they are all periodic at the fundamental frequency, therefore the sum of harmonics is also periodic at that frequency.

   a. 15 theorem
   b. BIBO stability
   c. BDDC
   d. Harmonic

30. _____ is the motion of a simple harmonic oscillator, a motion that is neither driven nor damped. The motion is periodic - as it repeats itself at standard intervals in a specific manner - and sinusoidal, with constant amplitude; the acceleration of a body executing _____ is directly proportional to the displacement of the body from the equilibrium position and is always directed towards the equilibrium position.

The motion is characterized by its amplitude (which is always positive), its period, the time for a single oscillation, its frequency, the reciprocal of the period (i.e. the number of cycles per unit time), and its phase, which determines the starting point on the sine wave.

   a. Simple harmonic motion
   b. 15 theorem
   c. Fundamental lemma in the calculus of variations
   d. Holonomic

31. In mathematics, an _____ is a generalization for the concept of a function in which the dependent variable has not been given 'explicitly' in terms of the independent variable. To give a function f explicitly is to provide a prescription for determining the output value of the function y in terms of the input value x:

   y = f(x.)

By contrast, the function is implicit if the value of y is obtained from x by solving an equation of the form:

   R(x,y) = 0.

   a. Implicit differentiation
   b. Automatic differentiation
   c. Ordinary differential equation
   d. Implicit function

32. In Geometry, the _____ is an algebraic curve defined by the equation

$$x^3 + y^3 - 3axy = 0$$

It forms a loop in the first quadrant with a double point at the origin and asymptote

$$x + y + a = 0$$

It is symmetrical about y = x.

a. Prolate cycloid
b. Folium of Descartes
c. Cochleoid
d. Curve

33. In calculus, a method called _____ can be applied to implicitly defined functions. This method is an application of the chain rule allowing one to calculate the derivative of a function given implicitly.

As explained in the introduction, y can be given as a function of x implicitly rather than explicitly. When we have an equation R(x,y) = 0, we may be able to solve it for y and then differentiate. However, sometimes it is simpler to differentiate R(x,y) with respect to x and then solve for dy / dx.

a. Ordinary differential equation
b. Automatic differentiation
c. Implicit function
d. Implicit differentiation

34. In mathematics, a _____ of a function of several variables is its derivative with respect to one of those variables with the others held constant (as opposed to the total derivative, in which all variables are allowed to vary.) Partial derivatives are useful in vector calculus and differential geometry.

The _____ of a function f with respect to the variable x is written as f'_x, $\partial_x f$, or $\partial f/\partial x$.

a. Level curve
b. Jacobian
c. Differentiation operator
d. Partial derivative

35. In geometry, a _____ is a special plane curve generated by the trace of a fixed point on a small circle that rolls within a larger circle. It is comparable to the cycloid but instead of the circle rolling along a line, it rolls within a circle. The red curve is a _____ traced as the smaller black circle rolls around inside the larger blue circle (parameters are R=3.0, r=1.0, and so k=3), giving a deltoid.

If the smaller circle has radius r, and the larger circle has radius R = kr, then the parametric equations for the curve can be given by either:

$$x(\theta) = (R - r)\cos\theta + r\cos\left(\frac{R-r}{r}\theta\right)$$
$$y(\theta) = (R - r)\sin\theta - r\sin\left(\frac{R-r}{r}\theta\right),$$

or:

$$x(\theta) = r(k-1)\cos\theta + r\cos((k-1)\theta)$$
$$y(\theta) = r(k-1)\sin\theta - r\sin((k-1)\theta).$$

If k is an integer, then the curve is closed, and has k cusps (i.e., sharp corners, where the curve is not differentiable.)

Chapter 3. THE DERIVATIVE

  a. Kappa curve
  c. Closed curve
  b. Bullet-nose curve
  d. Hypocycloid

36. In mathematics and elsewhere, the adjective _____ means 'fourth order', such as the function x^4. A _____ number is a number which equals the fourth power of an integer.
  a. 15 theorem
  c. Quartic
  b. Reduction
  d. BDDC

37. In mathematics, two vectors are _____ if they are perpendicular, i.e., they form a right angle. For example, a subway and the street above, although they do not physically intersect, are _____ if they cross at a right angle.
  a. ALGOR
  c. AUSM
  b. ACTRAN
  d. Orthogonal

38. In mathematics, _____ are a family of curves in the plane that intersect a given family of curves at right angles. The problem is classical, but is now understood by means of complex analysis; see for example harmonic conjugate.

For a family of level curves described by g(x,y) = C, where C is a constant, the _____ may be found as the level curves of a new function f(x,y) by solving the partial differential equation

$$\nabla f \cdot \nabla g = 0$$

for f(x,y).

  a. ACTRAN
  c. Infinitely near point
  b. ALGOR
  d. Orthogonal trajectories

39.

In differential calculus, _____ problems involve finding a rate that a quantity changes by relating the population of the earth. The rate of change is usually with respect to people who have died.

  a. Mean Value Theorem
  c. Visual Calculus
  b. Related rates
  d. Standard part function

40. In mathematics, a _____ is an approximation of a general function using a linear function (more precisely, an affine function.)

Given a differentiable function f of one real variable, Taylor's theorem for n=1 states that

$$f(x) = f(a) + f\,'(a)(x - a) + R_2$$

Chapter 3. THE DERIVATIVE

where R$_2$ is the remainder term. The _____ is obtained by dropping the remainder:

$$f(x) \approx f(a) + f'(a)(x-a)$$

which is true for x close to a.

a. Point of inflection
b. Lin-Tsien equation
c. Linear approximation
d. Smooth function

41. _____ is a property of functions that says -- roughly -- that if you zoom in on a point on the graph of the function (with equal scaling horizontally and vertically), the graph will eventually look like a straight line. More precisely, a function is locally linear at a point if and only if a tangent line exists at said point.

Thus, _____ is the graphical manifestation of differentiability.

a. 15 theorem
b. BDDC
c. Local linearity
d. BIBO stability

42. Integration is an important concept in mathematics, specifically in the field of calculus and, more broadly, mathematical analysis. Given a function f of a real variable x and an interval [a, b] of the real line, the _____

$$\int_a^b f(x)\, dx,$$

is defined informally to be the net signed area of the region in the xy-plane bounded by the graph of f, the x-axis, and the vertical lines x = a and x = b.

The term '_____' may also refer to the notion of antiderivative, a function F whose derivative is the given function f.

a. Integrand
b. Integral test for convergence
c. Indefinite integral
d. Integral

43. In infinitesimal calculus, a _____ is traditionally an infinitesimally small change in a variable. For example, if x is a variable, then a change in the value of x is often denoted Δx (or δx when this change is considered to be small.) The _____ dx represents such a change, but is infinitely small.

a. Local maximum
b. Differential
c. Dirichlet integral
d. The Method of Mechanical Theorems

44. The _____ in some data is the discrepancy between an exact value and some approximation to it. An _____ can occur because

1. the measurement of the data is not precise (due to the instruments), or
2. approximations are used instead of the real data (e.g., 3.14 instead of π.)

In the mathematical field of numerical analysis, the numerical stability of an algorithm in numerical analysis indicates how the error is propagated by the algorithm.

One commonly distinguishes between the relative error and the absolute error. The absolute error is the magnitude of the difference between the exact value and the approximation.

    a. AUSM   b. ALGOR
    c. ACTRAN   d. Approximation error

45. One commonly distinguishes between the _____ and the absolute error. The absolute error is the magnitude of the difference between the exact value and the approximation. The _____ is the absolute error divided by the magnitude of the exact value.

    a. Series acceleration   b. Numerical integration
    c. Meshfree methods   d. Relative error

46. The _____ of any solid, liquid, plasma, vacuum or theoretical object is how much three-dimensional space it occupies, often quantified numerically. One-dimensional figures (such as lines) and two-dimensional shapes (such as squares) are assigned zero _____ in the three-dimensional space. _____ is commonly presented in units such as mL or cm^3 (milliliters or cubic centimeters.)

    a. Dirac equation   b. Klein-Gordon equation
    c. Volume   d. Vector potential

Chapter 4. EXPONENTIAL, LOGARITHMIC, AND INVERSE TRIGONOMETRIC FUNCTIONS

1. In mathematics, the simplest case of _____ refers to the study of problems in which one seeks to minimize or maximize a real function by systematically choosing the values of real or integer variables from within an allowed set. This (a scalar real valued objective function) is actually a small subset of this field which comprises a large area of applied mathematics and generalizes to study of means to obtain 'best available' values of some objective function given a defined domain where the elaboration is on the types of functions and the conditions and nature of the objects in the problem domain.

   The first _____ technique, which is known as steepest descent, goes back to Gauss.

   a. AUSM
   b. ACTRAN
   c. ALGOR
   d. Optimization

2. In mathematics, the _____ of a function y = f(x) is a function that, in some fashion, 'undoes' the effect of f The _____ of f is denoted f^{-1}. The statements y=f(x) and x=f^{-1}(y) are equivalent.

   a. ACTRAN
   b. ALGOR
   c. AUSM
   d. Inverse

3. In mathematics, if f is a function from A to B then an _____ for f is a function in the opposite direction, from B to A, with the property that a round trip (a composition) from A to B to A (or from B to A to B) returns each element of the initial set to itself. Thus, if an input x into the function f produces an output y, then inputting y into the _____ f^{-1} (read f inverse, not to be confused with exponentiation) produces the output x. Not every function has an inverse; those that do are called invertible.

   a. Augustin Louis Cauchy
   b. Aristotle
   c. Augustin-Jean Fresnel
   d. Inverse function

4. The _____ of an angle is the ratio of the length of the opposite side to the length of the hypotenuse. In our case

   $$\sin A = \frac{\text{opposite}}{\text{hypotenuse}} = \frac{a}{h}.$$

   Note that this ratio does not depend on size of the particular right triangle chosen, as long as it contains the angle A, since all such triangles are similar.

   The cosine of an angle is the ratio of the length of the adjacent side to the length of the hypotenuse.

   a. Trigonometric
   b. Trigonometric functions
   c. Sine integral
   d. Sine

5. In vector calculus, the _____ is an operator that measures the magnitude of a vector field's source or sink at a given point; the _____ of a vector field is a (signed) scalar. For example, consider air as it is heated or cooled. The relevant vector field for this example is the velocity of the moving air at a point.

   a. Green's theorem
   b. Divergence
   c. Triple product
   d. Gradient theorem

6. In vector calculus, the _____ Ostrogradskye;s theorem the _____ states that the outward flux of a vector field through a surface is equal to the triple integral of the divergence on the region inside the surface. Intuitively, it states that the sum of all sources minus the sum of all sinks gives the net flow out of a region.

Chapter 4. EXPONENTIAL, LOGARITHMIC, AND INVERSE TRIGONOMETRIC FUNCTIONS

a. Del
b. Divergence
c. Divergence Theorem
d. Green's theorem

7. In mathematics, the _____ (or replacement set) of a given function is the set of 'input' values for which the function is defined. For instance, the _____ of cosine would be all real numbers, while the _____ of the square root would be only numbers greater than or equal to 0 (ignoring complex numbers in both cases.) In a representation of a function in a xy Cartesian coordinate system, the _____ is represented on the x axis (or abscissa.)
   a. Domain
   b. BDDC
   c. BIBO stability
   d. 15 theorem

8. In mathematics, the _____ of a function is the set of all 'output' values produced by that function. Sometimes it is called the image, or more precisely, the image of the domain of the function. If a function is a surjection then its _____ is equal to its codomain.
   a. Piecewise-defined function
   b. Constant function
   c. Surjective
   d. Range

9. In mathematics, a (topological) _____ is defined as follows: let I be an interval of real numbers (i.e. a non-empty connected subset of $\mathbb{R}$); then a _____ γ is a continuous mapping $\gamma : I \to X$, where X is a topological space. The _____ γ is said to be simple if it is injective, i.e. if for all x, y in I, we have $\gamma(x) = \gamma(y) \implies x = y$. If I is a closed bounded interval $[a, b]$, we also allow the possibility $\gamma(a) = \gamma(b)$ (this convention makes it possible to talk about closed simple _____.)
   a. Curve
   b. Prolate cycloid
   c. Closed curve
   d. Tractrix

10. In mathematics, the _____ is a test used to determine if a function is injective, surjective or bijective.

Suppose there is a function f : X → Y with a graph., and you have a horizontal line of X x Y :
$y_0 \in Y, \{(x, y_0) : x \in X\} = (X \times y_0)$.

- If the function is injective, then it can be visualized as one whose graph is never intersected by any horizontal line more than once.
- If and only if f is surjective, any horizontal line will intersect the graph at least at one point (when the horizontal line is in the codomain.)
- If f is bijective, any horizontal line will intersect the graph at exactly one point.

This test is also used to find whether or not the inverse of the function is indeed a function as well. This is due to the reflective properties of the function over y=x.

   a. Horizontal line test
   b. 15 theorem
   c. BDDC
   d. BIBO stability

11. Let S be a set with a binary operation * . If e is an identity element of (S, *) and a * b = e, then a is called a _____ of b and b is called a right inverse of a. If an element x is both a _____ and a right inverse of y, then x is called a two-sided inverse, or simply an inverse, of y.

Chapter 4. EXPONENTIAL, LOGARITHMIC, AND INVERSE TRIGONOMETRIC FUNCTIONS

a. Left inverse
b. Completing the square
c. Closed-form expression
d. Hurwitz quaternion order

12. An injective function is called an injection, and is also said to be a _____ function (not to be confused with _____ correspondence, i.e. a bijective function.)

A function f that is not injective is sometimes called many-to-one. (However, this terminology is also sometimes used to mean 'single-valued', i.e. each argument is mapped to at most one value.)

a. Onto
b. Injective function
c. One-to-one
d. One-to-one function

13. An injective function is called an injection, and is also said to be a _____ (not to be confused with one-to-one correspondence, i.e. a bijective function.)

A function f that is not injective is sometimes called many-to-one. (However, this terminology is also sometimes used to mean 'single-valued', i.e. each argument is mapped to at most one value.)

a. One-to-one
b. One-to-one function
c. Injective function
d. Onto

14. f'(x) is twice the absolute value function, and it does not have a derivative at zero. Similar examples show that a function can have k derivatives for any non-negative integer k but no (k + 1)-order derivative. A function that has k successive derivatives is called _____.

a. Differential calculus
b. K times differentiable
c. Power series
d. Differential coefficient

15. In calculus, a branch of mathematics, the _____ is a measurement of how a function changes when its input changes. Loosely speaking, a _____ can be thought of as how much a quantity is changing at some given point. For example, the _____ of the position (or distance) of a vehicle with respect to time is the instantaneous velocity (respectively, instantaneous speed) at which the vehicle is traveling.

The process of finding a _____ is called differentiation. The fundamental theorem of calculus states that differentiation is the reverse process to integration.

a. Derivative
b. Stationary phase approximation
c. Bounded function
d. Semi-differentiability

16. In mathematics, a _____ of a function of several variables is its derivative with respect to one of those variables with the others held constant (as opposed to the total derivative, in which all variables are allowed to vary.) Partial derivatives are useful in vector calculus and differential geometry.

The _____ of a function f with respect to the variable x is written as f'_x, $\partial_x f$, or $\partial f/\partial x$.

44   Chapter 4. EXPONENTIAL, LOGARITHMIC, AND INVERSE TRIGONOMETRIC FUNCTIONS

a. Jacobian
c. Level curve

b. Differentiation operator
d. Partial derivative

17. The _____ is a function in mathematics. The application of this function to a value x is written as exp(x). Equivalently, this can be written in the form e^x, where e is a mathematical constant, the base of the natural logarithm, which equals approximately 2.718281828, and is also known as Euler's number.

a. ACTRAN
c. Area hyperbolic functions

b. Exponential function
d. Integral part

18. The _____, formerly known as the hyperbolic logarithm, is the logarithm to the base e, where e is an irrational constant approximately equal to 2.718281828. It is also sometimes referred to as the Napierian logarithm, although the original meaning of this term is slightly different. In simple terms, the _____ of a number x is the power to which e would have to be raised to equal x -- for example the natural log of e itself is 1 because e^1 = e, while the _____ of 1 would be 0, since $e^0 = 1$.

a. 15 theorem
c. BIBO stability

b. BDDC
d. Natural logarithm

19. The function $\log_b(x)$ depends on both b and x, but the term _____ in standard usage refers to a function of the form $\log_b(x)$ in which the base b is fixed and so the only argument is x. Thus there is one _____ for each value of the base b (which must be positive and must differ from 1.) Viewed in this way, the base-b _____ is the inverse function of the exponential function b^x.

a. BDDC
c. BIBO stability

b. 15 theorem
d. Logarithm function

20. _____ (including exponential decay) occurs when the growth rate of a mathematical function is proportional to the function's current value. In the case of a discrete domain of definition with equal intervals it is also called geometric growth or geometric decay (the function values form a geometric progression.)

_____ is said to follow an exponential law; the simple-_____ model is known as the Malthusian growth model.

a. Oscillating
c. Inseparable differential equation

b. Exponential growth
d. Isomonodromic deformation

21. In mathematics, specifically in calculus and complex analysis, the _____ of a function f is defined by the formula

$$\frac{f'}{f}$$

where f ' is the derivative of f.

When f is a function f(x) of a real variable x, and takes real, strictly positive values, this is indeed the formula for (log f)', that is, the derivative of the natural logarithm of f, as follows directly from the chain rule.

Many properties of the real logarithm also apply to the _____, even when the function does not take values in the positive reals.

Chapter 4. EXPONENTIAL, LOGARITHMIC, AND INVERSE TRIGONOMETRIC FUNCTIONS

a. Lin-Tsien equation
c. Directional derivative
b. Point of inflection
d. Logarithmic derivative

22. This article will state and prove the _____ for differentiation, and then use it to prove these two formulas.

The _____ for differentiation states that for every natural number n, the derivative of $f(x) = x^n$ is $f'(x) = nx^{n-1}$, that is,

$$(x^n)' = nx^{n-1}.$$

The _____ for integration

$$\int x^n \, dx = \frac{x^{n+1}}{n+1} + C$$

for natural n is then an easy consequence. One just needs to take the derivative of this equality and use the _____ and linearity of differentiation on the right-hand side.

a. Test for Divergence
c. Leibniz rule
b. Functional integration
d. Power rule

23. In calculus, _____ gives a sequence of approximations of a differentiable function around a given point by polynomials (the Taylor polynomials of that function) whose coefficients depend only on the derivatives of the function at that point. The theorem also gives precise estimates on the size of the error in the approximation. The theorem is named after the mathematician Brook Taylor, who stated it in 1712, though the result was first discovered 41 years earlier in 1671 by James Gregory.

a. Local minimum
c. Fresnel integrals
b. Related rates
d. Taylor's theorem

24. The _____ of an angle is the ratio of the length of the adjacent side to the length of the hypotenuse. In our case

$$\cos A = \frac{\text{adjacent}}{\text{hypotenuse}} = \frac{b}{h}.$$

The tangent of an angle is the ratio of the length of the opposite side to the length of the adjacent side. In our case

$$\tan A = \frac{\text{opposite}}{\text{adjacent}} = \frac{a}{b}.$$

The remaining three functions are best defined using the above three functions.

46   *Chapter 4. EXPONENTIAL, LOGARITHMIC, AND INVERSE TRIGONOMETRIC FUNCTIONS*

a. Cosine
b. Sine integral
c. Trigonometric functions
d. Trigonometric

25. In mathematics, the _____ or cyclometric functions are the inverse functions of the trigonometric functions. The principal inverses are listed in the following table.

If x is allowed to be a complex number, then the range of y applies only to its real part.

a. AUSM
b. Inverse trigonometric functions
c. ACTRAN
d. ALGOR

26. Trigonometry is a branch of mathematics that deals with triangles, particularly those plane triangles in which one angle has 90 degrees (right triangles.) Trigonometry deals with relationships between the sides and the angles of triangles and with the _____ functions, which describe those relationships.

Trigonometry has applications in both pure mathematics and in applied mathematics, where it is essential in many branches of science and technology.

a. Trigonometric integrals
b. Trigonometric
c. Sine
d. Trigonometric functions

27. In mathematics, the _____ are functions of an angle. They are important in the study of triangles and modeling periodic phenomena, among many other applications. _____ are commonly defined as ratios of two sides of a right triangle containing the angle, and can equivalently be defined as the lengths of various line segments from a unit circle.

a. Trigonometric
b. Trigonometric integrals
c. Trigonometric functions
d. Sine integral

28. In geometry, the _____ (or simply the tangent) to a curve at a given point is the straight line that 'just touches' the curve at that point (in the sense explained more precisely below.) As it passes through the point of tangency, the _____ is 'going in the same direction' as the curve, and in this sense it is the best straight-line approximation to the curve at that point. The same definition applies to space curves and curves in n-dimensional Euclidean space.

a. Tangent line
b. North pole
c. Lie derivative
d. Minimal surface

29. In calculus and other branches of mathematical analysis, an _____ is an algebraic expression obtained in the context of limits. Limits involving algebraic operations are often performed by replacing subexpressions by their limits; if the expression obtained after this substitution does not give enough information to determine the original limit, it is known as an _____. The indeterminate forms include 0^0, $0/0$, 1^∞, $\infty - \infty$, ∞/∞, $0\times\infty$, and ∞^0.

a. AUSM
b. Indeterminate form
c. ALGOR
d. ACTRAN

30. _____ is a type of motion in which the velocity of an object changes equal amounts in equal time periods. An example of an object having _____ would be a ball rolling down a ramp. The object picks up velocity as it goes down the ramp with equal changes in time.

Chapter 4. EXPONENTIAL, LOGARITHMIC, AND INVERSE TRIGONOMETRIC FUNCTIONS

a. ACTRAN
c. AUSM
b. Uniform Acceleration
d. ALGOR

31. In mathematics, a _____ is a function whose values do not vary and thus are constant. For example, if we have the function f(x) = 4, then f is constant since f maps any value to 4. More formally, a function f : A → B is a _____ if f(x) = f(y) for all x and y in A.
   a. Range
   c. Surjective
   b. Constant function
   d. Piecewise-defined function

32. In mathematics, a _____ is a function which preserves the given order. This concept first arose in calculus, and was later generalized to the more abstract setting of order theory.

In calculus, a function f defined on a subset of the real numbers with real values is called monotonic (also monotonically increasing or non-decreasing), if for all x and y such that x >≤ y one has f(x) >≤ f(y), so f preserves the order.

   a. Pettis integral
   c. Monotonic function
   b. 15 theorem
   d. Pseudo-differential operator

33. In differential calculus, an inflection point, or _____ (or inflexion) is a point on a curve at which the curvature changes sign. The curve changes from being concave upwards (positive curvature) to concave downwards (negative curvature), or vice versa. If one imagines driving a vehicle along the curve, it is a point at which the steering-wheel is momentarily 'straight', being turned from left to right or vice versa.
   a. Lin-Tsien equation
   c. Logarithmic derivative
   b. Derivative of a constant
   d. Point of inflection

34. In mathematics, _____ and minima, known collectively as extrema, are the largest value (maximum) or smallest value (minimum), that a function takes in a point either within a given neighbourhood (local extremum) or on the function domain in its entirety (global extremum.)

Throughout, a point refers to an input (x), while a value refers to an output (y): one distinguishing between the maximum value and the point (or points) at which it occurs.

A real-valued function f defined on the real line is said to have a local maximum point at the point x^*, if there exists some ε > 0, such that $f(x^*) \geq f(x)$ when $|x - x^*| < ε$.

   a. Leibniz formula
   c. Maxima
   b. Racetrack principle
   d. Related rates

35. A _____ in biology generally concerns a measured property such as population size, body height or biomass. Values for the measured property can be plotted on a graph as a function of time.
   a. Variation of parameters
   c. Spectral theory of ordinary differential equations
   b. Cauchy-Euler equation
   d. Growth curve

Chapter 5. THE DERIVATIVE IN GRAPHING AND APPLICATIONS

1. In mathematics, a _____ is an ordered list of objects (or events). Like a set, it contains members (also called elements or terms), and the number of terms (possibly infinite) is called the length of the _____. Unlike a set, order matters, and the exact same elements can appear multiple times at different positions in the _____.

   a. 15 theorem
   b. Y-intercept
   c. Slope
   d. Sequence

2. In mathematics, a _____ (or critical number) is a point on the domain of a function where:

   - one dimension: the derivative (or slope of the line when visualized) is equal to zero or a point where the function ceases to be differentiable.
   - in general: there are two distinct concepts: either the derivative (Jacobian) vanishes, or it is not of full rank (or, in either case, the function is not differentiable); these agree in one dimension.

   Note that in one dimension, a critical value or critical number x of function f is the domain element at which the derivative is zero or undefined, whereas the associated ordered pair (x, y) is the _____. In higher dimensions a critical value is in the range whereas a _____ is in the domain.

   There are two situations in which a point becomes a _____ of a function of one variable. The first of which is that the value of the first derivative is equal to zero.

   a. Multivariable calculus
   b. Critical point
   c. Differentiation operator
   d. Total derivative

3. The _____ of an angle is the ratio of the length of the opposite side to the length of the hypotenuse. In our case

   $$\sin A = \frac{\text{opposite}}{\text{hypotenuse}} = \frac{a}{h}.$$

   Note that this ratio does not depend on size of the particular right triangle chosen, as long as it contains the angle A, since all such triangles are similar.

   The cosine of an angle is the ratio of the length of the adjacent side to the length of the hypotenuse.

   a. Sine integral
   b. Trigonometric
   c. Trigonometric functions
   d. Sine

4. In mathematics, particularly in calculus, a _____ is an input to a function where the derivative is zero (equivalently, the gradient is zero): where the function 'stops' increasing or decreasing (hence the name.)

   For the graph of a one-dimensional function, this corresponds to a point on the graph where the tangent is parallel to the x-axis. For the graph of a two-dimensional function, this corresponds to a point on the graph where the tangent plane is parallel to the xy plane.

   a. Continuously differentiable
   b. Stationary point
   c. Second derivative test
   d. Functional derivative

Chapter 5. THE DERIVATIVE IN GRAPHING AND APPLICATIONS

5. In calculus, a branch of mathematics, the _____ is a measurement of how a function changes when its input changes. Loosely speaking, a _____ can be thought of as how much a quantity is changing at some given point. For example, the _____ of the position (or distance) of a vehicle with respect to time is the instantaneous velocity (respectively, instantaneous speed) at which the vehicle is traveling.

The process of finding a _____ is called differentiation. The fundamental theorem of calculus states that differentiation is the reverse process to integration.

   a. Semi-differentiability
   b. Stationary phase approximation
   c. Bounded function
   d. Derivative

6. In calculus, the _____ determines whether a given critical point of a function is a maximum, a minimum, or neither.

Suppose that f is a function and we want to determine if f has a maximum or minimum at x. If f is increasing to the left of x and decreasing to the right of x, then x is a local maximum of f.

   a. Partial sum
   b. Continuous function
   c. Test for Divergence
   d. First derivative test

7. Let f be a differentiable function, and let f'(x) be its derivative. The derivative of f'(x) (if it has one) is written f''(x) and is called the _____ of f. Similarly, the derivative of a _____, if it exists, is written f'''(x) and is called the third derivative of f.

   a. Stationary phase approximation
   b. Slant asymptote
   c. Vertical asymptote
   d. Second derivative

8. In calculus, a branch of mathematics, the _____ is a criterion often useful for determining whether a given stationary point of a function is a local maximum or a local minimum.

The test states: If the function f is twice differentiable at a stationary point x, meaning that $f'(x) = 0$, then:

- If $f''(x) < 0$ then f has a local maximum at x.
- If $f''(x) > 0$ then f has a local minimum at x.
- If $f''(x) = 0$, the _____ says nothing about the point x, has a possible inflection point.

In the last case, the function may have a local maximum or minimum there, but the function is sufficiently 'flat' that this is undetected by the second derivative. In this case one has to examine the third derivative. Such an example is f(x) = x^4.

   a. Second derivative test
   b. Linearity of differentiation
   c. Stationary point
   d. Symmetric derivative

Chapter 5. THE DERIVATIVE IN GRAPHING AND APPLICATIONS

9. In differential calculus, an inflection point, or _____ (or inflexion) is a point on a curve at which the curvature changes sign. The curve changes from being concave upwards (positive curvature) to concave downwards (negative curvature), or vice versa. If one imagines driving a vehicle along the curve, it is a point at which the steering-wheel is momentarily 'straight', being turned from left to right or vice versa.

   a. Logarithmic derivative
   b. Lin-Tsien equation
   c. Derivative of a constant
   d. Point of inflection

10. In computer science and information science, _____ could also be a method or an algorithm. Again, an example will illustrate: There are systems of counting, as with Roman numerals, and various systems for filing papers, or catalogues, and various library systems, of which the Dewey Decimal _____ is an example. This still fits with the definition of components which are connected together (in this case in order to facilitate the flow of information.)

   a. BDDC
   b. System
   c. 15 theorem
   d. BIBO stability

11. An _____ of a real-valued function y = f(x) is a curve which describes the behavior of f as either x or y tends to infinity.

In other words, as one moves along the graph of f(x) in some direction, the distance between it and the _____ eventually becomes smaller than any distance that one may specify.

   a. AUSM
   b. Asymptote
   c. ALGOR
   d. ACTRAN

12. In mathematics, a (topological) _____ is defined as follows: let I be an interval of real numbers (i.e. a non-empty connected subset of $\mathbb{R}$); then a _____ γ is a continuous mapping $\gamma : I \to X$, where X is a topological space. The _____ γ is said to be simple if it is injective, i.e. if for all x, y in I, we have $\gamma(x) = \gamma(y) \implies x = y$. If I is a closed bounded interval $[a, b]$, we also allow the possibility $\gamma(a) = \gamma(b)$ (this convention makes it possible to talk about closed simple _____.)

   a. Closed curve
   b. Prolate cycloid
   c. Tractrix
   d. Curve

13. In mathematics, a _____ of a function of several variables is its derivative with respect to one of those variables with the others held constant (as opposed to the total derivative, in which all variables are allowed to vary.) Partial derivatives are useful in vector calculus and differential geometry.

The _____ of a function f with respect to the variable x is written as f'$_x$, $\partial_x f$, or $\partial f/\partial x$.

   a. Differentiation operator
   b. Jacobian
   c. Level curve
   d. Partial derivative

14. In mathematics, _____ and minima, known collectively as extrema, are the largest value (maximum) or smallest value (minimum), that a function takes in a point either within a given neighbourhood (local extremum) or on the function domain in its entirety (global extremum.)

Chapter 5. THE DERIVATIVE IN GRAPHING AND APPLICATIONS

Throughout, a point refers to an input (x), while a value refers to an output (y): one distinguishing between the maximum value and the point (or points) at which it occurs.

A real-valued function f defined on the real line is said to have a local maximum point at the point x^*, if there exists some $\varepsilon > 0$, such that $f(x^*) \geq f(x)$ when $|x - x^*| < \varepsilon$.

    a. Maxima
    b. Related rates
    c. Racetrack principle
    d. Leibniz formula

15. _____ generally conveys two primary meanings. The first is an imprecise sense of harmonious or aesthetically-pleasing proportionality and balance; such that it reflects beauty or perfection. The second meaning is a precise and well-defined concept of balance or 'patterned self-similarity' that can be demonstrated or proved according to the rules of a formal system: by geometry, through physics or otherwise.

    a. BDDC
    b. BIBO stability
    c. 15 theorem
    d. Symmetry

16. In coordinate geometry, the _____ is the y-value of the point where the graph of a function or relation intercepts the y-axis of the coordinate system.

In other words, the _____ of a function is the y-value of the point at which it intersects the line x=0 (the y-axis.) Thus, if the function is specified in form y = f(x), the _____ is easy to find by calculating f.

    a. Y-intercept
    b. 15 theorem
    c. Sequence
    d. Slope

17. In mathematics, a _____ is any function which can be written as the ratio of two polynomial functions.

$$y = \frac{x^2 - 3x - 2}{x^2 - 4}$$

In the case of one variable, x, a _____ is a function of the form

$$f(x) = \frac{P(x)}{Q(x)}$$

where P and Q are polynomial function in x and Q is not the zero polynomial. The domain of f is the set of all points x for which the denominator Q(x) is not zero.

    a. BDDC
    b. BIBO stability
    c. 15 theorem
    d. Rational function

Chapter 5. THE DERIVATIVE IN GRAPHING AND APPLICATIONS

18. In geometry, the _____ (or simply the tangent) to a curve at a given point is the straight line that 'just touches' the curve at that point (in the sense explained more precisely below.) As it passes through the point of tangency, the _____ is 'going in the same direction' as the curve, and in this sense it is the best straight-line approximation to the curve at that point. The same definition applies to space curves and curves in n-dimensional Euclidean space.

   a. Lie derivative
   b. Minimal surface
   c. Tangent line
   d. North pole

19. In mathematics, especially in order theory, an _____ of a subset S of some partially ordered set (P, >≤) is an element of P which is greater than or equal to every element of S. The term lower bound is defined dually as an element of P which is lesser than or equal to every element of S. A set with an _____ is said to be bounded from above by that bound, a set with a lower bound is said to be bounded from below by that bound.

A subset S of a partially ordered set P may fail to have any bounds or may have many different upper and lower bounds. By transitivity, any element greater than or equal to an _____ of S is again an _____ of S, and any element lesser than or equal to any lower bound of S is again a lower bound of S. This leads to the consideration of least upper bounds: (or suprema) and greatest lower bounds (or infima.)

   a. Upper bound
   b. ACTRAN
   c. ALGOR
   d. AUSM

20. The _____ is a function in mathematics. The application of this function to a value x is written as exp(x). Equivalently, this can be written in the form e^x, where e is a mathematical constant, the base of the natural logarithm, which equals approximately 2.718281828, and is also known as Euler's number.

   a. Exponential function
   b. Integral part
   c. ACTRAN
   d. Area hyperbolic functions

21. In physics, _____ is defined as the rate of change of position. it is vector physical quantity; both speed and direction are required to define it. In the SI (metric) system, it is measured in meters per second: (m/s) or ms^{-1}.

   a. BDDC
   b. 15 theorem
   c. BIBO stability
   d. Velocity

22. In physics, and more specifically kinematics, _____ is the change in velocity over time. Because velocity is a vector, it can change in two ways: a change in magnitude and/or a change in direction. In one dimension, _____ is the rate at which something speeds up or slows down.

   a. AUSM
   b. ACTRAN
   c. ALGOR
   d. Acceleration

23. In a totally ordered set all elements are mutually comparable, so such a set can have at most one minimal element and at most one maximal element. Then, due to mutual comparability, the minimal element will also be the least element and the maximal element will also be the greatest element. Thus in a totally ordered set we can simply use the terms minimum and _____.

   a. Nth term
   b. Leibniz rule
   c. Racetrack principle
   d. Maximum

Chapter 5. THE DERIVATIVE IN GRAPHING AND APPLICATIONS

24. In a totally ordered set all elements are mutually comparable, so such a set can have at most one minimal element and at most one maximal element. Then, due to mutual comparability, the minimal element will also be the least element and the maximal element will also be the greatest element. Thus in a totally ordered set we can simply use the terms _____ and maximum.

   a. Minimum
   b. Nth term
   c. Maximum
   d. Ghosts of departed quantities

25. In calculus, _____, was originally the use of expressions such as dx and dy and to represent 'infinitely small' (or infinitesimal) increments of quantities x and y, just as >Δx and >Δy represent finite increments of x and y respectively. So for y being a function of x, or

   the derivative of y with respect to x, which later came to be viewed as

   was, according to Leibniz, the quotient of an infinitesimal increment of y by an infinitesimal increment of x, or

   where the right hand side is Lagrange's notation for the derivative of f at x.

   Similarly, although mathematicians usually now view an integral

   as a limit

   where >Δx is an interval containing x_i, Leibniz viewed it as the sum (the integral sign denoting summation) of infinitely many infinitesimal quantities f(x) dx.

   a. Stationary point
   b. Smooth function
   c. Time derivative
   d. Leibniz's notation

26. The largest and the smallest element of a set are called extreme values, absolute extrema, or extreme records.

Chapter 5. THE DERIVATIVE IN GRAPHING AND APPLICATIONS

For a differentiable function f, if $f(x_0)$ is an _____ for the set of all values f(x), and if x_0 is in the interior of the domain of f, then x_0 is a critical point, by Fermat's theorem.

In the case of a general partial order one should not confuse a least element (smaller than all other) and a minimal element (nothing is smaller.)

    a. Infinitesimal
    c. Integration by substitution
    b. Extreme Value Theorem
    d. Extreme value

27. In mathematics, an _____ is a theorem with a statement beginning 'there exist(s) ..' y, ... there exist(s) ...'. That is, in more formal terms of symbolic logic, it is a theorem with a statement involving the existential quantifier.
    a. ALGOR
    c. AUSM
    b. ACTRAN
    d. Existence theorem

28. Cantor defined two kinds of _____ numbers, the ordinal numbers and the cardinal numbers. Ordinal numbers may be identified with well-ordered sets, or counting carried on to any stopping point, including points after an _____ number have already been counted. Generalizing finite and the ordinary _____ sequences which are maps from the positive integers leads to mappings from ordinal numbers, and transfinite sequences.
    a. ACTRAN
    c. ALGOR
    b. AUSM
    d. Infinite

29. In metric topology and related fields of mathematics, a set U is called _____ if, intuitively speaking, starting from any point x in U one can move by a small amount in any direction and still be in the set U. In other words, the distance between any point x in U and the edge of U is always greater than zero.

As an example, consider the _____ interval (0, 1) consisting of all real numbers x with 0 < x < 1. Here, the topology is the usual topology on the real line. We can look at this in two ways.

    a. AUSM
    c. Open
    b. ACTRAN
    d. ALGOR

30. In mathematics, _____ are a method of defining a curve. A simple kinematical example is when one uses a time parameter to determine the position, velocity, and other information about a body in motion.

Abstractly, a relation is given in the form of an equation, and it is shown also to be the image of functions from items such as R^n.

    a. Shift theorem
    c. Partial derivative
    b. Critical point
    d. Parametric equations

Chapter 5. THE DERIVATIVE IN GRAPHING AND APPLICATIONS

31. In mathematics, the simplest case of _____ refers to the study of problems in which one seeks to minimize or maximize a real function by systematically choosing the values of real or integer variables from within an allowed set. This (a scalar real valued objective function) is actually a small subset of this field which comprises a large area of applied mathematics and generalizes to study of means to obtain 'best available' values of some objective function given a defined domain where the elaboration is on the types of functions and the conditions and nature of the objects in the problem domain.

The first _____ technique, which is known as steepest descent, goes back to Gauss.

a. ALGOR
b. AUSM
c. ACTRAN
d. Optimization

32. The method of _____ or ordinary _____ is used to solve overdetermined systems. _____ is often applied in statistical contexts, particularly regression analysis.

_____ can be interpreted as a method of fitting data. The best fit in the _____ sense is that instance of the model for which the sum of squared residuals has its least value, a residual being the difference between an observed value and the value given by the model.

a. 15 theorem
b. BDDC
c. BIBO stability
d. Least squares

33. In mathematics, a _____ is a method for approximating the total area underneath a curve on a graph, otherwise known as an integral. It may also be used to define the integration operation.

Consider a function $f: D \to \mathbf{R}$, where D is a subset of the real numbers $\mathbf{R}$, and let $I = [a, b]$ be a closed interval contained in D. A finite set of points $\{x_0, x_1, x_2, ... x_n\}$ such that $a = x_0 < x_1 < x_2 ... < x_n = b$ creates a partition

$$P = \{[x_0, x_1), [x_1, x_2), ... [x_{n-1}, x_n]\}$$

of I.

a. Risch algorithm
b. Signed measure
c. Solid of revolution
d. Riemann sum

34. A quadratic equation with real or complex coefficients has two solutions (or roots), not necessarily distinct, which may or may not be real, given by the _____:

$$\frac{-b \pm \sqrt{b^2 - 4ac}}{2a}$$

Example discriminant signsâ– <0: $x^2+\frac{1}{2}$â– =0: $-\frac{4}{3}x^2+\frac{4}{3}x-\frac{1}{3}$â– >0: $\frac{3}{2}x^2+\frac{1}{2}x-\frac{4}{3}$

In the above formula, the expression underneath the square root sign

$$D = b^2 - 4ac,$$

is called the discriminant of the quadratic equation.

A quadratic equation with real coefficients can have either one or two distinct real roots, or two distinct complex roots. In this case the discriminant determines the number and nature of the roots.

a. Cubic function
b. Quadratic formula
c. Linear equation
d. Quartic function

35. Integration is an important concept in mathematics, specifically in the field of calculus and, more broadly, mathematical analysis. Given a function f of a real variable x and an interval [a, b] of the real line, the _____

$$\int_a^b f(x)\,dx,$$

is defined informally to be the net signed area of the region in the xy-plane bounded by the graph of f, the x-axis, and the vertical lines x = a and x = b.

The term '_____' may also refer to the notion of antiderivative, a function F whose derivative is the given function f.

a. Integrand
b. Indefinite integral
c. Integral test for convergence
d. Integral

36. _____ is a type of motion in which the velocity of an object changes equal amounts in equal time periods. An example of an object having _____ would be a ball rolling down a ramp. The object picks up velocity as it goes down the ramp with equal changes in time.
a. AUSM
b. ALGOR
c. ACTRAN
d. Uniform Acceleration

Chapter 6. INTEGRATION

1. In the branch of mathematics known as real analysis, the _____, created by Bernhard Riemann, was the first rigorous definition of the integral of a function on an interval. While the _____ is unsuitable for many theoretical purposes, it is one of the easiest integrals to define. Some of these technical deficiencies can be remedied by the Riemann-Stieltjes integral, and most of them disappear in the Lebesgue integral.
    a. Riemann integral
    b. Lebesgue integration
    c. Skorokhod integral
    d. Regulated integral

2. In infinitesimal calculus, a _____ is traditionally an infinitesimally small change in a variable. For example, if x is a variable, then a change in the value of x is often denoted Δx (or δx when this change is considered to be small.) The _____ dx represents such a change, but is infinitely small.
    a. Dirichlet integral
    b. Differential
    c. Local maximum
    d. The Method of Mechanical Theorems

3. _____, a field in mathematics, is the study of how functions change when their inputs change. The primary object of study in _____ is the derivative. A closely related notion is the differential.
    a. Ramp function
    b. Differential calculus
    c. Concave downwards
    d. Slant asymptote

4. Integration is an important concept in mathematics, specifically in the field of calculus and, more broadly, mathematical analysis. Given a function f of a real variable x and an interval [a, b] of the real line, the _____

$$\int_a^b f(x)\,dx,$$

is defined informally to be the net signed area of the region in the xy-plane bounded by the graph of f, the x-axis, and the vertical lines x = a and x = b.

The term '_____' may also refer to the notion of antiderivative, a function F whose derivative is the given function f.

    a. Integral
    b. Indefinite integral
    c. Integral test for convergence
    d. Integrand

5. In mathematics, a (topological) _____ is defined as follows: let I be an interval of real numbers (i.e. a non-empty connected subset of $\mathbb{R}$); then a _____ γ is a continuous mapping $\gamma : I \to X$, where X is a topological space. The _____ γ is said to be simple if it is injective, i.e. if for all x, y in I, we have $\gamma(x) = \gamma(y) \implies x = y$. If I is a closed bounded interval $[a, b]$, we also allow the possibility $\gamma(a) = \gamma(b)$ (this convention makes it possible to talk about closed simple _____.)
    a. Closed curve
    b. Prolate cycloid
    c. Tractrix
    d. Curve

6. The _____ is a method of finding the area of a shape by inscribing inside it a sequence of polygons whose areas converge to the area of the containing shape. If the sequence is correctly constructed, the difference in area between the nth polygon and the containing shape will become arbitrarily small as n becomes large. As this difference becomes arbitrarily small, the possible values for the area of the shape are systematically 'exhausted' by the lower bound areas successively established by the sequence members.

a. BDDC
b. 15 theorem
c. Method of exhaustion
d. BIBO stability

7. In mathematics, _____, first defined by the mathematician Daniel Bernoulli and generalized by Friedrich Bessel, are canonical solutions y(x) of Bessel's differential equation:

$$x^2 \frac{d^2y}{dx^2} + x\frac{dy}{dx} + (x^2 - \alpha^2)y = 0$$

for an arbitrary real or complex number α (the order of the Bessel function.) The most common and important special case is where α is an integer n.

Although α and −α produce the same differential equation, it is conventional to define different _____ for these two orders (e.g., so that the _____ are mostly smooth functions of α.)

a. Multiplication theorem
b. Logarithmic integral function
c. 15 theorem
d. Bessel functions

8. In calculus, an _____, primitive or indefinite integral of a function f is a function F whose derivative is equal to f, i.e., F >' = f. The process of solving for antiderivatives is antidifferentiation (or indefinite integration.) Antiderivatives are related to definite integrals through the fundamental theorem of calculus: the definite integral of a function over an interval is equal to the difference between the values of an _____ evaluated at the endpoints of the interval.

a. Indefinite integral
b. Integrand
c. Order of integration
d. Antiderivative

9. In mathematics, specifically in integral calculus, the _____ computes an approximation to a definite integral, made by finding the area of a collection of rectangles whose heights are determined by the values of the function.

Specifically, the interval over which the function is to be integrated is divided into n equal subintervals of length Δ = / n. The rectangles are then drawn so that either their left or right corners, or the middle of their top line lies on the graph of the function, with bases running along the x-axis.

a. Rectangle method
b. Trigonometric substitution
c. Solid of revolution
d. Riemann sum

10. The _____ specifies the relationship between the two central operations of calculus, differentiation and integration.

The first part of the theorem, sometimes called the first _____, shows that an indefinite integration can be reversed by a differentiation.

The second part, sometimes called the second _____, allows one to compute the definite integral of a function by using any one of its infinitely many antiderivatives.

Chapter 6. INTEGRATION

a. Fundamental Theorem of Calculus
b. Limits of integration
c. Periodic function
d. Leibniz formula

11. In mathematics, a _____ is a method for approximating the total area underneath a curve on a graph, otherwise known as an integral. It may also be used to define the integration operation.

Consider a function $f: D \to R$, where D is a subset of the real numbers R, and let $I = [a, b]$ be a closed interval contained in D. A finite set of points $\{x_0, x_1, x_2, \ldots x_n\}$ such that $a = x_0 < x_1 < x_2 \ldots < x_n = b$ creates a partition

$$P = \{[x_0, x_1), [x_1, x_2), \ldots [x_{n-1}, x_n]\}$$

of I.

a. Solid of revolution
b. Signed measure
c. Risch algorithm
d. Riemann sum

12. _____ is a type of motion in which the velocity of an object changes equal amounts in equal time periods. An example of an object having _____ would be a ball rolling down a ramp. The object picks up velocity as it goes down the ramp with equal changes in time.
a. ALGOR
b. AUSM
c. ACTRAN
d. Uniform Acceleration

13. In calculus, the indefinite integral of a given function (i.e. the set of all antiderivatives of the function) is always written with a constant, the _____. This constant expresses an ambiguity inherent in the construction of antiderivatives. If a function f(x) is defined on an interval and F(x) is an antiderivative of f(x), then the set of all antiderivatives of f(x) is given by the functions F(x) + C, where C is an arbitrary constant.
a. Sum rule in integration
b. Nonelementary integral
c. Disk integration
d. Constant of integration

14. In calculus, an antiderivative, primitive or _____ of a function f is a function F whose derivative is equal to f, i.e., F ' = f. The process of solving for antiderivatives is antidifferentiation (or indefinite integration.) Antiderivatives are related to definite integrals through the fundamental theorem of calculus: the definite integral of a function over an interval is equal to the difference between the values of an antiderivative evaluated at the endpoints of the interval.
a. Integration by parts operator
b. Arc length
c. Indefinite integral
d. Integral test for convergence

15. If a function has an integral, it is said to be integrable. The function for which the integral is calculated is called the _____. The region over which a function is being integrated is called the domain of integration.
a. Integration by parts
b. Order of integration
c. Integral test for convergence
d. Integrand

16. In calculus, _____ gives a sequence of approximations of a differentiable function around a given point by polynomials (the Taylor polynomials of that function) whose coefficients depend only on the derivatives of the function at that point. The theorem also gives precise estimates on the size of the error in the approximation. The theorem is named after the mathematician Brook Taylor, who stated it in 1712, though the result was first discovered 41 years earlier in 1671 by James Gregory.

    a. Fresnel integrals   b. Local minimum
    c. Taylor's theorem   d. Related rates

17. In mathematics, the _____ of a function y = f(x) is a function that, in some fashion, 'undoes' the effect of f The _____ of f is denoted f^{-1}. The statements y=f(x) and $x=f^{-1}(y)$ are equivalent.

    a. Inverse   b. AUSM
    c. ACTRAN   d. ALGOR

18. In mathematics, the _____ or cyclometric functions are the inverse functions of the trigonometric functions. The principal inverses are listed in the following table.

If x is allowed to be a complex number, then the range of y applies only to its real part.

    a. ALGOR   b. AUSM
    c. ACTRAN   d. Inverse trigonometric functions

19. Trigonometry is a branch of mathematics that deals with triangles, particularly those plane triangles in which one angle has 90 degrees (right triangles.) Trigonometry deals with relationships between the sides and the angles of triangles and with the _____ functions, which describe those relationships.

Trigonometry has applications in both pure mathematics and in applied mathematics, where it is essential in many branches of science and technology.

    a. Trigonometric integrals   b. Trigonometric
    c. Sine   d. Trigonometric functions

20. In mathematics, the _____ are functions of an angle. They are important in the study of triangles and modeling periodic phenomena, among many other applications. _____ are commonly defined as ratios of two sides of a right triangle containing the angle, and can equivalently be defined as the lengths of various line segments from a unit circle.

    a. Trigonometric functions   b. Trigonometric
    c. Sine integral   d. Trigonometric integrals

21. A _____ is a mathematical equation for an unknown function of one or several variables that relates the values of the function itself and of its derivatives of various orders. they play a prominent role in engineering, physics, economics and other disciplines.

A simplified real world example of a _____ is modeling the acceleration of a ball falling through the air (considering only gravity and air resistance.)

Chapter 6. INTEGRATION

a. Structural stability
c. Phase line

b. Differential equation
d. Caloric polynomial

22. In mathematics, a _____ (or direction field) is a graphical representation of the solutions of a first-order differential equation. It is achieved without solving the differential equation analytically, and thence it is useful. The representation may be used to qualitatively visualise solutions, or to numerically approximate them.

a. Visual Calculus
c. Slope field

b. Continuous function
d. Leibniz function

23. In differential calculus, an inflection point, or _____ (or inflexion) is a point on a curve at which the curvature changes sign. The curve changes from being concave upwards (positive curvature) to concave downwards (negative curvature), or vice versa. If one imagines driving a vehicle along the curve, it is a point at which the steering-wheel is momentarily 'straight', being turned from left to right or vice versa.

a. Lin-Tsien equation
c. Point of inflection

b. Derivative of a constant
d. Logarithmic derivative

24. In mathematics, in the field of differential equations, an initial value problem is an ordinary differential equation together with specified value, called the _____, of the unknown function at a given point in the domain of the solution. In physics or other sciences, modeling a system frequently amounts to solving an initial value problem; in this context, the differential equation is an evolution equation specifying how, given initial conditions, the system will evolve with time.

An initial value problem is a differential equation

$$y'(t) = f(t, y(t)) \quad \text{with} \quad f : \mathbb{R} \times \mathbb{R} \to \mathbb{R}$$

together with a point in the domain of f

$$(t_0, y_0) \in \mathbb{R} \times \mathbb{R},$$

called the _____.

a. Initial condition
c. ACTRAN

b. AUSM
d. ALGOR

25. In mathematics, in the field of differential equations, an _____ is an ordinary differential equation together with specified value, called the initial condition, of the unknown function at a given point in the domain of the solution. In physics or other sciences, modeling a system frequently amounts to solving an _____; in this context, the differential equation is an evolution equation specifying how, given initial conditions, the system will evolve with time.

An _____ is a differential equation

$$y'(t) = f(t, y(t)) \quad \text{with} \quad f : \mathbb{R} \times \mathbb{R} \to \mathbb{R}$$

together with a point in the domain of f

$$(t_0, y_0) \in \mathbb{R} \times \mathbb{R},$$

called the initial condition.

- a. ALGOR
- b. AUSM
- c. ACTRAN
- d. Initial value problem

26. _____ is used to describe the steepness, incline, gradient, or grade of a straight line. A higher _____ value indicates a steeper incline. The _____ is defined as the ratio of the 'rise' divided by the 'run' between two points on a line, or in other words, the ratio of the altitude change to the horizontal distance between any two points on the line.
- a. Y-intercept
- b. 15 theorem
- c. Slope
- d. Sequence

27. The formula is used to transform one integral into another integral that is easier to compute. Thus, the formula can be used from left to right or from right to left in order to simplify a given integral. When used in the former manner, it is sometimes known as _____.
- a. Integration by substitution
- b. Extreme value
- c. U-substitution
- d. Extreme Value Theorem

28. The _____ is a fractal named after the Polish mathematician Wacław Sierpiński who described it in 1915.

Originally constructed as a curve, this is one of the basic examples of self-similar sets, i.e. it is a mathematically generated pattern that can be reproducible at any magnification or reduction.

Comparing the _____ or the Sierpinski carpet to equivalent repetitive tiling arrangements, it is evident that similar structures can be built into any rep-tile arrangements.

- a. BDDC
- b. 15 theorem
- c. BIBO stability
- d. Sierpinski triangle

29. A _____ is one of the most curvilinear basic geometric shapes: It has two faces, zero vertices, and zero edges. The surface formed by the points at a fixed distance from a given straight line, the axis of the _____. The solid enclosed by this surface and by two planes perpendicular to the axis is also called a _____.
- a. BDDC
- b. 15 theorem
- c. Right circular cylinder
- d. Cylinder

30. In mathematics, the concept of a '_____' is used to describe the behavior of a function as its argument or input either 'gets close' to some point, or as the argument becomes arbitrarily large; or the behavior of a sequence's elements as their index increases indefinitely. Limits are used in calculus and other branches of mathematical analysis to define derivatives and continuity.

In formulas, _____ is usually abbreviated as lim

a. BIBO stability
b. BDDC
c. 15 theorem
d. Limit

31. _____ is the addition of a set of numbers; the result is their sum or total. An interim or present total of a _____ process is termed the running total. The 'numbers' to be summed may be natural numbers, complex numbers, matrices, or still more complicated objects.

a. BIBO stability
b. Summation
c. 15 theorem
d. BDDC

32. In mathematics, a _____ is an informal expression referring to a series whose sum can be found by exploiting the circumstance that nearly every term cancels with either a succeeding or preceding term. Such a technique is also known as the method of differences.

For example, the series

$$\sum_{n=1}^{\infty} \frac{1}{n(n+1)}$$

simplifies as

$$\sum_{n=1}^{\infty} \frac{1}{n(n+1)} = \sum_{n=1}^{\infty} \left(\frac{1}{n} - \frac{1}{n+1}\right)$$
$$= \left(1 - \frac{1}{2}\right) + \left(\frac{1}{2} - \frac{1}{3}\right) + \cdots$$
$$= 1 + \left(-\frac{1}{2} + \frac{1}{2}\right) + \left(-\frac{1}{3} + \frac{1}{3}\right) + \cdots = 1.$$

Although telescoping can be a useful technique, there are pitfalls to watch out for:

$$0 = \sum_{n=1}^{\infty} 0 = \sum_{n=1}^{\infty}(1-1) = 1 + \sum_{n=1}^{\infty}(-1+1) = 1$$

is not correct because regrouping of terms is invalid unless the individual terms converge to 0; see Grandi's series.

a. Converge absolutely
b. Sequence transformation
c. Geometric series
d. Telescoping series

33. In calculus, _____, was originally the use of expressions such as dx and dy and to represent 'infinitely small' (or infinitesimal) increments of quantities x and y, just as >Δx and >Δy represent finite increments of x and y respectively. So for y being a function of x, or

the derivative of y with respect to x, which later came to be viewed as

was, according to Leibniz, the quotient of an infinitesimal increment of y by an infinitesimal increment of x, or

where the right hand side is Lagrange's notation for the derivative of f at x.

Similarly, although mathematicians usually now view an integral

as a limit

where $>\Delta x$ is an interval containing x_i, Leibniz viewed it as the sum (the integral sign denoting summation) of infinitely many infinitesimal quantities f(x) dx.

    a. Time derivative
    b. Smooth function
    c. Stationary point
    d. Leibniz's notation

34. In mathematics, the _____ is a representation of a function as an infinite sum of terms calculated from the values of its derivatives at a single point. It may be regarded as the limit of the Taylor polynomials. If the series is centered at zero, the series is also called a Maclaurin series.
    a. BDDC
    b. 15 theorem
    c. BIBO stability
    d. Taylor series

35. In mathematics, especially vector calculus and differential topology, a _____ is a differential form α whose differential is zero (dα = 0), and an exact form is a differential form that is the differential of another differential form β, a 'potential form' or 'primitive' for α, (α = dβ for some differential form β of one-step lower order. Since $d^2 = 0$, β is not unique, but can be modified by the addition of the differential of a two-step-lower-order form. This is called gauge transformation.)
    a. Soldering
    b. Hodge dual
    c. Differential ideal
    d. Closed form

36. In metric topology and related fields of mathematics, a set U is called _____ if, intuitively speaking, starting from any point x in U one can move by a small amount in any direction and still be in the set U. In other words, the distance between any point x in U and the edge of U is always greater than zero.

Chapter 6. INTEGRATION

As an example, consider the _____ interval (0, 1) consisting of all real numbers x with 0 < x < 1. Here, the topology is the usual topology on the real line. We can look at this in two ways.

   a. AUSM
   c. ALGOR
   b. Open
   d. ACTRAN

37. In mathematics, the _____, named after German mathematician Bernhard Riemann, is a prominent function of great significance in number theory because of its relation to the distribution of prime numbers. It also has applications in other areas such as physics, probability theory, and applied statistics.

The Riemann hypothesis, a conjecture about the distribution of the zeros of the _____, is considered by many mathematicians to be the most important unsolved problem in pure mathematics.

   a. Riemann zeta function
   c. 15 theorem
   b. BIBO stability
   d. BDDC

38. In numerical analysis, _____ constitutes a broad family of algorithms for calculating the numerical value of a definite integral, and by extension, the term is also sometimes used to describe the numerical solution of differential equations The term numerical quadrature is more or less a synonym for _____, especially as applied to one-dimensional integrals.

   a. Meshfree methods
   c. Galerkin methods
   b. Multigrid method
   d. Numerical integration

39. _____ is usually defined as the activity of using and developing computer technology, computer hardware and software. It is the computer-specific part of information technology. Computer science (or _____ science) is the study and the science of the theoretical foundations of information and computation and their implementation and application in computer systems.

   a. BIBO stability
   c. 15 theorem
   b. BDDC
   d. Computing

40. In mathematics, a _____ is the graph of the system of parametric equations

$$x = A\sin(at + \delta), \quad y = B\sin(bt),$$

which describes complex harmonic motion. This family of curves was investigated by Nathaniel Bowditch in 1815, and later in more detail by Jules Antoine Lissajous in 1857.

The appearance of the figure is highly sensitive to the ratio a/b.

   a. BDDC
   c. BIBO stability
   b. 15 theorem
   d. Lissajous curve

41. In mathematics, an _____ is a function whose integral exists. Unless specifically stated, the integral in question is usually the Lebesgue integral. Otherwise, one can say that the function is 'Riemann-integrable' (i.e., its Riemann integral exists), 'Henstock-Kurzweil-integrable,' etc.

   a. ACTRAN   b. Integrable function
   c. AUSM   d. ALGOR

42. In calculus and mathematical analysis the _____ of the integral

$$\int_a^b f(x)\,dx$$

of a Riemann integrable function f defined on a closed and bounded interval [a, b] are the real numbers a and b.

_____ can also be defined for improper integrals, with the _____ of both

$$\lim_{z \to a^+} \int_z^b f(x)\,dx$$

and

$$\lim_{z \to b^-} \int_a^z f(x)\,dx$$

again being a and b. For an improper integral

$$\int_a^\infty f(x)\,dx$$

or

$$\int_{-\infty}^b f(x)\,dx$$

the _____ are a and ∞, or −∞ and b, respectively.

   a. Maxima   b. Differential
   c. Limits of integration   d. Test for Divergence

43. In mathematics, a function f defined on some set X with real or complex values is a _____ function, if the set of its values is _____. In other words, there exists a number M>0 such that

$$|f(x)| \le M$$

for all x in X.

Sometimes, if $f(x) \leq A$ for all x in X, then the function is said to be _____ above by A.

a. Differential coefficient
b. Stationary phase approximation
c. Bounded
d. Concave upwards

44. In mathematics, a function f defined on some set X with real or complex values is a _____, if the set of its values is bounded. In other words, there exists a number M>0 such that

$$\boxed{} >$$

for all x in X.

Sometimes, if $\boxed{} >$ for all x in X, then the function is said to be bounded above by A.

a. Concave downwards
b. Bounded function
c. Concave upwards
d. Power series

45. The _____ of an angle is the ratio of the length of the opposite side to the length of the hypotenuse. In our case

$$\sin A = \frac{\text{opposite}}{\text{hypotenuse}} = \frac{a}{h}.$$

Note that this ratio does not depend on size of the particular right triangle chosen, as long as it contains the angle A, since all such triangles are similar.

The cosine of an angle is the ratio of the length of the adjacent side to the length of the hypotenuse.

a. Trigonometric functions
b. Trigonometric
c. Sine integral
d. Sine

46. In vector calculus, the _____ is an operator that measures the magnitude of a vector field's source or sink at a given point; the _____ of a vector field is a (signed) scalar. For example, consider air as it is heated or cooled. The relevant vector field for this example is the velocity of the moving air at a point.
a. Green's theorem
b. Triple product
c. Gradient theorem
d. Divergence

47. In vector calculus, the _____ Ostrogradskye;s theorem the _____ states that the outward flux of a vector field through a surface is equal to the triple integral of the divergence on the region inside the surface. Intuitively, it states that the sum of all sources minus the sum of all sinks gives the net flow out of a region.
a. Divergence
b. Divergence Theorem
c. Green's theorem
d. Del

Chapter 6. INTEGRATION

48. In calculus, a branch of mathematics, the _____ is a measurement of how a function changes when its input changes. Loosely speaking, a _____ can be thought of as how much a quantity is changing at some given point. For example, the _____ of the position (or distance) of a vehicle with respect to time is the instantaneous velocity (respectively, instantaneous speed) at which the vehicle is traveling.

The process of finding a _____ is called differentiation. The fundamental theorem of calculus states that differentiation is the reverse process to integration.

    a. Bounded function
    b. Semi-differentiability
    c. Stationary phase approximation
    d. Derivative

49. _____ is any physical or virtual entity that is owned by an individual or jointly by a group of individuals. An owner of _____ has the right to consume, sell, rent, mortgage, transfer and exchange his or her _____. Important widely-recognized types of _____ include real _____, personal _____ (other physical possessions), and intellectual _____ (rights over artistic creations, inventions, etc.), although the latter is not always as widely recognized or enforced.

    a. Property
    b. 15 theorem
    c. BIBO stability
    d. BDDC

50. A _____ is a set of standard clothing worn by members of an organization while participating in that organization's activity. Modern uniforms are worn by armed forces and paramilitary organisations such as police, emergency services, security guards, in some workplaces and schools and by inmates in prisons. In some countries, some other officials also wear uniforms in their duties; such is the case of the Commissioned Corps of the United States Public Health Service or the French prefects.

    a. ALGOR
    b. AUSM
    c. ACTRAN
    d. Uniform

51. _____ is the long dimension of any object. The _____ of a thing is the distance between its ends, its linear extent as measured from end to end. This may be distinguished from height, which is vertical extent, and width or breadth, which are the distance from side to side, measuring across the object at right angles to the _____.

    a. Length
    b. BDDC
    c. BIBO stability
    d. 15 theorem

52. In elementary mathematics, physics, and engineering, a _____ is a geometric object that has both a magnitude (or length), direction and sense, (i.e., orientation along the given direction.) A _____ is frequently represented by a line segment with a definite direction, or graphically as an arrow, connecting an initial point A with a terminal point B, and denoted by

$\boxed{\times}\!\!\!\rightarrow$.

The magnitude of the _____ is the length of the segment and the direction characterizes the displacement of B relative to A: how much one should move the point A to 'carry' it to the point B.

Many algebraic operations on real numbers have close analogues for vectors.

Chapter 6. INTEGRATION

    a. 15 theorem   b. BDDC
    c. Linear partial differential operator   d. Vector

53. In physics, _____ is defined as the rate of change of position. it is vector physical quantity; both speed and direction are required to define it. In the SI (metric) system, it is measured in meters per second: (m/s) or ms^{-1}.
    a. Velocity   b. BDDC
    c. BIBO stability   d. 15 theorem

54. In mathematics and statistics, the _____ of a list of numbers is the sum of all of the list divided by the number of items in the list. If the list is a statistical population, then the mean of that population is called a population mean. If the list is a statistical sample, we call the resulting statistic a sample mean.
    a. Arithmetic mean   b. AUSM
    c. ACTRAN   d. ALGOR

55. In mathematics, a _____ is a function for which, intuitively, small changes in the input result in small changes in the output. Otherwise, a function is said to be discontinuous. A _____ with a continuous inverse function is called bicontinuous. An intuitive though imprecise (and inexact) idea of continuity is given by the common statement that a _____ is a function whose graph can be drawn without lifting the chalk from the blackboard.
    a. Hyperbolic angle   b. Visual Calculus
    c. Continuous function   d. Binomial series

56. In probability theory and statistics, the _____ (or expectation value or mean and for continuous random variables with a density function it is the probability density -weighted integral of the possible values.

The term '_____' can be misleading.

    a. Expected value   b. AUSM
    c. ACTRAN   d. ALGOR

57. In physics, and more specifically kinematics, _____ is the change in velocity over time. Because velocity is a vector, it can change in two ways: a change in magnitude and/or a change in direction. In one dimension, _____ is the rate at which something speeds up or slows down.
    a. AUSM   b. Acceleration
    c. ACTRAN   d. ALGOR

58. A _____ is a statement of the meaning of a word or phrase. The term to be defined is known as the definiendum. The words which define it are known as the definiens.
    a. BIBO stability   b. BDDC
    c. 15 theorem   d. Definition

59. _____ is the study of algorithms for the problems of continuous mathematics (as distinguished from discrete mathematics.)

One of the earliest mathematical writings is the Babylonian tablet YBC 7289, which gives a sexagesimal numerical approximation of $\sqrt{2}$, the length of the diagonal in a unit square. Being able to compute the sides of a triangle (and hence, being able to compute square roots) is extremely important, for instance, in carpentry and construction.

    a. Numerical analysis   b. 15 theorem
    c. BIBO stability   d. BDDC

60. The _____ is a function in mathematics. The application of this function to a value x is written as exp(x). Equivalently, this can be written in the form e^x, where e is a mathematical constant, the base of the natural logarithm, which equals approximately 2.718281828, and is also known as Euler's number.

    a. Integral part   b. ACTRAN
    c. Exponential function   d. Area hyperbolic functions

61. A _____ officer is an officer of high military rank. The term or equivalent is used by nearly every country in the world. _____ can be used as a generic term for all grades of _____ officer, or it can specifically refer to a single rank that is just called _____.

    a. BDDC   b. 15 theorem
    c. General   d. BIBO stability

62. In mathematics, an _____ is a function built from a finite number of exponentials, logarithms, constants, one variable, and nth roots through composition and combinations using the four elementary operations (+ - × ÷.) The trigonometric functions and their inverses are assumed to be included in the elementary functions by using complex variables and the relations between the trigonometric functions and the exponential and logarithm functions.

Elementary functions are considered a subset of special functions.

    a. AUSM   b. ALGOR
    c. Elementary function   d. ACTRAN

63. The _____ of an angle is the ratio of the length of the adjacent side to the length of the hypotenuse. In our case

$$\cos A = \frac{\text{adjacent}}{\text{hypotenuse}} = \frac{b}{h}.$$

The tangent of an angle is the ratio of the length of the opposite side to the length of the adjacent side. In our case

$$\tan A = \frac{\text{opposite}}{\text{adjacent}} = \frac{a}{b}.$$

The remaining three functions are best defined using the above three functions.

a. Sine integral
c. Cosine

b. Trigonometric functions
d. Trigonometric

64. In mathematics, the _____ of a function is the set of all 'output' values produced by that function. Sometimes it is called the image, or more precisely, the image of the domain of the function. If a function is a surjection then its _____ is equal to its codomain.

a. Constant function
c. Piecewise-defined function

b. Surjective
d. Range

Chapter 7. APPLICATIONS OF THE DEFINITE INTEGRAL IN GEOMETRY, SCIENCE, AND ENGINEERING

1. In computer science and information science, _____ could also be a method or an algorithm. Again, an example will illustrate: There are systems of counting, as with Roman numerals, and various systems for filing papers, or catalogues, and various library systems, of which the Dewey Decimal _____ is an example. This still fits with the definition of components which are connected together (in this case in order to facilitate the flow of information.)
   a. BDDC
   b. 15 theorem
   c. BIBO stability
   d. System

2. In mathematics, the _____, named after German mathematician Bernhard Riemann, is a prominent function of great significance in number theory because of its relation to the distribution of prime numbers. It also has applications in other areas such as physics, probability theory, and applied statistics.

   The Riemann hypothesis, a conjecture about the distribution of the zeros of the _____, is considered by many mathematicians to be the most important unsolved problem in pure mathematics.

   a. 15 theorem
   b. BDDC
   c. BIBO stability
   d. Riemann zeta function

3. A _____ is one of the most curvilinear basic geometric shapes: It has two faces, zero vertices, and zero edges. The surface formed by the points at a fixed distance from a given straight line, the axis of the _____. The solid enclosed by this surface and by two planes perpendicular to the axis is also called a _____.
   a. Right circular cylinder
   b. Cylinder
   c. BDDC
   d. 15 theorem

4. In mathematics, a _____ is a method for approximating the total area underneath a curve on a graph, otherwise known as an integral. It may also be used to define the integration operation.

   Consider a function $f: D \to \mathbf{R}$, where D is a subset of the real numbers $\mathbf{R}$, and let $I = [a, b]$ be a closed interval contained in D. A finite set of points $\{x_0, x_1, x_2, \ldots x_n\}$ such that $a = x_0 < x_1 < x_2 \ldots < x_n = b$ creates a partition

   $$P = \{[x_0, x_1), [x_1, x_2), \ldots [x_{n-1}, x_n]\}$$

   of I.

   a. Risch algorithm
   b. Signed measure
   c. Solid of revolution
   d. Riemann sum

5. The _____ of an angle is the ratio of the length of the opposite side to the length of the hypotenuse. In our case

   $$\sin A = \frac{\text{opposite}}{\text{hypotenuse}} = \frac{a}{h}.$$

   Note that this ratio does not depend on size of the particular right triangle chosen, as long as it contains the angle A, since all such triangles are similar.

Chapter 7. APPLICATIONS OF THE DEFINITE INTEGRAL IN GEOMETRY, SCIENCE, AND ENGINEERING

The cosine of an angle is the ratio of the length of the adjacent side to the length of the hypotenuse.

a. Trigonometric
b. Trigonometric functions
c. Sine integral
d. Sine

6. If a particular point on a sphere is (arbitrarily) designated as its _____, then the corresponding antipodal point is called the south pole and the equator is the great circle that is equidistant to them. Great circles through the two poles are called lines (or meridians) of longitude, and the line connecting the two poles is called the axis of rotation. Circles on the sphere that are parallel to the equator are lines of latitude.

a. Tangent line
b. Minimal surface
c. Sphere
d. North pole

7. A _____ is a statement of the meaning of a word or phrase. The term to be defined is known as the definiendum. The words which define it are known as the definiens.

a. BIBO stability
b. BDDC
c. 15 theorem
d. Definition

8. _____ is the long dimension of any object. The _____ of a thing is the distance between its ends, its linear extent as measured from end to end. This may be distinguished from height, which is vertical extent, and width or breadth, which are the distance from side to side, measuring across the object at right angles to the _____.

a. BIBO stability
b. 15 theorem
c. Length
d. BDDC

9. In mathematics, a (topological) _____ is defined as follows: let I be an interval of real numbers (i.e. a non-empty connected subset of $\mathbb{R}$); then a _____ γ is a continuous mapping $\gamma : I \to X$, where X is a topological space. The _____ γ is said to be simple if it is injective, i.e. if for all x, y in I, we have $\gamma(x) = \gamma(y) \implies x = y$. If I is a closed bounded interval $[a, b]$, we also allow the possibility $\gamma(a) = \gamma(b)$ (this convention makes it possible to talk about closed simple _____.)

a. Prolate cycloid
b. Tractrix
c. Closed curve
d. Curve

10. A _____ is a type of manifold that is locally similar enough to Euclidean space to allow one to do calculus Any manifold can be described by a collection of charts, also known as an atlas.

a. Tangent line
b. Sphere
c. Minimal surface
d. Differentiable manifold

11. Smooth functions with given closed support are used in the construction of smooth partitions of unity ; these are essential in the study of smooth manifolds, for example to show that Riemannian metrics can be defined globally starting from their local existence. A simple case is that of a bump function on the real line, that is, a _____ f that takes the value 0 outside an interval [a,b] and such that

f(x) > 0 for a < x < b.

Chapter 7. APPLICATIONS OF THE DEFINITE INTEGRAL IN GEOMETRY, SCIENCE, AND ENGINEERING

Given a number of overlapping intervals on the line, bump functions can be constructed on each of them, and on semi-infinite intervals (->∞, c] and [d,+>∞) to cover the whole line, such that the sum of the functions is always 1.

a. Continuously differentiable
b. Symmetric derivative
c. Smooth function
d. Gradient

12. For some curves there is a smallest number L that is an upper bound on the length of any polygonal approximation. If such a number exists, then the curve is said to be rectifiable and the curve is defined to have _____ L.

Let C be a curve in Euclidean (or, generally, a metric) space X = R^n, so C is the image of a continuous function f : [a, b] → X of the interval [a, b] into X.

a. Integration by parametric derivatives
b. Order of integration
c. Integrand
d. Arc length

13. In mathematics, _____ are a method of defining a curve. A simple kinematical example is when one uses a time parameter to determine the position, velocity, and other information about a body in motion.

Abstractly, a relation is given in the form of an equation, and it is shown also to be the image of functions from items such as R^n.

a. Parametric equations
b. Critical point
c. Shift theorem
d. Partial derivative

14. In mathematics, an _____ is a particular type of curve: a hypocycloid with four cusps. Astroids are also superellipses: all astroids are scaled versions of the curve specified by the equation

$$x^{2/3} + y^{2/3} = 1$$

Its modern name comes from the Greek word for 'star'.

a. Astroid
b. ACTRAN
c. Epicycloid
d. ALGOR

15. In geometry, a _____ is a special plane curve generated by the trace of a fixed point on a small circle that rolls within a larger circle. It is comparable to the cycloid but instead of the circle rolling along a line, it rolls within a circle. The red curve is a _____ traced as the smaller black circle rolls around inside the larger blue circle (parameters are R=3.0, r=1.0, and so k=3), giving a deltoid.

Chapter 7. APPLICATIONS OF THE DEFINITE INTEGRAL IN GEOMETRY, SCIENCE, AND ENGINEERING

If the smaller circle has radius r, and the larger circle has radius R = kr, then the parametric equations for the curve can be given by either:

$$x(\theta) = (R-r)\cos\theta + r\cos\left(\frac{R-r}{r}\theta\right)$$
$$y(\theta) = (R-r)\sin\theta - r\sin\left(\frac{R-r}{r}\theta\right),$$

or:

$$x(\theta) = r(k-1)\cos\theta + r\cos((k-1)\theta)$$
$$y(\theta) = r(k-1)\sin\theta - r\sin((k-1)\theta).$$

If k is an integer, then the curve is closed, and has k cusps (i.e., sharp corners, where the curve is not differentiable.)

 a. Closed curve
 b. Kappa curve
 c. Bullet-nose curve
 d. Hypocycloid

16. In numerical analysis, _____ constitutes a broad family of algorithms for calculating the numerical value of a definite integral, and by extension, the term is also sometimes used to describe the numerical solution of differential equations The term numerical quadrature is more or less a synonym for _____, especially as applied to one-dimensional integrals.
 a. Meshfree methods
 b. Multigrid method
 c. Galerkin methods
 d. Numerical integration

17. A _____ is a surface created by rotating a curve lying on some plane (the generatrix) around a straight line (the axis of rotation) that lies on the same plane.

Examples of surfaces generated by a straight line are the cylindrical and conical surfaces. A circle that is rotated about a (coplanar) axis through the center generates a sphere.

 a. Surface of revolution
 b. Shell integration
 c. Riemann sum
 d. Constant of integration

18. A _____ is perfectly round geometrical object in three-dimensional space, such as the shape of a round ball. Like a circle in two dimensions, a perfect _____ is completely symmetrical around its center, with all points on the surface lying the same distance r from the center point. This distance r is known as the radius of the _____.
 a. Tangent line
 b. Sphere
 c. North pole
 d. Minimal surface

Chapter 7. APPLICATIONS OF THE DEFINITE INTEGRAL IN GEOMETRY, SCIENCE, AND ENGINEERING

19. Integration is an important concept in mathematics, specifically in the field of calculus and, more broadly, mathematical analysis. Given a function f of a real variable x and an interval [a, b] of the real line, the _____

$$\int_a^b f(x)\,dx,$$

is defined informally to be the net signed area of the region in the xy-plane bounded by the graph of f, the x-axis, and the vertical lines x = a and x = b.

The term '_____' may also refer to the notion of antiderivative, a function F whose derivative is the given function f.

   a. Integrand
   b. Integral test for convergence
   c. Indefinite integral
   d. Integral

20. In vector calculus, the _____ is an operator that measures the magnitude of a vector field's source or sink at a given point; the _____ of a vector field is a (signed) scalar. For example, consider air as it is heated or cooled. The relevant vector field for this example is the velocity of the moving air at a point.
   a. Green's theorem
   b. Triple product
   c. Divergence
   d. Gradient theorem

21. In vector calculus, the _____ Ostrogradskye;s theorem the _____ states that the outward flux of a vector field through a surface is equal to the triple integral of the divergence on the region inside the surface. Intuitively, it states that the sum of all sources minus the sum of all sinks gives the net flow out of a region.
   a. Divergence
   b. Green's theorem
   c. Del
   d. Divergence Theorem

22. In vector calculus, the _____ is shorthand for either the _____ matrix or its determinant, the _____ determinant.

In algebraic geometry the _____ of a curve means the _____ variety: a group variety associated to the curve, in which the curve can be embedded.

These concepts are all named after the mathematician Carl Gustav Jacob Jacobi.

   a. Vector Laplacian
   b. Saddle surface
   c. Critical point
   d. Jacobian

23. If a function has an integral, it is said to be integrable. The function for which the integral is calculated is called the _____. The region over which a function is being integrated is called the domain of integration.
   a. Order of integration
   b. Integration by parts
   c. Integrand
   d. Integral test for convergence

Chapter 7. APPLICATIONS OF THE DEFINITE INTEGRAL IN GEOMETRY, SCIENCE, AND ENGINEERING

24. _____ is a type of motion in which the velocity of an object changes equal amounts in equal time periods. An example of an object having _____ would be a ball rolling down a ramp. The object picks up velocity as it goes down the ramp with equal changes in time.

   a. ALGOR
   b. AUSM
   c. ACTRAN
   d. Uniform Acceleration

25. In physics, the _____ is a unit of force specified in the centimetre-gram-second (CGS) system of units, a predecessor of the modern SI. One _____ is equal to exactly 10 micronewtons. Equivalently, the _____ is defined as 'the force required to accelerate a mass of one gram at a rate of one centimetre per second squared':

1 dyn = 1 g·cm/s² = 10⁻⁵ kg·m/s² = 10 μN

The _____ per centimetre is the unit usually associated with measuring surface tension.

   a. BDDC
   b. Dyne
   c. 15 theorem
   d. BIBO stability

26. The _____ is the derived unit of energy in the International System of Units. It is defined as:

$$1\,\text{J} = 1\,\text{kg} \cdot \text{m}^2 \cdot \text{s}^{-2}$$

One _____ is the amount of energy required to perform the following physical actions:

- The work done by a force of one newton travelling through a distance of one metre;
- The work required to move an electric charge of one coulomb through an electrical potential difference of one volt; or one coulomb volt, with the symbol C·V;
- The work done to produce the power of one watt continuously for one second; or one watt second (compare kilowatt hour), with the symbol W·s. Thus a kilowatt hour is 3,600,000 joules or 3.6 megajoules;

Chapter 7. APPLICATIONS OF THE DEFINITE INTEGRAL IN GEOMETRY, SCIENCE, AND ENGINEERING

1 _____ is equal to:

- 1×10^7 ergs (exactly)
- 1.6022×10^{19} eV (electronvolts)
- 0.2390 cal (gram calories or small calories)
- 2.3901×10^{-4} kcal (kilocalories, kilogram calories, large calories or food calories)
- 9.4782×10^{-4} BTU (British thermal unit)
- 0.7376 ftÂ·lbf (foot-pound force)
- 23.7 ftÂ·pdl (foot-poundals)
- 2.7778×10^{-7} kilowatt-hour
- 2.7778×10^{-4} watt-hour
- 9.8692×10^{-3} litre-atmosphere
- 1×10^{-44} Foe (exactly)

Units defined in terms of the _____ include:

- 1 thermochemical calorie = 4.184 J
- 1 International Table calorie = 4.1868 J
- 1 watt hour = 3600 J
- 1 kilowatt hour = 3.6×10^6 J (or 3.6 MJ)
- 1 ton TNT exploding = 4.184 GJ

Useful to remember:

- 1 _____ = 1 newton × 1 meter = 1 watt × 1 second

One _____ in everyday life is approximately:

- the energy required to lift a small apple one metre straight up.
- the energy released when that same apple falls one meter to the ground.
- the energy released as heat by a quiet person, every hundredth of a second.
- the energy required to heat one gram of dry, cool air by 1 degree Celsius.
- one hundredth of the energy a person can receive by drinking a drop of beer.
- the kinetic energy of an adult human moving a distance of about a handspan every second.

- Conversion of units
- Orders of magnitude (energy)
- Fluence

Chapter 7. APPLICATIONS OF THE DEFINITE INTEGRAL IN GEOMETRY, SCIENCE, AND ENGINEERING

a. 15 theorem
b. BIBO stability
c. Joule
d. BDDC

27. The _____ of an object is the extra energy which it possesses due to its motion. It is defined as the work needed to accelerate a body of a given mass from rest to its current velocity. Having gained this energy during its acceleration, the body maintains this _____ unless its speed changes.

   a. Law of Conservation of Energy
   b. 15 theorem
   c. Kinetic energy
   d. BDDC

28. In mathematics, _____ and minima, known collectively as extrema, are the largest value (maximum) or smallest value (minimum), that a function takes in a point either within a given neighbourhood (local extremum) or on the function domain in its entirety (global extremum.)

Throughout, a point refers to an input (x), while a value refers to an output (y): one distinguishing between the maximum value and the point (or points) at which it occurs.

A real-valued function f defined on the real line is said to have a local maximum point at the point x^*, if there exists some $\varepsilon > 0$, such that $f(x^*) \geq f(x)$ when $|x - x^*| < \varepsilon$.

   a. Maxima
   b. Leibniz formula
   c. Related rates
   d. Racetrack principle

29. The most commonly encountered form of Hooke's law is probably the spring equation, which relates the force exerted by a spring to the distance it is stretched by a _____, k, measured in force per length.

$$F = -kx$$

The negative sign indicates that the force exerted by the spring is in direct opposition to the direction of displacement. It is called a 'restoring force', as it tends to restore the system to equilibrium.

   a. Spring constant
   b. Spring equation
   c. Polar moment of inertia
   d. Navier-Stokes equations

30. In mathematics, the _____ is an extension of the factorial function to real and complex numbers. For a complex number z with positive real part the _____ is defined by

$$\Gamma(z) = \int_0^\infty t^{z-1} e^{-t}\, dt .$$

This definition can be extended to the rest of the complex plane, excepting the non-positive integers.

Chapter 7. APPLICATIONS OF THE DEFINITE INTEGRAL IN GEOMETRY, SCIENCE, AND ENGINEERING

If n is a positive integer, then

Γ(n) = (n − 1)!,

showing the connection to the factorial function.

a. Pochhammer k-symbol
b. Digamma function
c. Gamma function
d. Multivariate gamma function

31. In mathematics, a _____ is an ordered list of objects (or events). Like a set, it contains members (also called elements or terms), and the number of terms (possibly infinite) is called the length of the _____. Unlike a set, order matters, and the exact same elements can appear multiple times at different positions in the _____.

a. Slope
b. 15 theorem
c. Y-intercept
d. Sequence

32. In mathematics, a _____ is the graph of the system of parametric equations

$$x = A\sin(at + \delta), \quad y = B\sin(bt),$$

which describes complex harmonic motion. This family of curves was investigated by Nathaniel Bowditch in 1815, and later in more detail by Jules Antoine Lissajous in 1857.

The appearance of the figure is highly sensitive to the ratio a/b.

a. BDDC
b. 15 theorem
c. BIBO stability
d. Lissajous curve

33. The _____ of a material is defined as its mass per unit volume. The symbol of _____ is ρ '>rho.)

Mathematically:

$$d = \frac{m}{V}$$

where:

    d is the _____,
    m is the mass,
    V is the volume.

Chapter 7. APPLICATIONS OF THE DEFINITE INTEGRAL IN GEOMETRY, SCIENCE, AND ENGINEERING

a. BIBO stability
b. BDDC
c. 15 theorem
d. Density

34. In physics, and more specifically kinematics, _____ is the change in velocity over time. Because velocity is a vector, it can change in two ways: a change in magnitude and/or a change in direction. In one dimension, _____ is the rate at which something speeds up or slows down.
   a. Acceleration
   b. ACTRAN
   c. ALGOR
   d. AUSM

35. The _____ of an angle is the ratio of the length of the adjacent side to the length of the hypotenuse. In our case

$$\cos A = \frac{\text{adjacent}}{\text{hypotenuse}} = \frac{b}{h}.$$

The tangent of an angle is the ratio of the length of the opposite side to the length of the adjacent side. In our case

$$\tan A = \frac{\text{opposite}}{\text{adjacent}} = \frac{a}{b}.$$

The remaining three functions are best defined using the above three functions.

   a. Trigonometric
   b. Cosine
   c. Sine integral
   d. Trigonometric functions

36. In mathematics, the hyperbolic functions are analogs of the ordinary trigonometric functions. The basic hyperbolic functions are the hyperbolic sine 'sinh', and the _____ 'cosh', from which are derived the hyperbolic tangent 'tanh', etc., in analogy to the derived trigonometric functions. The inverse hyperbolic functions are the area hyperbolic sine 'arsinh' (also called 'asinh', or sometimes by the misnomer of 'arcsinh') and so on.
   a. Step function
   b. Square root function
   c. Hyperbolic tangent
   d. Hyperbolic cosine

37. In mathematics, the _____ are analogs of the ordinary trigonometric or circular functions. The basic _____ are the hyperbolic sine 'sinh', and the hyperbolic cosine 'cosh', from which are derived the hyperbolic tangent 'tanh', etc., in analogy to the derived trigonometric functions. The inverse _____ are the area hyperbolic sine 'arsinh' (also called 'asinh', or sometimes by the misnomer of 'arcsinh') and so on.
   a. Signum function
   b. Hyperbolic cosine
   c. Hyperbolic functions
   d. Multiplicative inverse

38. In mathematics, the hyperbolic functions are analogs of the ordinary trigonometric functions. The basic hyperbolic functions are the _____ 'sinh', and the hyperbolic cosine 'cosh', from which are derived the hyperbolic tangent 'tanh', etc., in analogy to the derived trigonometric functions. The inverse hyperbolic functions are the area _____ 'arsinh' (also called 'asinh', or sometimes by the misnomer of 'arcsinh') and so on.

Chapter 7. APPLICATIONS OF THE DEFINITE INTEGRAL IN GEOMETRY, SCIENCE, AND ENGINEERING

a. Hyperbolic tangent
b. Hyperbolic sine
c. Signum function
d. Square root function

39. In mathematics, the hyperbolic functions are analogs of the ordinary trigonometric functions. The basic hyperbolic functions are the hyperbolic sine 'sinh', and the hyperbolic cosine 'cosh', from which are derived the _____ 'tanh', etc., in analogy to the derived trigonometric functions. The inverse hyperbolic functions are the area hyperbolic sine 'arsinh' (also called 'asinh', or sometimes by the misnomer of 'arcsinh') and so on.
   a. Step function
   b. Signum function
   c. Hyperbolic sine
   d. Hyperbolic tangent

40. In geometry, the _____ (or simply the tangent) to a curve at a given point is the straight line that 'just touches' the curve at that point (in the sense explained more precisely below.) As it passes through the point of tangency, the _____ is 'going in the same direction' as the curve, and in this sense it is the best straight-line approximation to the curve at that point. The same definition applies to space curves and curves in n-dimensional Euclidean space.
   a. North pole
   b. Tangent line
   c. Lie derivative
   d. Minimal surface

41. An _____ of a real-valued function y = f(x) is a curve which describes the behavior of f as either x or y tends to infinity.

In other words, as one moves along the graph of f(x) in some direction, the distance between it and the _____ eventually becomes smaller than any distance that one may specify.

   a. ALGOR
   b. ACTRAN
   c. AUSM
   d. Asymptote

42. In physics and geometry, the _____ is the theoretical shape of a hanging flexible chain or cable when supported at its ends and acted upon by a uniform gravitational force (its own weight) and in equilibrium. The curve has a U shape that is similar in appearance to the parabola, though it is a different curve.
   a. Catenary
   b. 15 theorem
   c. BDDC
   d. BIBO stability

43. In calculus, a branch of mathematics, the _____ is a measurement of how a function changes when its input changes. Loosely speaking, a _____ can be thought of as how much a quantity is changing at some given point. For example, the _____ of the position (or distance) of a vehicle with respect to time is the instantaneous velocity (respectively, instantaneous speed) at which the vehicle is traveling.

The process of finding a _____ is called differentiation. The fundamental theorem of calculus states that differentiation is the reverse process to integration.

   a. Derivative
   b. Stationary phase approximation
   c. Bounded function
   d. Semi-differentiability

Chapter 7. APPLICATIONS OF THE DEFINITE INTEGRAL IN GEOMETRY, SCIENCE, AND ENGINEERING

44. In mathematics, the _____ of a function y = f(x) is a function that, in some fashion, 'undoes' the effect of f The _____ of f is denoted f^{-1}. The statements y=f(x) and x=f^{-1}(y) are equivalent.
    a. ALGOR
    b. ACTRAN
    c. AUSM
    d. Inverse

45. Any formula written in terms of logarithms may be said to be in _____.

In contexts including complex manifolds and algebraic geometry, a logarithmic differential form is a 1-form that, locally at least, can be written

$$\frac{df}{f}$$

for some meromorphic function (resp. rational function) f.

   a. Holomorphic sheaf
   b. Bifurcation locus
   c. Cayley transform
   d. Logarithmic form

46. _____ is the curve along which a small object moves, under the influence of friction, when pulled on a horizontal plane by a piece of thread and a puller that moves at a right angle to the initial line between the object and the puller at an infinitesimal speed. It is therefore a curve of pursuit. It was first introduced by Claude Perrault in 1670, and later studied by Sir Isaac Newton and Christian Huygens (1692.)
    a. Curve
    b. Folium of Descartes
    c. Bullet-nose curve
    d. Tractrix

Chapter 8. PRINCIPLES OF INTEGRAL EVALUATION

1. In calculus, _____ gives a sequence of approximations of a differentiable function around a given point by polynomials (the Taylor polynomials of that function) whose coefficients depend only on the derivatives of the function at that point. The theorem also gives precise estimates on the size of the error in the approximation. The theorem is named after the mathematician Brook Taylor, who stated it in 1712, though the result was first discovered 41 years earlier in 1671 by James Gregory.

   a. Related rates
   b. Fresnel integrals
   c. Local minimum
   d. Taylor's theorem

2. If a function has an integral, it is said to be integrable. The function for which the integral is calculated is called the _____. The region over which a function is being integrated is called the domain of integration.

   a. Integration by parts
   b. Integral test for convergence
   c. Order of integration
   d. Integrand

3. The formula is used to transform one integral into another integral that is easier to compute. Thus, the formula can be used from left to right or from right to left in order to simplify a given integral. When used in the former manner, it is sometimes known as _____.

   a. U-substitution
   b. Integration by substitution
   c. Extreme Value Theorem
   d. Extreme value

4. In calculus, and more generally in mathematical analysis, _____ is a rule that transforms the integral of products of functions into other, hopefully simpler, integrals. The rule arises from the product rule of differentiation.

   If u = f(x), v = g(x), and the differentials du = f '(x) dx and dv = g'(x) dx; then in its simplest form the product rule is:

   $$\int u\,dv = uv - \int v\,du.$$

   Suppose f(x) and g(x) are two continuously differentiable functions.

   a. Integration by parametric derivatives
   b. Integrand
   c. Arc length
   d. Integration by parts

5. In calculus, the _____ is a formula used to find the derivatives of products of functions. It may be stated thus:

   $$(f \cdot g)' = f' \cdot g + f \cdot g'$$

   or in the Leibniz notation thus:

   $$\frac{d}{dx}(u \cdot v) = u \cdot \frac{dv}{dx} + v \cdot \frac{du}{dx}.$$

   Discovery of this rule is credited to Gottfried Leibniz, who demonstrated it using differentials. Here is Leibniz's argument: Let u and v be two differentiable functions of x.

Chapter 8. PRINCIPLES OF INTEGRAL EVALUATION

a. Differentiation rules
b. Constant factor rule in differentiation
c. Quotient Rule
d. Product rule

6. Integration is an important concept in mathematics, specifically in the field of calculus and, more broadly, mathematical analysis. Given a function f of a real variable x and an interval [a, b] of the real line, the _____

$$\int_a^b f(x)\,dx,$$

is defined informally to be the net signed area of the region in the xy-plane bounded by the graph of f, the x-axis, and the vertical lines x = a and x = b.

The term '_____' may also refer to the notion of antiderivative, a function F whose derivative is the given function f.

a. Integrand
b. Indefinite integral
c. Integral test for convergence
d. Integral

7. In mathematics, _____ refers to the rewriting of an expression into a simpler form. For example, the process of rewriting a fraction into one with the smallest whole-number denominator possible (while keeping the numerator an integer) is called 'reducing a fraction'. Rewriting a radical (or 'root') expression with the smallest possible whole number under the radical symbol is called 'reducing a radical'.

a. 15 theorem
b. BDDC
c. Quartic
d. Reduction

8. Trigonometry is a branch of mathematics that deals with triangles, particularly those plane triangles in which one angle has 90 degrees (right triangles.) Trigonometry deals with relationships between the sides and the angles of triangles and with the _____ functions, which describe those relationships.

Trigonometry has applications in both pure mathematics and in applied mathematics, where it is essential in many branches of science and technology.

a. Sine
b. Trigonometric integrals
c. Trigonometric functions
d. Trigonometric

9. In mathematics, the _____ are functions of an angle. They are important in the study of triangles and modeling periodic phenomena, among many other applications. _____ are commonly defined as ratios of two sides of a right triangle containing the angle, and can equivalently be defined as the lengths of various line segments from a unit circle.

a. Trigonometric
b. Trigonometric functions
c. Trigonometric integrals
d. Sine integral

10. In mathematics, the _____ are a family of integrals which involve trigonometric functions. A number of the basic _____ are discussed at the list of integrals of trigonometric functions.

Chapter 8. PRINCIPLES OF INTEGRAL EVALUATION

The different sine integral definitions are:

$$\text{Si}(x) = \int_0^x \frac{\sin t}{t} \, dt$$

$$\text{si}(x) = -\int_x^\infty \frac{\sin t}{t} \, dt$$

Si(x) is the primitive of sinx / x which is zero for x = 0; si(x) is the primitive of sinx / x which is zero for $x = \infty$.

a. Sine
b. Trigonometric
c. Trigonometric functions
d. Trigonometric integrals

11. The _____ of an angle is the ratio of the length of the adjacent side to the length of the hypotenuse. In our case

$$\cos A = \frac{\text{adjacent}}{\text{hypotenuse}} = \frac{b}{h}.$$

The tangent of an angle is the ratio of the length of the opposite side to the length of the adjacent side. In our case

$$\tan A = \frac{\text{opposite}}{\text{adjacent}} = \frac{a}{b}.$$

The remaining three functions are best defined using the above three functions.

a. Cosine
b. Trigonometric
c. Sine integral
d. Trigonometric functions

12. The _____ of an angle is the ratio of the length of the opposite side to the length of the hypotenuse. In our case

$$\sin A = \frac{\text{opposite}}{\text{hypotenuse}} = \frac{a}{h}.$$

Note that this ratio does not depend on size of the particular right triangle chosen, as long as it contains the angle A, since all such triangles are similar.

The cosine of an angle is the ratio of the length of the adjacent side to the length of the hypotenuse.

a. Sine integral
b. Trigonometric functions
c. Sine
d. Trigonometric

13. In mathematics, _____ is the substitution of trigonometric functions for other expressions. One may use the trigonometric identities to simplify certain integrals containing radical expressions:

- If the integrand contains

$$\sqrt{a^2 - x^2},$$

let

$$x = a \sin \theta$$

and use the identity

$1 - \sin^2\theta = \cos^2\theta.$

- If the integrand contains

$$\sqrt{a^2 + x^2}$$

let $x = a \tan \theta$
and use the identity

$$1 + \tan^2 \theta = \sec^2 \theta.$$

- If the integrand contains

$$\sqrt{x^2 - a^2}$$

let

$$x = a \sec \theta$$

and use the identity

$$\sec^2 \theta - 1 = \tan^2 \theta.$$

In the integral

$$\int \frac{dx}{\sqrt{a^2 - x^2}}$$

we may use

$$x = a\sin(\theta), \; dx = a\cos(\theta)\,d\theta$$
$$\theta = \arcsin\left(\frac{x}{a}\right)$$

so that the integral becomes

$$\int \frac{dx}{\sqrt{a^2 - x^2}} = \int \frac{a\cos(\theta)\,d\theta}{\sqrt{a^2 - a^2\sin^2(\theta)}} = \int \frac{a\cos(\theta)\,d\theta}{\sqrt{a^2(1 - \sin^2(\theta))}}$$
$$= \int \frac{a\cos(\theta)\,d\theta}{\sqrt{a^2\cos^2(\theta)}} = \int d\theta = \theta + C = \arcsin\left(\frac{x}{a}\right) + C$$

Note that the above step requires that a > 0 and cos(θ) > 0; we can choose the a to be the positive square root of a^2; and we impose the restriction on θ to be −π/2 < θ < π/2 by using the arcsin function.

For a definite integral, one must figure out how the bounds of integration change. For example, as x goes from 0 to a/2, then sin (θ) goes from 0 to 1/2, so θ goes from 0 to π/6.

a. Rectangle method
b. Surface of revolution
c. Riemann sum
d. Trigonometric substitution

14. In physics, and more specifically kinematics, _____ is the change in velocity over time. Because velocity is a vector, it can change in two ways: a change in magnitude and/or a change in direction. In one dimension, _____ is the rate at which something speeds up or slows down.
   a. Acceleration
   b. AUSM
   c. ALGOR
   d. ACTRAN

15. In mathematics, a _____ is the graph of the system of parametric equations

$$x = A\sin(at + \delta), \quad y = B\sin(bt),$$

which describes complex harmonic motion. This family of curves was investigated by Nathaniel Bowditch in 1815, and later in more detail by Jules Antoine Lissajous in 1857.

The appearance of the figure is highly sensitive to the ratio a/b.

a. BIBO stability
b. 15 theorem
c. Lissajous curve
d. BDDC

Chapter 8. PRINCIPLES OF INTEGRAL EVALUATION

16. In mathematics, a (topological) _____ is defined as follows: let I be an interval of real numbers (i.e. a non-empty connected subset of $\mathbb{R}$); then a _____ γ is a continuous mapping $\gamma : I \to X$, where X is a topological space. The _____ γ is said to be simple if it is injective, i.e. if for all x, y in I, we have $\gamma(x) = \gamma(y) \implies x = y$. If I is a closed bounded interval $[a, b]$, we also allow the possibility $\gamma(a) = \gamma(b)$ (this convention makes it possible to talk about closed simple _____.)

   a. Closed curve
   c. Prolate cycloid
   b. Curve
   d. Tractrix

17. In calculus, a branch of mathematics, the _____ is a measurement of how a function changes when its input changes. Loosely speaking, a _____ can be thought of as how much a quantity is changing at some given point. For example, the _____ of the position (or distance) of a vehicle with respect to time is the instantaneous velocity (respectively, instantaneous speed) at which the vehicle is traveling.

The process of finding a _____ is called differentiation. The fundamental theorem of calculus states that differentiation is the reverse process to integration.

   a. Stationary phase approximation
   c. Derivative
   b. Semi-differentiability
   d. Bounded function

18. In mathematics, a _____ of a function of several variables is its derivative with respect to one of those variables with the others held constant (as opposed to the total derivative, in which all variables are allowed to vary.) Partial derivatives are useful in vector calculus and differential geometry.

The _____ of a function f with respect to the variable x is written as f'_x, $\partial_x f$, or $\partial f/\partial x$.

   a. Differentiation operator
   c. Level curve
   b. Jacobian
   d. Partial derivative

19. In integral calculus we would want to write a fractional algebraic expression as the sum of its _____ in order to take the integral of each simple fraction separately. Once the original denominator, D_0, has been factored we set up a fraction for each factor in the denominator. We may use a subscripted D to represent the denominator of the respective _____ which are the factors in D_0.

   a. Closed-form expression
   c. Left inverse
   b. Multinomial theorem
   d. Partial fractions

20. In mathematics, a _____ is any function which can be written as the ratio of two polynomial functions.

$$y = \frac{x^2 - 3x - 2}{x^2 - 4}$$

Chapter 8. PRINCIPLES OF INTEGRAL EVALUATION

In the case of one variable, x, a _____ is a function of the form

$$f(x) = \frac{P(x)}{Q(x)}$$

where P and Q are polynomial function in x and Q is not the zero polynomial. The domain of f is the set of all points x for which the denominator Q(x) is not zero.

a. 15 theorem
b. BIBO stability
c. BDDC
d. Rational function

21. In computer science and information science, _____ could also be a method or an algorithm. Again, an example will illustrate: There are systems of counting, as with Roman numerals, and various systems for filing papers, or catalogues, and various library systems, of which the Dewey Decimal _____ is an example. This still fits with the definition of components which are connected together (in this case in order to facilitate the flow of information.)

a. 15 theorem
b. BDDC
c. BIBO stability
d. System

22. In mathematics, a _____ is a method for approximating the total area underneath a curve on a graph, otherwise known as an integral. It may also be used to define the integration operation.

Consider a function $f: D \longrightarrow \mathbf{R}$, where D is a subset of the real numbers $\mathbf{R}$, and let $I = [a, b]$ be a closed interval contained in D. A finite set of points $\{x_0, x_1, x_2, ... x_n\}$ such that $a = x_0 < x_1 < x_2 ... < x_n = b$ creates a partition

$$P = \{[x_0, x_1), [x_1, x_2), ... [x_{n-1}, x_n]\}$$

of I.

a. Riemann sum
b. Solid of revolution
c. Risch algorithm
d. Signed measure

23. In mathematics, the _____, named after German mathematician Bernhard Riemann, is a prominent function of great significance in number theory because of its relation to the distribution of prime numbers. It also has applications in other areas such as physics, probability theory, and applied statistics.

The Riemann hypothesis, a conjecture about the distribution of the zeros of the _____, is considered by many mathematicians to be the most important unsolved problem in pure mathematics.

a. BIBO stability
b. 15 theorem
c. BDDC
d. Riemann zeta function

Chapter 8. PRINCIPLES OF INTEGRAL EVALUATION

24. In numerical analysis, _____ constitutes a broad family of algorithms for calculating the numerical value of a definite integral, and by extension, the term is also sometimes used to describe the numerical solution of differential equations The term numerical quadrature is more or less a synonym for _____, especially as applied to one-dimensional integrals.
   a. Meshfree methods
   b. Numerical integration
   c. Galerkin methods
   d. Multigrid method

25. In geometry, the _____ (or simply the tangent) to a curve at a given point is the straight line that 'just touches' the curve at that point (in the sense explained more precisely below.) As it passes through the point of tangency, the _____ is 'going in the same direction' as the curve, and in this sense it is the best straight-line approximation to the curve at that point. The same definition applies to space curves and curves in n-dimensional Euclidean space.
   a. Minimal surface
   b. Lie derivative
   c. North pole
   d. Tangent line

26. _____ is the study of algorithms for the problems of continuous mathematics (as distinguished from discrete mathematics.)

One of the earliest mathematical writings is the Babylonian tablet YBC 7289, which gives a sexagesimal numerical approximation of $\sqrt{2}$, the length of the diagonal in a unit square. Being able to compute the sides of a triangle (and hence, being able to compute square roots) is extremely important, for instance, in carpentry and construction.

   a. 15 theorem
   b. BIBO stability
   c. BDDC
   d. Numerical analysis

27. Cantor defined two kinds of _____ numbers, the ordinal numbers and the cardinal numbers. Ordinal numbers may be identified with well-ordered sets, or counting carried on to any stopping point, including points after an _____ number have already been counted. Generalizing finite and the ordinary _____ sequences which are maps from the positive integers leads to mappings from ordinal numbers, and transfinite sequences.
   a. ACTRAN
   b. ALGOR
   c. AUSM
   d. Infinite

28. In calculus, an _____ is the limit of a definite integral as an endpoint of the interval of integration approaches either a specified real number or ∞ or −∞ or, in some cases, as both endpoints approach limits.

Specifically, an _____ is a limit of the form

$$\lim_{b \to \infty} \int_a^b f(x)\, dx, \qquad \lim_{a \to -\infty} \int_a^b f(x)\, dx,$$

or of the form

$$\lim_{c \to b^-} \int_a^c f(x)\, dx, \qquad \lim_{c \to a^+} \int_c^b f(x)\, dx,$$

Chapter 8. PRINCIPLES OF INTEGRAL EVALUATION

in which one takes a limit in one or the other (or sometimes both) endpoints. Improper integrals may also occur at an interior point of the domain of integration, or at multiple such points.

a. ACTRAN
b. ALGOR
c. AUSM
d. Improper integral

29. For some curves there is a smallest number L that is an upper bound on the length of any polygonal approximation. If such a number exists, then the curve is said to be rectifiable and the curve is defined to have _____ L.

Let C be a curve in Euclidean (or, generally, a metric) space $X = R^n$, so C is the image of a continuous function $f : [a, b] \to X$ of the interval [a, b] into X.

a. Integration by parametric derivatives
b. Integrand
c. Order of integration
d. Arc length

30. _____ is the long dimension of any object. The _____ of a thing is the distance between its ends, its linear extent as measured from end to end. This may be distinguished from height, which is vertical extent, and width or breadth, which are the distance from side to side, measuring across the object at right angles to the _____.

a. BDDC
b. BIBO stability
c. 15 theorem
d. Length

31. _____ is how much exposed area an object has. It is expressed in square units. If an object has flat faces, its _____ can be calculated by adding together the areas of its faces.

a. Vector area
b. Plane curve
c. Lipschitz domain
d. Surface area

32. In mathematics, the _____ is an extension of the factorial function to real and complex numbers. For a complex number z with positive real part the _____ is defined by

$$\Gamma(z) = \int_0^\infty t^{z-1} e^{-t}\, dt\ .$$

This definition can be extended to the rest of the complex plane, excepting the non-positive integers.

If n is a positive integer, then

$$\Gamma(n) = (n - 1)!,$$

showing the connection to the factorial function.

a. Multivariate gamma function
b. Digamma function
c. Pochhammer k-symbol
d. Gamma function

Chapter 9. MATHEMATICAL MODELING WITH DIFFERENTIAL EQUATIONS

1. In infinitesimal calculus, a _____ is traditionally an infinitesimally small change in a variable. For example, if x is a variable, then a change in the value of x is often denoted Δx (or δx when this change is considered to be small.) The _____ dx represents such a change, but is infinitely small.
   a. Dirichlet integral
   b. The Method of Mechanical Theorems
   c. Local maximum
   d. Differential

2. A _____ is a mathematical equation for an unknown function of one or several variables that relates the values of the function itself and of its derivatives of various orders. they play a prominent role in engineering, physics, economics and other disciplines.

   A simplified real world example of a _____ is modeling the acceleration of a ball falling through the air (considering only gravity and air resistance.)

   a. Phase line
   b. Differential equation
   c. Structural stability
   d. Caloric polynomial

3. In mathematics, a (topological) _____ is defined as follows: let I be an interval of real numbers (i.e. a non-empty connected subset of $\mathbb{R}$); then a _____ γ is a continuous mapping $\gamma : I \to X$, where X is a topological space. The _____ γ is said to be simple if it is injective, i.e. if for all x, y in I, we have $\gamma(x) = \gamma(y) \implies x = y$. If I is a closed bounded interval $[a, b]$, we also allow the possibility $\gamma(a) = \gamma(b)$ (this convention makes it possible to talk about closed simple _____.)
   a. Closed curve
   b. Curve
   c. Prolate cycloid
   d. Tractrix

4. A _____ officer is an officer of high military rank. The term or equivalent is used by nearly every country in the world. _____ can be used as a generic term for all grades of _____ officer, or it can specifically refer to a single rank that is just called _____.
   a. 15 theorem
   b. BIBO stability
   c. General
   d. BDDC

5. In mathematics, a _____ to an ordinary or partial differential equation is a function for which the derivatives appearing in the equation may not all exist but which is nonetheless deemed to satisfy the equation in some precisely defined sense. There are many different definitions of _____, appropriate for different classes of equations. One of the most important is based on the notion of distributions.
   a. Structural stability
   b. Weak solution
   c. Conserved quantity
   d. Singular perturbation

6. In mathematics, a _____ is an ordered list of objects (or events). Like a set, it contains members (also called elements or terms), and the number of terms (possibly infinite) is called the length of the _____. Unlike a set, order matters, and the exact same elements can appear multiple times at different positions in the _____.
   a. Slope
   b. Y-intercept
   c. 15 theorem
   d. Sequence

Chapter 9. MATHEMATICAL MODELING WITH DIFFERENTIAL EQUATIONS

7. In differential calculus, an inflection point, or _____ (or inflexion) is a point on a curve at which the curvature changes sign. The curve changes from being concave upwards (positive curvature) to concave downwards (negative curvature), or vice versa. If one imagines driving a vehicle along the curve, it is a point at which the steering-wheel is momentarily 'straight', being turned from left to right or vice versa.

   a. Lin-Tsien equation
   b. Point of inflection
   c. Derivative of a constant
   d. Logarithmic derivative

8. In mathematics, in the field of differential equations, an initial value problem is an ordinary differential equation together with specified value, called the _____, of the unknown function at a given point in the domain of the solution. In physics or other sciences, modeling a system frequently amounts to solving an initial value problem; in this context, the differential equation is an evolution equation specifying how, given initial conditions, the system will evolve with time.

An initial value problem is a differential equation

$$y'(t) = f(t, y(t)) \quad \text{with} \quad f : \mathbb{R} \times \mathbb{R} \to \mathbb{R}$$

together with a point in the domain of f

$$(t_0, y_0) \in \mathbb{R} \times \mathbb{R},$$

called the _____.

   a. Initial condition
   b. ALGOR
   c. ACTRAN
   d. AUSM

9. In mathematics, in the field of differential equations, an _____ is an ordinary differential equation together with specified value, called the initial condition, of the unknown function at a given point in the domain of the solution. In physics or other sciences, modeling a system frequently amounts to solving an _____; in this context, the differential equation is an evolution equation specifying how, given initial conditions, the system will evolve with time.

An _____ is a differential equation

$$y'(t) = f(t, y(t)) \quad \text{with} \quad f : \mathbb{R} \times \mathbb{R} \to \mathbb{R}$$

together with a point in the domain of f

$$(t_0, y_0) \in \mathbb{R} \times \mathbb{R},$$

called the initial condition.

   a. ACTRAN
   b. ALGOR
   c. Initial value problem
   d. AUSM

Chapter 9. MATHEMATICAL MODELING WITH DIFFERENTIAL EQUATIONS

10. Integration is an important concept in mathematics, specifically in the field of calculus and, more broadly, mathematical analysis. Given a function f of a real variable x and an interval [a, b] of the real line, the _____

$$\int_a^b f(x)\, dx,$$

is defined informally to be the net signed area of the region in the xy-plane bounded by the graph of f, the x-axis, and the vertical lines x = a and x = b.

The term '_____' may also refer to the notion of antiderivative, a function F whose derivative is the given function f.

a. Integral test for convergence
b. Integrand
c. Indefinite integral
d. Integral

11. In mathematics, an _____ is a function that is chosen to facilitate the solving of a given ordinary differential equation.

Consider an ordinary differential equation of the form

$$y' + a(x)y = b(x) \qquad (1)$$

where y = y(x) is an unknown function of x, and a(x) and b(x) are given functions.

The _____ method works by turning the left hand side into the form of the derivative of a product.

a. Integrating factor
b. Isomonodromic deformation
c. Oscillating
d. Exponential growth

12. In mathematics, a _____ is a differential equation of the form

$$Ly = f$$

where the differential operator L is a linear operator, y is the unknown function, and the right hand side f is a given function (called the source term.) The linearity condition on L rules out operations such as taking the square of the derivative of y; but permits, for example, taking the second derivative of y. Therefore a fairly general form of such an equation would be

$$a_n(x)D^n y(x) + a_{n-1}(x)D^{n-1}y(x) + \cdots + a_1(x)Dy(x) + a_0(x)y(x) = f(x)$$

where D is the differential operator d/dx (i.e. Dy = y', D^2y = y',...), and the a_i are given functions.

a. Stochastic differential equation
b. Petrovsky lacuna
c. Method of undetermined coefficients
d. Linear differential equation

13. In mathematics, a _____ differential equation may refer to one of two related things, both of which are differential equations that can be attacked by a method of separation of variables.

- For ordinary differential equations, it describes a class of equations that can be separated into a pair of integrals. See: Examples of differential equations

- For partial differential equations, it describes a class of equations that can be broken down into differential equations in fewer independent variables. See _____ partial differential equation.

a. Separable
b. Method of undetermined coefficients
c. Lax pair
d. Differential equation

14. In mathematics, _____ is any of several methods for solving ordinary and partial differential equations, in which algebra allows one to rewrite an equation so that each of two variables occurs on a different side of the equation.

Suppose a differential equation can be written in the form

$$\frac{d}{dx}f(x) = g(x)h(f(x)), \qquad (1)$$

which we can write more simply by letting y = f(x):

$$\frac{dy}{dx} = g(x)h(y).$$

As long as h(y) ≠ 0, we can rearrange terms to obtain:

$$\frac{dy}{h(y)} = g(x)dx,$$

so that the two variables x and y have been separated.

Some who dislike Leibniz's notation may prefer to write this as

$$\frac{1}{h(y)}\frac{dy}{dx} = g(x),$$

but that fails to make it quite as obvious why this is called '_____'.

Chapter 9. MATHEMATICAL MODELING WITH DIFFERENTIAL EQUATIONS

a. Sturm separation theorem
b. Power series method
c. Damping ratio
d. Separation of variables

15. In vector calculus, the _____ is an operator that measures the magnitude of a vector field's source or sink at a given point; the _____ of a vector field is a (signed) scalar. For example, consider air as it is heated or cooled. The relevant vector field for this example is the velocity of the moving air at a point.
    a. Divergence
    b. Triple product
    c. Green's theorem
    d. Gradient theorem

16. In vector calculus, the _____ Ostrogradskye;s theorem the _____ states that the outward flux of a vector field through a surface is equal to the triple integral of the divergence on the region inside the surface. Intuitively, it states that the sum of all sources minus the sum of all sinks gives the net flow out of a region.
    a. Divergence Theorem
    b. Del
    c. Green's theorem
    d. Divergence

17. In physics, _____ is defined as the rate of change of position. it is vector physical quantity; both speed and direction are required to define it. In the SI (metric) system, it is measured in meters per second: (m/s) or ms^{-1}.
    a. BDDC
    b. 15 theorem
    c. Velocity
    d. BIBO stability

18. The _____ of an angle is the ratio of the length of the opposite side to the length of the hypotenuse. In our case

$$\sin A = \frac{\text{opposite}}{\text{hypotenuse}} = \frac{a}{h}.$$

Note that this ratio does not depend on size of the particular right triangle chosen, as long as it contains the angle A, since all such triangles are similar.

The cosine of an angle is the ratio of the length of the adjacent side to the length of the hypotenuse.

a. Sine integral
b. Sine
c. Trigonometric
d. Trigonometric functions

19. In mathematics, a _____ (or direction field) is a graphical representation of the solutions of a first-order differential equation. It is achieved without solving the differential equation analytically, and thence it is useful. The representation may be used to qualitatively visualise solutions, or to numerically approximate them.
    a. Leibniz function
    b. Visual Calculus
    c. Slope field
    d. Continuous function

20. _____ is used to describe the steepness, incline, gradient, or grade of a straight line. A higher _____ value indicates a steeper incline. The _____ is defined as the ratio of the 'rise' divided by the 'run' between two points on a line, or in other words, the ratio of the altitude change to the horizontal distance between any two points on the line.
    a. 15 theorem
    b. Y-intercept
    c. Sequence
    d. Slope

21. In mathematics, an autonomous system or _____ is a system of ordinary differential equations which does not depend on the independent variable.

Many laws in physics, where the independent variable is usually assumed to be time, are expressed as autonomous systems because it is assumed the laws of nature which hold now are identical to those for any point in the past or future.

Autonomous systems are closely related to dynamical systems.

    a. Autonomous differential equation
    b. Integro-differential equation
    c. Algebraic differential equation
    d. Annihilator method

22. _____ is the change in population over time, and can be quantified as the change in the number of individuals in a population using 'per unit time' for measurement. The term _____ can technically refer to any species, but almost always refers to humans, and it is often used informally for the more specific demographic term _____ rate, and is often used to refer specifically to the growth of the population of the world.

Simple models of _____ include the Malthusian Growth Model and the logistic model.

    a. 15 theorem
    b. Population growth
    c. BIBO stability
    d. BDDC

23. The _____ of a biological species in an environment is the population size of the species that the environment can sustain in the long term, given the food, habitat, water and other necessities available in the environment. For the human population, more complex variables such as sanitation and medical care are sometimes considered as part of the necessary infrastructure.

As population density increases, birth rate often increases and death rate typically decreases.

    a. 15 theorem
    b. BIBO stability
    c. BDDC
    d. Carrying capacity

24. The _____ is a polynomial mapping of degree 2, often cited as an archetypal example of how complex, chaotic behaviour can arise from very simple non-linear dynamical equations. The map was popularized in a seminal 1976 paper by the biologist Robert May, in part as a discrete-time demographic model analogous to the logistic equation first created by Pierre François Verhulst. Mathematically, the _____ is written

$$(1) \quad x_{n+1} = r x_n (1 - x_n)$$

where:

    x_n is a number between zero and one, and represents the population at year n, and hence x_0 represents the initial population (at year 0)
    r is a positive number, and represents a combined rate for reproduction and starvation.

Chapter 9. MATHEMATICAL MODELING WITH DIFFERENTIAL EQUATIONS

a. BIBO stability
c. BDDC
b. 15 theorem
d. Logistic map

25. _____ is a type of motion in which the velocity of an object changes equal amounts in equal time periods. An example of an object having _____ would be a ball rolling down a ramp. The object picks up velocity as it goes down the ramp with equal changes in time.
   a. Uniform Acceleration
   c. AUSM
   b. ACTRAN
   d. ALGOR

26. A quantity is said to be subject to _____ if it decreases at a rate proportional to its value. Symbolically, this can be expressed as the following differential equation, where N is the quantity and λ is a positive number called the decay constant.

$$\frac{dN}{dt} = -\lambda N.$$

The solution to this equation is:

$$N(t) = N_0 e^{-\lambda t}.$$

Here N(t) is the quantity at time t, and $N_0 = N(0)$ is the initial quantity, i.e. the quantity at time t = 0.

   a. Exponential sum
   c. ALGOR
   b. ACTRAN
   d. Exponential decay

27. _____ (including exponential decay) occurs when the growth rate of a mathematical function is proportional to the function's current value. In the case of a discrete domain of definition with equal intervals it is also called geometric growth or geometric decay (the function values form a geometric progression.)

_____ is said to follow an exponential law; the simple-_____ model is known as the Malthusian growth model.

   a. Oscillating
   c. Inseparable differential equation
   b. Isomonodromic deformation
   d. Exponential growth

28. In computer science and information science, _____ could also be a method or an algorithm. Again, an example will illustrate: There are systems of counting, as with Roman numerals, and various systems for filing papers, or catalogues, and various library systems, of which the Dewey Decimal _____ is an example. This still fits with the definition of components which are connected together (in this case in order to facilitate the flow of information.)
   a. BDDC
   c. 15 theorem
   b. BIBO stability
   d. System

29. The _____ of a quantity whose value decreases with time is the interval required for the quantity to decay to half of its initial value. The concept originated in describing how long it takes atoms to undergo radioactive decay but also applies in a wide variety of other situations.

Chapter 9. MATHEMATICAL MODELING WITH DIFFERENTIAL EQUATIONS

The term '_____' dates to 1907.

a. BDDC
c. 15 theorem

b. BIBO stability
d. Half-life

30. In mathematics, _____ and minima, known collectively as extrema, are the largest value (maximum) or smallest value (minimum), that a function takes in a point either within a given neighbourhood (local extremum) or on the function domain in its entirety (global extremum.)

Throughout, a point refers to an input (x), while a value refers to an output (y): one distinguishing between the maximum value and the point (or points) at which it occurs.

A real-valued function f defined on the real line is said to have a local maximum point at the point x^*, if there exists some $\varepsilon > 0$, such that $f(x^*) \geq f(x)$ when $|x - x^*| < \varepsilon$.

a. Related rates
c. Racetrack principle

b. Leibniz formula
d. Maxima

31. A _____ has several distinct meanings.

One meaning is that a first-order ordinary differential equation is homogeneous if it has the form

$$\frac{dy}{dx} = F(y/x).$$

To solve such equations, one makes the change of variables u = y/x, which will transform such an equation into separable one.

Another meaning is a linear _____, which is a differential equation of the form

$$Ly = 0$$

where the differential operator L is a linear operator, and y is the unknown function.

a. Homogeneous differential equation
c. Structural stability

b. Differential algebraic equations
d. Nahm equations

32. In acoustics and telecommunication, a _____ of a wave is a component frequency of the signal that is an integer multiple of the fundamental frequency. For example, if the fundamental frequency is f, the harmonics have frequencies f, 2f, 3f, 4f, etc. The harmonics have the property that they are all periodic at the fundamental frequency, therefore the sum of harmonics is also periodic at that frequency.

Chapter 9. MATHEMATICAL MODELING WITH DIFFERENTIAL EQUATIONS

- a. Harmonic
- b. 15 theorem
- c. BIBO stability
- d. BDDC

33. In mathematics, especially in order theory, an upper bound of a subset S of some partially ordered set (P, ≤) is an element of P which is greater than or equal to every element of S. The term _____ is defined dually as an element of P which is lesser than or equal to every element of S. A set with an upper bound is said to be bounded from above by that bound, a set with a _____ is said to be bounded from below by that bound.

A subset S of a partially ordered set P may fail to have any bounds or may have many different upper and lower bounds. By transitivity, any element greater than or equal to an upper bound of S is again an upper bound of S, and any element lesser than or equal to any _____ of S is again a _____ of S. This leads to the consideration of least upper bounds: (or suprema) and greatest lower bounds (or infima.)

- a. BIBO stability
- b. BDDC
- c. Lower bound
- d. 15 theorem

34. The most commonly encountered form of Hooke's law is probably the spring equation, which relates the force exerted by a spring to the distance it is stretched by a _____, k, measured in force per length.

$$F = -kx$$

The negative sign indicates that the force exerted by the spring is in direct opposition to the direction of displacement. It is called a 'restoring force', as it tends to restore the system to equilibrium.

- a. Spring equation
- b. Navier-Stokes equations
- c. Polar moment of inertia
- d. Spring constant

35. _____ is any effect, either deliberately engendered or inherent to a system, that tends to reduce the amplitude of oscillations of an oscillatory system.

In physics and engineering, _____ may be mathematically modelled as a force synchronous with the velocity of the object but opposite in direction to it. If such force is also proportional to the velocity, as for a simple mechanical viscous damper (dashpot), the force F may be related to the velocity v by

$$\mathbf{F} = -c\mathbf{v}$$

where c is the viscous _____ coefficient, given in units of newton-seconds per meter.

- a. BDDC
- b. BIBO stability
- c. 15 theorem
- d. Damping

Chapter 10. INFINITE SERIES

1. Cantor defined two kinds of _____ numbers, the ordinal numbers and the cardinal numbers. Ordinal numbers may be identified with well-ordered sets, or counting carried on to any stopping point, including points after an _____ number have already been counted. Generalizing finite and the ordinary _____ sequences which are maps from the positive integers leads to mappings from ordinal numbers, and transfinite sequences.
   - a. AUSM
   - b. ALGOR
   - c. ACTRAN
   - d. Infinite

2. The terms of the series are often produced according to a certain rule, such as by a formula, by an algorithm, by a sequence of measurements, or even by a random number generator. As there are an infinite number of terms, this notion is often called an _____. Unlike finite summations, series need tools from mathematical analysis to be fully understood and manipulated.
   - a. Extreme Value Theorem
   - b. Integration by substitution
   - c. Infinite series
   - d. Extreme value

3. In calculus, _____ gives a sequence of approximations of a differentiable function around a given point by polynomials (the Taylor polynomials of that function) whose coefficients depend only on the derivatives of the function at that point. The theorem also gives precise estimates on the size of the error in the approximation. The theorem is named after the mathematician Brook Taylor, who stated it in 1712, though the result was first discovered 41 years earlier in 1671 by James Gregory.
   - a. Taylor's theorem
   - b. Fresnel integrals
   - c. Local minimum
   - d. Related rates

4. In mathematics, a _____ is an approximation of a general function using a linear function (more precisely, an affine function.)

Given a differentiable function f of one real variable, Taylor's theorem for n=1 states that

$$f(x) = f(a) + f\,'(a)(x - a) + R_2$$

where R_2 is the remainder term. The _____ is obtained by dropping the remainder:

$$f(x) \approx f(a) + f\,'(a)(x - a)$$

which is true for x close to a.

   - a. Point of inflection
   - b. Lin-Tsien equation
   - c. Smooth function
   - d. Linear approximation

5. In mathematics, the _____ of a non-negative integer n, denoted by n!, is the product of all positive integers less than or equal to n. For example,

$$5! = 1 \times 2 \times 3 \times 4 \times 5 = 120$$

and

$$6! = 1 \times 2 \times 3 \times 4 \times 5 \times 6 = 720.$$

The notation n! was introduced by Christian Kramp in 1808.

The _____ function is formally defined by

$$n! = \prod_{k=1}^{n} k \qquad \forall n \in \mathbb{N}$$

or recursively defined by

$$n! = \begin{cases} n \leq 1 & 1 \\ n > 1 & n(n-1)! \end{cases} \qquad \forall n \in \mathbb{N}.$$

Both of the above definitions incorporate the instance

$$0! = 1$$

as an instance of the fact that the product of no numbers at all is 1.

   a. BDDC   b. Constraint counting
   c. 15 theorem   d. Factorial

   6. _____ is the addition of a set of numbers; the result is their sum or total. An interim or present total of a _____ process is termed the running total. The 'numbers' to be summed may be natural numbers, complex numbers, matrices, or still more complicated objects.
     a. Summation   b. 15 theorem
     c. BIBO stability   d. BDDC

   7. In mathematics, a _____ is an ordered list of objects (or events). Like a set, it contains members (also called elements or terms), and the number of terms (possibly infinite) is called the length of the _____. Unlike a set, order matters, and the exact same elements can appear multiple times at different positions in the _____.
     a. Slope   b. Y-intercept
     c. 15 theorem   d. Sequence

Chapter 10. INFINITE SERIES

8. In mathematics, a (topological) _____ is defined as follows: let I be an interval of real numbers (i.e. a non-empty connected subset of $\mathbb{R}$); then a _____ γ is a continuous mapping $\gamma : I \to X$, where X is a topological space. The _____ γ is said to be simple if it is injective, i.e. if for all x, y in I, we have $\gamma(x) = \gamma(y) \implies x = y$. If I is a closed bounded interval $[a, b]$, we also allow the possibility $\gamma(a) = \gamma(b)$ (this convention makes it possible to talk about closed simple _____.)

   a. Prolate cycloid
   b. Curve
   c. Closed curve
   d. Tractrix

9. A _____ officer is an officer of high military rank. The term or equivalent is used by nearly every country in the world. _____ can be used as a generic term for all grades of _____ officer, or it can specifically refer to a single rank that is just called _____.

   a. BIBO stability
   b. BDDC
   c. General
   d. 15 theorem

10. In mathematics, the concept of a '_____' is used to describe the behavior of a function as its argument or input either 'gets close' to some point, or as the argument becomes arbitrarily large; or the behavior of a sequence's elements as their index increases indefinitely. Limits are used in calculus and other branches of mathematical analysis to define derivatives and continuity.

   In formulas, _____ is usually abbreviated as lim

   a. Limit
   b. BIBO stability
   c. 15 theorem
   d. BDDC

11. In mathematics, especially in order theory, an _____ of a subset S of some partially ordered set (P, >≤) is an element of P which is greater than or equal to every element of S. The term lower bound is defined dually as an element of P which is lesser than or equal to every element of S. A set with an _____ is said to be bounded from above by that bound, a set with a lower bound is said to be bounded from below by that bound.

   A subset S of a partially ordered set P may fail to have any bounds or may have many different upper and lower bounds. By transitivity, any element greater than or equal to an _____ of S is again an _____ of S, and any element lesser than or equal to any lower bound of S is again a lower bound of S. This leads to the consideration of least upper bounds: (or suprema) and greatest lower bounds (or infima.)

   a. Upper bound
   b. AUSM
   c. ACTRAN
   d. ALGOR

12. In calculus, a branch of mathematics, the _____ is a measurement of how a function changes when its input changes. Loosely speaking, a _____ can be thought of as how much a quantity is changing at some given point. For example, the _____ of the position (or distance) of a vehicle with respect to time is the instantaneous velocity (respectively, instantaneous speed) at which the vehicle is traveling.

   The process of finding a _____ is called differentiation. The fundamental theorem of calculus states that differentiation is the reverse process to integration.

a. Bounded function
c. Stationary phase approximation
b. Derivative
d. Semi-differentiability

13. In mathematics the infimum of a subset of some set is the greatest element, not necessarily in the subset, that is less than or equal to all elements of the subset. Consequently the term _____ is also commonly used. Infima of real numbers are a common special case that is especially important in analysis.
   a. Greatest lower bound
   c. BIBO stability
   b. 15 theorem
   d. BDDC

14. In mathematics, given a subset S of a partially ordered set T, the _____ (sup) of S, if it exists, is the least element of T that is greater than or equal to each element of S. Consequently, the _____ is also referred to as the least upper bound, lub or LUB. If the _____ exists, it may or may not belong to S.
   a. BDDC
   c. Supremum
   b. BIBO stability
   d. 15 theorem

15. In mathematics, especially in order theory, an upper bound of a subset S of some partially ordered set (P, ≤) is an element of P which is greater than or equal to every element of S. The term _____ is defined dually as an element of P which is lesser than or equal to every element of S. A set with an upper bound is said to be bounded from above by that bound, a set with a _____ is said to be bounded from below by that bound.

A subset S of a partially ordered set P may fail to have any bounds or may have many different upper and lower bounds. By transitivity, any element greater than or equal to an upper bound of S is again an upper bound of S, and any element lesser than or equal to any _____ of S is again a _____ of S. This leads to the consideration of least upper bounds: (or suprema) and greatest lower bounds (or infima.)

   a. Lower bound
   c. BDDC
   b. 15 theorem
   d. BIBO stability

16. In mathematics, a _____ of a function of several variables is its derivative with respect to one of those variables with the others held constant (as opposed to the total derivative, in which all variables are allowed to vary.) Partial derivatives are useful in vector calculus and differential geometry.

The _____ of a function f with respect to the variable x is written as f'_x, $\partial_x f$, or $\partial f/\partial x$.

   a. Differentiation operator
   c. Partial derivative
   b. Level curve
   d. Jacobian

17. In mathematics, the _____ is a representation of a function as an infinite sum of terms calculated from the values of its derivatives at a single point. It may be regarded as the limit of the Taylor polynomials. If the series is centered at zero, the series is also called a Maclaurin series.
   a. BDDC
   c. BIBO stability
   b. 15 theorem
   d. Taylor series

18. In mathematics, a _____ is the graph of the system of parametric equations

$$x = A\sin(at + \delta), \quad y = B\sin(bt),$$

which describes complex harmonic motion. This family of curves was investigated by Nathaniel Bowditch in 1815, and later in more detail by Jules Antoine Lissajous in 1857.

The appearance of the figure is highly sensitive to the ratio a/b.

a. BDDC
b. BIBO stability
c. 15 theorem
d. Lissajous curve

19. Call S_N the _____ to N of the sequence {a_n}, or _____ of the series. A series is the sequence of partial sums, {S_N}.

When talking about series, one can refer either to the sequence {S_N} of the partial sums, or to the sum of the series,

$$\sum_{n=0}^{\infty} a_n$$

i.e., the limit of the sequence of partial sums - it is clear which one is meant from context.

a. Dirichlet integral
b. Maxima
c. The Method of Mechanical Theorems
d. Partial sum

20. In mathematics, a _____ is a series with a constant ratio between successive terms. For example, the series

$$\frac{1}{2} + \frac{1}{4} + \frac{1}{8} + \frac{1}{16} + \cdots$$

is geometric, because each term is equal to half of the previous term. The sum of this series is 1, as illustrated in the following picture:

_____ are one of the simplest examples of infinite series with finite sums.

a. Sequence transformation
b. Conditionally convergent
c. Converge absolutely
d. Geometric series

21. A _____ is an expression which compares quantities relative to each other. The most common examples involve two quantities, but in theory any number of quantities can be compared. In mathematical terms, they are represented by separating each quantity with a colon, for example the _____ 2:3, which is read as the _____ 'two to three'.

a. Ratio
b. Y-intercept
c. 15 theorem
d. Sequence

22. In acoustics and telecommunication, a _____ of a wave is a component frequency of the signal that is an integer multiple of the fundamental frequency. For example, if the fundamental frequency is f, the harmonics have frequencies f, 2f, 3f, 4f, etc. The harmonics have the property that they are all periodic at the fundamental frequency, therefore the sum of harmonics is also periodic at that frequency.

a. BDDC
b. BIBO stability
c. 15 theorem
d. Harmonic

23. In mathematics, the _____ is the infinite series

$$\sum_{k=1}^{\infty} \frac{1}{k} = 1 + \frac{1}{2} + \frac{1}{3} + \frac{1}{4} + \cdots.$$

Its name derives from the concept of overtones, or harmonics, in music: the wavelengths of the overtones of a vibrating string are 1/2, 1/3, 1/4, etc., of the string's fundamental wavelength. Every term of the series after the first is the harmonic mean of the neighboring terms; the term harmonic mean likewise derives from music.

The _____ diverges to infinity, albeit rather slowly (the first 10^{43} terms sum to less than 100 .)

a. BDDC
b. 15 theorem
c. Harmonic series
d. BIBO stability

24. If a particular point on a sphere is (arbitrarily) designated as its _____, then the corresponding antipodal point is called the south pole and the equator is the great circle that is equidistant to them. Great circles through the two poles are called lines (or meridians) of longitude, and the line connecting the two poles is called the axis of rotation. Circles on the sphere that are parallel to the equator are lines of latitude.

a. Tangent line
b. Minimal surface
c. Sphere
d. North pole

25. In vector calculus, the _____ is an operator that measures the magnitude of a vector field's source or sink at a given point; the _____ of a vector field is a (signed) scalar. For example, consider air as it is heated or cooled. The relevant vector field for this example is the velocity of the moving air at a point.

a. Divergence
b. Triple product
c. Green's theorem
d. Gradient theorem

26. In the branch of mathematics known as real analysis, the _____, created by Bernhard Riemann, was the first rigorous definition of the integral of a function on an interval. While the _____ is unsuitable for many theoretical purposes, it is one of the easiest integrals to define. Some of these technical deficiencies can be remedied by the Riemann-Stieltjes integral, and most of them disappear in the Lebesgue integral.

a. Riemann integral
b. Lebesgue integration
c. Skorokhod integral
d. Regulated integral

27. Integration is an important concept in mathematics, specifically in the field of calculus and, more broadly, mathematical analysis. Given a function f of a real variable x and an interval [a, b] of the real line, the _____

$$\int_a^b f(x)\,dx,$$

is defined informally to be the net signed area of the region in the xy-plane bounded by the graph of f, the x-axis, and the vertical lines x = a and x = b.

The term '_____' may also refer to the notion of antiderivative, a function F whose derivative is the given function f.

a. Integral
c. Integral test for convergence
b. Indefinite integral
d. Integrand

28. In mathematics, the _____ for convergence is a method used to test infinite series of non-negative terms for convergence. An early form of the test of convergence was developed in India by Madhava in the 14th century, and by his followers at the Kerala School. In Europe, it was later developed by Maclaurin and Cauchy and is sometimes known as the Maclaurin-Cauchy test.

a. Integral test
c. ACTRAN
b. ALGOR
d. AUSM

29. In mathematics, the _____, sometimes called the direct _____ is a criterion for convergence or divergence of a series whose terms are real or complex numbers. The test determines convergence by comparing the terms of the series in question with those of a series whose convergence properties are known.

The _____ states that if the series

$$\sum_{n=1}^{\infty} b_n$$

is an absolutely convergent series and

$$|a_n| \le |b_n|$$

for sufficiently large n , then the series

$$\sum_{n=1}^{\infty} a_n$$

converges absolutely.

a. Conditionally convergent
c. Ratio test
b. Telescoping series
d. Comparison test

30. _____ is how much exposed area an object has. It is expressed in square units. If an object has flat faces, its _____ can be calculated by adding together the areas of its faces.
   a. Lipschitz domain
   b. Vector area
   c. Surface area
   d. Plane curve

31. In mathematics, the _____ is a test (or 'criterion') for the convergence of a series

$$\sum_{n=0}^{\infty} a_n$$

whose terms are real or complex numbers. The test was first published by Jean le Rond d'Alembert and is sometimes known as d'Alembert's _____. The test makes use of the number

$$()$$

in the cases where this limit exists.

   a. Telescoping series
   b. Geometric series
   c. Converge absolutely
   d. Ratio test

32. In mathematics, the _____ is a criterion for the convergence (a convergence test) of an infinite series

$$\sum_{n=1}^{\infty} a_n.$$

It is particularly useful in connection with power series.

The _____ was developed first by Cauchy and so is sometimes known as the Cauchy _____ or Cauchy's radical test.
The _____ uses the number

$$C = \limsup_{n \to \infty} \sqrt[n]{|a_n|},$$

where 'lim sup' denotes the limit superior, possibly ∞.

   a. Root test
   b. Mean Value Theorem
   c. Related rates
   d. Racetrack principle

33. In mathematics, _____, first defined by the mathematician Daniel Bernoulli and generalized by Friedrich Bessel, are canonical solutions y(x) of Bessel's differential equation:

$$x^2\frac{d^2y}{dx^2} + x\frac{dy}{dx} + (x^2 - \alpha^2)y = 0$$

for an arbitrary real or complex number α (the order of the Bessel function.) The most common and important special case is where α is an integer n.

Although α and −α produce the same differential equation, it is conventional to define different _____ for these two orders (e.g., so that the _____ are mostly smooth functions of α.)

    a. Logarithmic integral function
    b. 15 theorem
    c. Multiplication theorem
    d. Bessel functions

34. In mathematics, an _____ is an infinite series of the form

$$\sum_{n=0}^{\infty}(-1)^n a_n,$$

with $a_n \geq 0$ (or $a_n \leq 0$) for all n. A finite sum of this kind is an alternating sum. An _____ converges if the terms a_n converge to 0 monotonically.

    a. Uniform convergence
    b. Infinite series
    c. Extreme value
    d. Alternating series

35. The _____ converges:

$$\sum_{k=1}^{\infty}\frac{(-1)^{k+1}}{k} = 1 - \frac{1}{2} + \frac{1}{3} - \frac{1}{4} + \cdots = \ln 2 = 0.693\,147\,180\ldots.$$

This equality is a consequence of the Mercator series, the Taylor series for the natural logarithm. Another equality, similar in form to Mercator's series, is:

$$\sum_{k=0}^{\infty}\frac{(-1)^k}{2k+1} = 1 - \frac{1}{3} + \frac{1}{5} - \frac{1}{7} + \cdots = \arctan(1) = \frac{\pi}{4}.$$

This is a consequence of the Taylor series representation of the inverse tangent function (which has a radius of convergence of 1.)

The nth partial sum of the diverging harmonic series,

$$H_n = \sum_{k=1}^{n}\frac{1}{k},$$

is called the nth harmonic number.

a. ACTRAN
c. Alternating harmonic series

b. ALGOR
d. AUSM

36. In mathematics, a series (or sometimes also an integral) is said to converge absolutely if the sum (or integral) of the absolute value of the summand or integrand is finite.

More precisely, a real or complex-valued series $\sum_{n=0}^{\infty} a_n$ is said to converge absolutely if $\sum_{n=0}^{\infty} |a_n| < \infty$.

_____ is vitally important to the study of infinite series because on the one hand, it is strong enough that such series retain certain basic properties of finite sums -- the most important ones being rearrangement of the terms and convergence of products of two infinite series -- that are unfortunately not possessed by all convergent series. On the other hand _____ is weak enough to occur very often in practice.

a. ACTRAN
c. Absolute convergence

b. Eisenstein series
d. Alternating series test

37. In mathematics, a series or integral is said to be _____ if it converges, but it does not converge absolutely.

More precisely, a series $\sum_{n=0}^{\infty} a_n$ is said to converge conditionally if $\lim_{m \to \infty} \sum_{n=0}^{m} a_n$ exists and is a finite number (not ∞ or −∞), but $\sum_{n=0}^{\infty} |a_n| = \infty$.

A classical example is given by

$$1 - \frac{1}{2} + \frac{1}{3} - \frac{1}{4} + \frac{1}{5} - \cdots = \sum_{n=1}^{\infty} \frac{(-1)^{n+1}}{n}$$

which converges to ln 2 , but is not absolutely convergent

The simplest examples of _____ series (including the one above) are the alternating series.

a. Converge absolutely
c. Geometric series

b. Ratio test
d. Conditionally convergent

38. The _____ is a method used to prove that infinite series of terms converge. It was discovered by Gottfried Leibniz and is sometimes known as Leibniz's test or the Leibniz criterion.

A series of the form

$$\sum_{n=1}^{\infty} (-1)^n a_n$$

where all the a_n are positive or 0, is called an alternating series.

a. Absolute convergence
b. ACTRAN
c. Alternating series test
d. Eisenstein series

39. In mathematics, a _____ (in one variable) is an infinite series of the form

$$f(x) = \sum_{n=0}^{\infty} a_n (x - c)^n = a_0 + a_1(x - c)^1 + a_2(x - c)^2 + a_3(x - c)^3 + \cdots$$

where a_n represents the coefficient of the nth term, c is a constant, and x varies around c (for this reason one sometimes speaks of the series as being centered at c

In many situations c is equal to zero, for instance when considering a Maclaurin series.

a. Differential calculus
b. Stationary phase approximation
c. Differential coefficient
d. Power series

40. In mathematics, the _____ of a power series is a non-negative quantity, either a real number or ∞, that represents a domain (within the radius) in which the series will converge. Within the _____, a power series converges absolutely and uniformly on compacta as well. If the series converges, it is the Taylor series of the analytic function to which it converges inside its _____.

a. Blaschke product
b. Radius of convergence
c. Branch point
d. Holomorphically separable

41. The _____ of an angle is the ratio of the length of the opposite side to the length of the hypotenuse. In our case

$$\sin A = \frac{\text{opposite}}{\text{hypotenuse}} = \frac{a}{h}.$$

Note that this ratio does not depend on size of the particular right triangle chosen, as long as it contains the angle A, since all such triangles are similar.

The cosine of an angle is the ratio of the length of the adjacent side to the length of the hypotenuse.

a. Trigonometric
b. Trigonometric functions
c. Sine integral
d. Sine

42. Trigonometry is a branch of mathematics that deals with triangles, particularly those plane triangles in which one angle has 90 degrees (right triangles.) Trigonometry deals with relationships between the sides and the angles of triangles and with the _____ functions, which describe those relationships.

Trigonometry has applications in both pure mathematics and in applied mathematics, where it is essential in many branches of science and technology.

   a. Trigonometric functions
   b. Sine
   c. Trigonometric integrals
   d. Trigonometric

43. In mathematics, the _____ are functions of an angle. They are important in the study of triangles and modeling periodic phenomena, among many other applications. _____ are commonly defined as ratios of two sides of a right triangle containing the angle, and can equivalently be defined as the lengths of various line segments from a unit circle.

   a. Trigonometric integrals
   b. Trigonometric
   c. Trigonometric functions
   d. Sine integral

44. The _____ is a function in mathematics. The application of this function to a value x is written as exp(x). Equivalently, this can be written in the form e^x, where e is a mathematical constant, the base of the natural logarithm, which equals approximately 2.718281828, and is also known as Euler's number.

   a. Area hyperbolic functions
   b. ACTRAN
   c. Integral part
   d. Exponential function

45. _____ is the study of algorithms for the problems of continuous mathematics (as distinguished from discrete mathematics.)

One of the earliest mathematical writings is the Babylonian tablet YBC 7289, which gives a sexagesimal numerical approximation of $\sqrt{2}$, the length of the diagonal in a unit square. Being able to compute the sides of a triangle (and hence, being able to compute square roots) is extremely important, for instance, in carpentry and construction.

   a. BIBO stability
   b. BDDC
   c. Numerical analysis
   d. 15 theorem

46. In elementary algebra, a _____ is a polynomial with two terms--the sum of two monomials--often bound by parenthesis or brackets when operated upon. It is the simplest kind of polynomial other than monomials.

- The _____ $a^2 - b^2$ can be factored as the product of two other binomials:

    $a^2 - b^2 = (a + b)(a - b.)$

    This is a special case of the more general formula:

    $$a^{n+1} - b^{n+1} = (a - b) \sum_{k=0}^{n} a^k b^{n-k}$$

- The product of a pair of linear binomials $(ax + b)$ and $(cx + d)$ is:

    $(ax + b)(cx + d) = acx^2 + axd + bcx + bd.$

- A _____ raised to the nth power, represented as

    $(a + b)^n$

    can be expanded by means of the _____ theorem or, equivalently, using Pascal's triangle. Taking a simple example, the perfect square _____ $(p + q)^2$ can be found by squaring the :first digit, adding twice the product of the first and second digit and finally adding the square of the second digit, to give $p^2 + 2pq + q^2$.

    a. Completing the square
    b. Binomial
    c. Partial fractions
    d. Multinomial theorem

47. In mathematics, the _____ generalizes the purely algebraic formula of the binomial theorem to complex values of α. It is also a special case of a Newton series. The _____ is the series

$$(1 + x)^\alpha = \sum_{k=0}^{\infty} \binom{\alpha}{k} x^k = \sum_{k=0}^{\infty} \frac{\prod_{a=0}^{k-1}(\alpha - a) \, x^k}{k!}$$

where α is a complex number and

$$\binom{\alpha}{k} = \frac{\alpha(\alpha - 1)(\alpha - 2) \cdots (\alpha - k + 1)}{k!}$$

is the (generalized) binomial coefficient (if α is a non negative integer, then the (α + 1) th term and all later terms in the series are zero, since each one contains a factor equal to (α − α): thus, in that case, the summation reduces to the algebraic binomial formula.)

a. Maxima
b. Fresnel integrals
c. Binomial series
d. Differential

48. In mathematics, the _____ $\binom{n}{k}$ is the coefficient of the x^k term in the polynomial expansion of the binomial power $(1 + x)^n$.

In combinatorics, $\binom{n}{k}$ is interpreted as the number of k-element subsets (the k-combinations) of an n-element set, that is the number of ways that k things can be 'chosen' from a set of n things. Hence, $\binom{n}{k}$ is often read as 'n choose k' and is called the choose function of n and k.

    a. 15 theorem
    c. BDDC
    b. Factorial
    d. Binomial coefficient

49. In mathematics, a _____ is a constant multiplicative factor of a certain object. For example, in the expression $9x^2$, the _____ of x^2 is 9.

The object can be such things as a variable, a vector, a function, etc.

    a. Binomial type
    c. Coefficient
    b. Resultant
    d. Degree of the polynomial

50. In mathematics and physics, a _____ associates a scalar value, which can be either mathematical in definition to every point in space. Scalar fields are often used in physics, for instance to indicate the temperature distribution throughout space or more specifically, differential geometry, the set of functions defined on a manifold define the commutative ring of functions.

    a. Symmetry of second derivatives
    c. Level curve
    b. Vector Laplacian
    d. Scalar field

51. The _____ of an object is the extra energy which it possesses due to its motion. It is defined as the work needed to accelerate a body of a given mass from rest to its current velocity. Having gained this energy during its acceleration, the body maintains this _____ unless its speed changes.

    a. Law of Conservation of Energy
    c. 15 theorem
    b. BDDC
    d. Kinetic energy

52. In mathematics, the _____, named after German mathematician Bernhard Riemann, is a prominent function of great significance in number theory because of its relation to the distribution of prime numbers. It also has applications in other areas such as physics, probability theory, and applied statistics.

The Riemann hypothesis, a conjecture about the distribution of the zeros of the _____, is considered by many mathematicians to be the most important unsolved problem in pure mathematics.

    a. BIBO stability
    c. Riemann zeta function
    b. 15 theorem
    d. BDDC

Chapter 11. ANALYTIC GEOMETRY IN CALCULUS

1. In mathematics and its applications, a _____ system is a system for assigning an n-tuple of numbers or scalars to each point in an n-dimensional space. This concept is part of the theory of manifolds. 'Scalars' in many cases means real numbers, but, depending on context, can mean complex numbers or elements of some other commutative ring.
   a. Spherical coordinate system
   b. 15 theorem
   c. Cylindrical coordinate system
   d. Coordinate

2. In mathematics, the _____ is a two-dimensional coordinate system in which each point on a plane is determined by an angle and a distance. The _____ is especially useful in situations where the relationship between two points is most easily expressed in terms of angles and distance; in the more familiar Cartesian or rectangular coordinate system, such a relationship can only be found through trigonometric formulation.

   As the coordinate system is two-dimensional, each point is determined by two polar coordinates: the radial coordinate and the angular coordinate.

   a. 15 theorem
   b. BIBO stability
   c. BDDC
   d. Polar coordinate system

3. In complex analysis, a mathematical discipline, a _____ of a meromorphic function is a certain type of singularity that behaves like the singularity of $\frac{1}{z^n}$ at z = 0. This means that, in particular, a _____ of the function f(z) is a point z = a such that f(z) approaches infinity uniformly as z approaches a.

   Formally, suppose U is an open subset of the complex plane C, a is an element of U and f : U {a} → C is a function which is holomorphic over its domain.

   a. Pole
   b. Lacunary function
   c. Complex logarithm
   d. Bieberbach conjecture

4. In mathematics, a (topological) _____ is defined as follows: let I be an interval of real numbers (i.e. a non-empty connected subset of $\mathbb{R}$); then a _____ γ is a continuous mapping $\gamma : I \to X$, where X is a topological space. The _____ γ is said to be simple if it is injective, i.e. if for all x, y in I, we have $\gamma(x) = \gamma(y) \implies x = y$. If I is a closed bounded interval $[a, b]$, we also allow the possibility $\gamma(a) = \gamma(b)$ (this convention makes it possible to talk about closed simple _____.)
   a. Tractrix
   b. Curve
   c. Prolate cycloid
   d. Closed curve

5. In mathematics, a _____ or rhodonea curve is a sinusoid plotted in polar coordinates. Up to similarity, these curves can all be expressed by a polar equation of the form

$$r = \cos(k\theta).$$

Chapter 11. ANALYTIC GEOMETRY IN CALCULUS

If k is an integer, the curve will be _____ shaped with

- 2k petals if k is even, and
- k petals if k is odd.

When k is even, the entire graph of the _____ will be traced out exactly once when the value of θ changes from 0 to 2π. When k is odd, this will happen on the interval between 0 and π. (More generally, this will happen on any interval of length 2π for k even, and π for k odd.)

a. Space curve	b. Curtate cycloid
c. Rose	d. Cochleoid

6. _____ generally conveys two primary meanings. The first is an imprecise sense of harmonious or aesthetically-pleasing proportionality and balance; such that it reflects beauty or perfection. The second meaning is a precise and well-defined concept of balance or 'patterned self-similarity' that can be demonstrated or proved according to the rules of a formal system: by geometry, through physics or otherwise.

a. BDDC	b. BIBO stability
c. 15 theorem	d. Symmetry

7. A _____ is closed curve with one cusp.

In geometry, the _____ is an epicycloid with one cusp.

Rolling circle around another fixed circle produces _____ (red curve) Conformal mapping from circle to _____

- epicycloid produced as the path (or locus) of a point on the circumference of a circle as that circle rolls around another fixed circle with the same radius.

- limaçon with one cusp. The cusp is formed when the ratio of a to b in the equation is equal to one.

a. 15 theorem	b. BDDC
c. BIBO stability	d. Cardioid

8. In calculus, _____, was originally the use of expressions such as dx and dy and to represent 'infinitely small' (or infinitesimal) increments of quantities x and y, just as >Δx and >Δy represent finite increments of x and y respectively. So for y being a function of x, or

118 *Chapter 11. ANALYTIC GEOMETRY IN CALCULUS*

the derivative of y with respect to x, which later came to be viewed as

$$$$

was, according to Leibniz, the quotient of an infinitesimal increment of y by an infinitesimal increment of x, or

$$$$

where the right hand side is Lagrange's notation for the derivative of f at x.

Similarly, although mathematicians usually now view an integral

$$$$

as a limit

$$$$

where $>\Delta x$ is an interval containing x_i, Leibniz viewed it as the sum (the integral sign denoting summation) of infinitely many infinitesimal quantities f(x) dx.

    a. Time derivative   b. Stationary point
    c. Leibniz's notation   d. Smooth function

9.   In calculus, a branch of mathematics, the _____ is a measurement of how a function changes when its input changes. Loosely speaking, a _____ can be thought of as how much a quantity is changing at some given point. For example, the _____ of the position (or distance) of a vehicle with respect to time is the instantaneous velocity (respectively, instantaneous speed) at which the vehicle is traveling.

The process of finding a _____ is called differentiation. The fundamental theorem of calculus states that differentiation is the reverse process to integration.

    a. Bounded function   b. Stationary phase approximation
    c. Semi-differentiability   d. Derivative

10.   In mathematics, a _____ of a function of several variables is its derivative with respect to one of those variables with the others held constant (as opposed to the total derivative, in which all variables are allowed to vary.) Partial derivatives are useful in vector calculus and differential geometry.

The _____ of a function f with respect to the variable x is written as f'_x, $\partial_x f$, or $\partial f / \partial x$.

a. Partial derivative
b. Differentiation operator
c. Level curve
d. Jacobian

11. In mathematics, a _____ is the graph of the system of parametric equations

$$x = A\sin(at + \delta), \quad y = B\sin(bt),$$

which describes complex harmonic motion. This family of curves was investigated by Nathaniel Bowditch in 1815, and later in more detail by Jules Antoine Lissajous in 1857.

The appearance of the figure is highly sensitive to the ratio a/b.

a. BIBO stability
b. Lissajous curve
c. 15 theorem
d. BDDC

12. In mathematics, a _____ is a set (or locus) of points in the plane such that each point p on the oval bears a special relation to two other, fixed points q_1 and q_2: the product of the distance from p to q_1 and the distance from p to q_2 is constant. That is, if we define the function dist(x,y) to be the distance from a point x to a point y, then all points p on a _____ satisfy the equation

$$\text{dist}(q_1, p) \times \text{dist}(q_2, p) = b^2$$

where b is a constant.

The points q_1 and q_2 are called the foci of the oval.

a. Folium of Descartes
b. Secant line
c. Tractrix
d. Cassini oval

13. In geometry, the _____ or Gutschoven's curve is a two-dimensional algebraic curve resembling the Greek letter κ (kappa.)

Using the Cartesian coordinate system it can be expressed as:

$$x^2(x^2 + y^2) = a^2 y^2$$

or, using parametric equations:

$$\begin{aligned} x &= a\cos t \cot t \\ y &= a\cos t \end{aligned}$$

Chapter 11. ANALYTIC GEOMETRY IN CALCULUS

In polar coordinates its equation is even simpler:

r = atanθ

It has two vertical asymptotes at $x = \pm a$, shown as dashed blue lines in the figure at right.

The _____'s curvature:

$$\kappa(\theta) = \frac{8\left(3 - \sin^2 \theta\right) \sin^4 \theta}{a \left[\sin^2(2\theta) + 4\right]^{\frac{3}{2}}}$$

Tangential angle:

$$\phi(\theta) = -\arctan\left[\frac{1}{2}\sin(2\theta)\right]$$

The _____ was first studied by Gérard van Gutschoven around 1662.

   a. Witch of Agnesi
   c. Prolate cycloid
   b. Tractrix
   d. Kappa curve

14. In mathematics, _____ are a method of defining a curve. A simple kinematical example is when one uses a time parameter to determine the position, velocity, and other information about a body in motion.

Abstractly, a relation is given in the form of an equation, and it is shown also to be the image of functions from items such as R^n.

   a. Shift theorem
   c. Partial derivative
   b. Critical point
   d. Parametric equations

15. Cantor defined two kinds of _____ numbers, the ordinal numbers and the cardinal numbers. Ordinal numbers may be identified with well-ordered sets, or counting carried on to any stopping point, including points after an _____ number have already been counted. Generalizing finite and the ordinary _____ sequences which are maps from the positive integers leads to mappings from ordinal numbers, and transfinite sequences.
   a. ACTRAN
   c. ALGOR
   b. AUSM
   d. Infinite

16. In mathematics, _____ and minima, known collectively as extrema, are the largest value (maximum) or smallest value (minimum), that a function takes in a point either within a given neighbourhood (local extremum) or on the function domain in its entirety (global extremum.)

Chapter 11. ANALYTIC GEOMETRY IN CALCULUS

Throughout, a point refers to an input (x), while a value refers to an output (y): one distinguishing between the maximum value and the point (or points) at which it occurs.

A real-valued function f defined on the real line is said to have a local maximum point at the point x^*, if there exists some $\varepsilon > 0$, such that $f(x^*) \geq f(x)$ when $|x - x^*| < \varepsilon$.

- a. Related rates
- b. Leibniz formula
- c. Racetrack principle
- d. Maxima

17. _____ is used to describe the steepness, incline, gradient, or grade of a straight line. A higher _____ value indicates a steeper incline. The _____ is defined as the ratio of the 'rise' divided by the 'run' between two points on a line, or in other words, the ratio of the altitude change to the horizontal distance between any two points on the line.
- a. 15 theorem
- b. Sequence
- c. Y-intercept
- d. Slope

18. In geometry, the _____ (or simply the tangent) to a curve at a given point is the straight line that 'just touches' the curve at that point (in the sense explained more precisely below.) As it passes through the point of tangency, the _____ is 'going in the same direction' as the curve, and in this sense it is the best straight-line approximation to the curve at that point. The same definition applies to space curves and curves in n-dimensional Euclidean space.
- a. Tangent line
- b. Minimal surface
- c. North pole
- d. Lie derivative

19. In mathematics, the _____ is a conic section, the intersection of a right circular conical surface and a plane parallel to a generating straight line of that surface. Given a point (the focus) and a line (the directrix) that lie in a plane, the locus of points in that plane that are equidistant to them is a _____.

A particular case arises when the plane is tangent to the conical surface of a circle.

- a. Parabola
- b. BIBO stability
- c. 15 theorem
- d. BDDC

20. For some curves there is a smallest number L that is an upper bound on the length of any polygonal approximation. If such a number exists, then the curve is said to be rectifiable and the curve is defined to have _____ L.

Let C be a curve in Euclidean (or, generally, a metric) space $X = R^n$, so C is the image of a continuous function f : [a, b] → X of the interval [a, b] into X.

- a. Order of integration
- b. Integration by parametric derivatives
- c. Integrand
- d. Arc length

21. _____ is the long dimension of any object. The _____ of a thing is the distance between its ends, its linear extent as measured from end to end. This may be distinguished from height, which is vertical extent, and width or breadth, which are the distance from side to side, measuring across the object at right angles to the _____.

a. BDDC
c. Length
b. BIBO stability
d. 15 theorem

22. A _____ is the curve defined by the path of a point on the edge of circular wheel as the wheel rolls along a straight line. It is an example of a roulette, a curve generated by a curve rolling on another curve.

The _____ is the solution to the brachistochrone problem (i.e. it is the curve of fastest descent under gravity) and the related tautochrone problem (i.e. the period of a ball rolling back and forth inside it does not depend on the ball's starting position.)

a. Curtate cycloid
c. Cycloid
b. Tractrix
d. Prolate cycloid

23. A _____ spheroid is a spheroid in which the polar diameter is greater than the equatorial diameter. A _____ spheroid

The _____ spheroid is the shape of the ball in several sports, such as Rugby Football and Australian Rules Football. American Football and Canadian Football use a pointed _____ spheroid (also resembling a rotated vesica piscis.)

a. Hyperbolic paraboloid
c. Prolate
b. Parametric surface
d. Normal vector

24. Several curves are related to the cycloid. When we relax the requirement that the fixed point be on the edge of the circle, we get the curtate cycloid and the _____. In the former case, the point tracing out the curve is inside the circle, and, in the latter case, it is outside.
a. Prolate cycloid
c. Rose
b. Cassini oval
d. Hypocycloid

25. In mathematics, a function f defined on some set X with real or complex values is a _____ function, if the set of its values is _____. In other words, there exists a number M>0 such that

$$|f(x)| \leq M$$

for all x in X.

Sometimes, if $f(x) \leq A$ for all x in X, then the function is said to be _____ above by A.

a. Differential coefficient
c. Concave upwards
b. Stationary phase approximation
d. Bounded

26. The _____ of an angle is the ratio of the length of the opposite side to the length of the hypotenuse. In our case

Chapter 11. ANALYTIC GEOMETRY IN CALCULUS

$$\sin A = \frac{\text{opposite}}{\text{hypotenuse}} = \frac{a}{h}.$$

Note that this ratio does not depend on size of the particular right triangle chosen, as long as it contains the angle A, since all such triangles are similar.

The cosine of an angle is the ratio of the length of the adjacent side to the length of the hypotenuse.

a. Trigonometric
b. Sine integral
c. Trigonometric functions
d. Sine

27. In Geometry, the _____ is an algebraic curve defined by the equation

$$x^3 + y^3 - 3axy = 0$$

It forms a loop in the first quadrant with a double point at the origin and asymptote

$$x + y + a = 0$$

It is symmetrical about y = x.

a. Prolate cycloid
b. Cochleoid
c. Curve
d. Folium of Descartes

28. In mathematics, a _____ (or just conic) is a curve obtained by intersecting a cone (more precisely, a circular conical surface) with a plane. A _____ is therefore a restriction of a quadric surface to the plane. The conic sections were named and studied as long ago as 200 BC, when Apollonius of Perga undertook a systematic study of their properties.

a. Conic section
b. BDDC
c. Latus rectum
d. 15 theorem

29. In mathematics, an _____, is the apparent shape of a circle viewed obliquely from outside it, as distinct from a hyperbola which is the shape seen from inside. It is the finite or bounded case of a conic section as a shape cut in a cone by a plane, the unbounded cases being the parabola, which like the _____ remains connected, and the hyperbola, which separates into two connected components or branches.

Equivalently an _____ can be defined as the locus of points, or path traced out, in a plane such that the sum of the distances from the moving point to two fixed points remains constant.

a. AUSM
b. ALGOR
c. ACTRAN
d. Ellipse

30. In mathematics, a _____ is a method for approximating the total area underneath a curve on a graph, otherwise known as an integral. It may also be used to define the integration operation.

Chapter 11. ANALYTIC GEOMETRY IN CALCULUS

Consider a function $f: D \rightarrowtail \mathbf{R}$, where D is a subset of the real numbers $\mathbf{R}$, and let $I = [a, b]$ be a closed interval contained in D. A finite set of points $\{x_0, x_1, x_2, \ldots x_n\}$ such that $a = x_0 < x_1 < x_2 \ldots < x_n = b$ creates a partition

$$P = \{[x_0, x_1], [x_1, x_2], \ldots [x_{n-1}, x_n]\}$$

of I.

- a. Risch algorithm
- b. Riemann sum
- c. Solid of revolution
- d. Signed measure

31. An _____ of a real-valued function $y = f(x)$ is a curve which describes the behavior of f as either x or y tends to infinity.

In other words, as one moves along the graph of f(x) in some direction, the distance between it and the _____ eventually becomes smaller than any distance that one may specify.

- a. Asymptote
- b. ACTRAN
- c. AUSM
- d. ALGOR

32. In geometry, the _____ (also semimajor axis) is used to describe the dimensions of ellipses and hyperbolae.

The major axis of an ellipse is its longest diameter, a line that runs through the centre and both foci, its ends being at the widest points of the shape. The _____ is one half of the major axis, and thus runs from the centre, through a focus, and to the edge of the ellipse.

- a. BIBO stability
- b. Semi-major axis
- c. 15 theorem
- d. BDDC

33. In mathematics, a _____ is an ordered list of objects (or events). Like a set, it contains members (also called elements or terms), and the number of terms (possibly infinite) is called the length of the _____. Unlike a set, order matters, and the exact same elements can appear multiple times at different positions in the _____.

- a. Y-intercept
- b. Slope
- c. 15 theorem
- d. Sequence

34. Integration is an important concept in mathematics, specifically in the field of calculus and, more broadly, mathematical analysis. Given a function f of a real variable x and an interval [a, b] of the real line, the _____

$$\int_a^b f(x)\, dx ,$$

is defined informally to be the net signed area of the region in the xy-plane bounded by the graph of f, the x-axis, and the vertical lines x = a and x = b.

The term '_____' may also refer to the notion of antiderivative, a function F whose derivative is the given function f.

a. Integrand
b. Integral test for convergence
c. Indefinite integral
d. Integral

35. In computer science and information science, _____ could also be a method or an algorithm. Again, an example will illustrate: There are systems of counting, as with Roman numerals, and various systems for filing papers, or catalogues, and various library systems, of which the Dewey Decimal _____ is an example. This still fits with the definition of components which are connected together (in this case in order to facilitate the flow of information.)

a. BDDC
b. 15 theorem
c. System
d. BIBO stability

36. In algebra, the _____ of a polynomial with real or complex coefficients is a certain expression in the coefficients of the polynomial which is a symmetric polynomial in the coefficients and gives information on the nature of the roots; in particular, it is equal to zero if and only if the polynomial has a multiple root (i.e. a root with multiplicity greater than one) in the complex numbers. For example, the _____ of the quadratic polynomial

$$ax^2 + bx + c \text{ is } b^2 - 4ac.$$

The _____ of the cubic polynomial

$$ax^3 + bx^2 + cx + d \text{ is } b^2c^2 - 4ac^3 - 4b^3d - 27a^2d^2 + 18abcd.$$

a. Quadratic polynomial
b. Resultant
c. Sheffer sequence
d. Discriminant

37. In mathematics, a _____ is a polynomial equation of the second degree. The general form is

$$ax^2 + bx + c = 0,$$

where a ≠ 0.

Students and teachers all over the world are familiar with the quadratic formula that can be derived by completing the square.

a. Stern-Brocot tree
b. Continued fraction
c. Quadratic equation
d. Lochs' theorem

38. _____ is any physical or virtual entity that is owned by an individual or jointly by a group of individuals. An owner of _____ has the right to consume, sell, rent, mortgage, transfer and exchange his or her _____. Important widely-recognized types of _____ include real _____, personal _____ (other physical possessions), and intellectual _____ (rights over artistic creations, inventions, etc.), although the latter is not always as widely recognized or enforced.

Chapter 11. ANALYTIC GEOMETRY IN CALCULUS

    a. BDDC
    b. 15 theorem
    c. Property
    d. BIBO stability

39. In mathematics and statistics, the _____ of a list of numbers is the sum of all of the list divided by the number of items in the list. If the list is a statistical population, then the mean of that population is called a population mean. If the list is a statistical sample, we call the resulting statistic a sample mean.
    a. ALGOR
    b. Arithmetic mean
    c. AUSM
    d. ACTRAN

40. In probability theory and statistics, the _____ (or expectation value or mean and for continuous random variables with a density function it is the probability density -weighted integral of the possible values.

The term '_____' can be misleading.

    a. Expected value
    b. AUSM
    c. ACTRAN
    d. ALGOR

41. The _____, in mathematics, is a type of mean or average, which indicates the central tendency or typical value of a set of numbers. It is similar to the arithmetic mean, which is what most people think of with the word 'average,' except that instead of adding the set of numbers and then dividing the sum by the count of numbers in the set, n, the numbers are multiplied and then the nth root of the resulting product is taken.

For instance, the _____ of two numbers, say 2 and 8, is just the square root (i.e., the second root) of their product, 16, which is 4.

    a. Standard deviation
    b. Geometric mean
    c. Continuous random variable
    d. Normal distribution

42. _____ was a German mathematician, astronomer and astrologer, and key figure in the 17th century scientific revolution. He is best known for his eponymous laws of planetary motion, codified by later astronomers based on his works Astronomia nova, Harmonices Mundi, and Epitome of Copernican Astronomy. They also provided one of the foundations for Isaac Newton's theory of universal gravitation.
    a. Niels Henrik David Bohr
    b. Johannes Kepler
    c. MÄ dhava of Sangamagrama
    d. Robin K. Bullough

43. In calculus, an antiderivative, primitive or _____ of a function f is a function F whose derivative is equal to f, i.e., F ' = f. The process of solving for antiderivatives is antidifferentiation (or indefinite integration.) Antiderivatives are related to definite integrals through the fundamental theorem of calculus: the definite integral of a function over an interval is equal to the difference between the values of an antiderivative evaluated at the endpoints of the interval.
    a. Integration by parts operator
    b. Integral test for convergence
    c. Arc length
    d. Indefinite integral

44. Derivative terms are used to identify the body being orbited. The most common are perigee and apogee, referring to orbits around the Earth , and perihelion and _____, referring to orbits around the Sun . During the Apollo program, the terms pericynthion and apocynthion were used when referring to the moon.

a. AUSM b. ACTRAN
c. Aphelion d. ALGOR

45. In mathematics, two vectors are _____ if they are perpendicular, i.e., they form a right angle. For example, a subway and the street above, although they do not physically intersect, are _____ if they cross at a right angle.
   a. ACTRAN b. ALGOR
   c. AUSM d. Orthogonal

46. In economics, the _____ functional form of production functions is widely used to represent the relationship of an output to inputs. It was proposed by Knut Wicksell (1851-1926), and tested against statistical evidence by Charles Cobb and Paul Douglas in 1900-1928.

For production, the function is

$$Y = AL^{\alpha}K^{\beta},$$

where:

- Y = total production (the monetary value of all goods produced in a year)
- L = labor input
- K = capital input
- A = total factor productivity
- α and β are the output elasticities of labor and capital, respectively. These values are constants determined by available technology.

Output elasticity measures the responsiveness of output to a change in levels of either labor or capital used in production, ceteris paribus. For example if α = 0.15, a 1% increase in labor would lead to approximately a 0.15% increase in output.

   a. 15 theorem b. Cobb-Douglas
   c. BIBO stability d. BDDC

Chapter 12. THREE-DIMENSIONAL SPACE; VECTORS

1. In mathematics, the _____ is used to determine each point uniquely in a plane through two numbers, usually called the x-coordinate or abscissa and the y-coordinate or ordinate of the point. To define the coordinates, two perpendicular directed lines, are specified, as well as the unit length, which is marked off on the two axes Cartesian coordinate systems are also used in space and in higher dimensions.

   a. Coordinate
   b. Cylindrical coordinate system
   c. 15 theorem
   d. Cartesian coordinate system

2. In mathematics, the _____, named after German mathematician Bernhard Riemann, is a prominent function of great significance in number theory because of its relation to the distribution of prime numbers. It also has applications in other areas such as physics, probability theory, and applied statistics.

   The Riemann hypothesis, a conjecture about the distribution of the zeros of the _____, is considered by many mathematicians to be the most important unsolved problem in pure mathematics.

   a. BDDC
   b. BIBO stability
   c. 15 theorem
   d. Riemann zeta function

3. In computer science and information science, _____ could also be a method or an algorithm. Again, an example will illustrate: There are systems of counting, as with Roman numerals, and various systems for filing papers, or catalogues, and various library systems, of which the Dewey Decimal _____ is an example. This still fits with the definition of components which are connected together (in this case in order to facilitate the flow of information.)

   a. BIBO stability
   b. 15 theorem
   c. System
   d. BDDC

4. In mathematics and its applications, a _____ system is a system for assigning an n-tuple of numbers or scalars to each point in an n-dimensional space. This concept is part of the theory of manifolds. 'Scalars' in many cases means real numbers, but, depending on context, can mean complex numbers or elements of some other commutative ring.

   a. 15 theorem
   b. Spherical coordinate system
   c. Coordinate
   d. Cylindrical coordinate system

5. In mathematics, the concept of a '_____' is used to describe the behavior of a function as its argument or input either 'gets close' to some point, or as the argument becomes arbitrarily large; or the behavior of a sequence's elements as their index increases indefinitely. Limits are used in calculus and other branches of mathematical analysis to define derivatives and continuity.

   In formulas, _____ is usually abbreviated as lim

   a. BDDC
   b. BIBO stability
   c. 15 theorem
   d. Limit

6. In calculus, a _____ is either of the two limits of a function f(x) of a real variable x as x approaches a specified point either from below or from above. One should write either:

$$\lim_{x \to a^+} f(x) \text{ or } \lim_{x \downarrow a} f(x)$$

for the limit as x decreases in value approaching a (x approaches a 'from above' or 'from the right'), and similarly

$$\lim_{x \to a^-} f(x) \text{ or } \lim_{x \uparrow a} f(x)$$

for the limit as x increases in value approaching a (x approaches a 'from below' or 'from the left'.)

The two one-sided limits exist and are equal if and only if the limit of f(x) as x approaches a exists.

a. ALGOR
b. AUSM
c. ACTRAN
d. One-sided limit

7. In mathematics, the _____ is a two-dimensional coordinate system in which each point on a plane is determined by an angle and a distance. The _____ is especially useful in situations where the relationship between two points is most easily expressed in terms of angles and distance; in the more familiar Cartesian or rectangular coordinate system, such a relationship can only be found through trigonometric formulation.

As the coordinate system is two-dimensional, each point is determined by two polar coordinates: the radial coordinate and the angular coordinate.

a. BIBO stability
b. BDDC
c. Polar coordinate system
d. 15 theorem

8. Someone who is _____ will prefer to use this hand for everyday activities, such as writing, maintaining personal hygiene, cooking and so forth. According to a variety of studies, anywhere from 70% to 90% of the world population is _____, while most of the remaining are left-handed. A small percentage of the population can use both hands equally well; a person with this ability is deemed to be ambidextrous (though such people may still have a personal preference of one hand over the other.)

a. BDDC
b. 15 theorem
c. BIBO stability
d. Right-handed

9. In mathematics, a _____ is an ordered list of objects (or events). Like a set, it contains members (also called elements or terms), and the number of terms (possibly infinite) is called the length of the _____. Unlike a set, order matters, and the exact same elements can appear multiple times at different positions in the _____.

a. Slope
b. Sequence
c. 15 theorem
d. Y-intercept

10. A _____ is perfectly round geometrical object in three-dimensional space, such as the shape of a round ball. Like a circle in two dimensions, a perfect _____ is completely symmetrical around its center, with all points on the surface lying the same distance r from the center point. This distance r is known as the radius of the _____.

a. Minimal surface
b. Tangent line
c. North pole
d. Sphere

Chapter 12. THREE-DIMENSIONAL SPACE; VECTORS

11. A _____ is one of the most curvilinear basic geometric shapes:It has two faces, zero vertices, and zero edges. The surface formed by the points at a fixed distance from a given straight line, the axis of the _____. The solid enclosed by this surface and by two planes perpendicular to the axis is also called a _____.
    a. BDDC
    b. Right circular cylinder
    c. Cylinder
    d. 15 theorem

12. A _____ is a lens which focuses light which passes through onto a line instead of onto a point, as a spherical lens would. The curved face or faces of a _____ are sections of a cylinder, and focus the image passing through it onto a line parallel to the intersection of the surface of the lens and a plane tangent to it. The lens compresses the image in the direction perpendicular to this line, and leaves it unaltered in the direction parallel to it (in the tangent plane.)
    a. BIBO stability
    b. BDDC
    c. 15 theorem
    d. Cylindrical lens

13. In elementary mathematics, physics, and engineering, a _____ is a geometric object that has both a magnitude (or length), direction and sense, (i.e., orientation along the given direction.) A _____ is frequently represented by a line segment with a definite direction, or graphically as an arrow, connecting an initial point A with a terminal point B, and denoted by

The magnitude of the _____ is the length of the segment and the direction characterizes the displacement of B relative to A: how much one should move the point A to 'carry' it to the point B.

Many algebraic operations on real numbers have close analogues for vectors.

    a. BDDC
    b. 15 theorem
    c. Linear partial differential operator
    d. Vector

14. Integration is an important concept in mathematics, specifically in the field of calculus and, more broadly, mathematical analysis. Given a function f of a real variable x and an interval [a, b] of the real line, the _____

$$\int_a^b f(x)\,dx,$$

is defined informally to be the net signed area of the region in the xy-plane bounded by the graph of f, the x-axis, and the vertical lines x = a and x = b.

The term '_____' may also refer to the notion of antiderivative, a function F whose derivative is the given function f.

    a. Integrand
    b. Indefinite integral
    c. Integral
    d. Integral test for convergence

15. The _____ of an angle is the ratio of the length of the adjacent side to the length of the hypotenuse. In our case

$$\cos A = \frac{\text{adjacent}}{\text{hypotenuse}} = \frac{b}{h}.$$

The tangent of an angle is the ratio of the length of the opposite side to the length of the adjacent side. In our case

$$\tan A = \frac{\text{opposite}}{\text{adjacent}} = \frac{a}{b}.$$

The remaining three functions are best defined using the above three functions.

- a. Trigonometric functions
- b. Trigonometric
- c. Sine integral
- d. Cosine

16. In physics, displacement is the vector that specifies the change in position of a point or a particle in reference to a previous position. When the previous point is the origin, this is better referred to as a position. _____ versus distance traveled along a path.
- a. BIBO stability
- b. Displacement vector
- c. 15 theorem
- d. BDDC

17. In differential calculus, an inflection point, or _____ (or inflexion) is a point on a curve at which the curvature changes sign. The curve changes from being concave upwards (positive curvature) to concave downwards (negative curvature), or vice versa. If one imagines driving a vehicle along the curve, it is a point at which the steering-wheel is momentarily 'straight', being turned from left to right or vice versa.
- a. Derivative of a constant
- b. Logarithmic derivative
- c. Lin-Tsien equation
- d. Point of inflection

18. A _____ is a reference from which measurements are made. In surveying and geodesy, a datum is a set of reference points on the earth's surface against which position measurements are made, and (often) an associated model of the shape of the earth (reference ellipsoid) to define a geographic coordinate system. Horizontal datums are used for describing a point on the earth's surface, in latitude and longitude or another coordinate system.
- a. BIBO stability
- b. Geodetic datum
- c. BDDC
- d. 15 theorem

19. _____ is the addition of a set of numbers; the result is their sum or total. An interim or present total of a _____ process is termed the running total. The 'numbers' to be summed may be natural numbers, complex numbers, matrices, or still more complicated objects.
- a. BIBO stability
- b. 15 theorem
- c. Summation
- d. BDDC

20. In physics, _____ is defined as the rate of change of position. it is vector physical quantity; both speed and direction are required to define it. In the SI (metric) system, it is measured in meters per second: (m/s) or ms^{-1}.

a. BDDC
c. 15 theorem
b. BIBO stability
d. Velocity

21. In linear algebra, the null vector or _____ is the vector (0, 0, …, 0) in Euclidean space, all of whose components are zero. It is usually written $\vec{0}$ or 0 or simply 0. A _____ has no direction.
   a. Scalar multiplication
   c. Homogeneous function
   b. Direction vector
   d. Zero vector

22. In mathematics, a _____ in a normed vector space is a vector (often a spatial vector) whose length is 1 (the unit length.) A _____ is often denoted by a lowercase letter with a superscribed caret or e;hate;, like this: $\hat{\imath}$.

In Euclidean space, the dot product of two unit vectors is simply the cosine of the angle between them.

   a. ALGOR
   c. Overdetermined
   b. ACTRAN
   d. Unit vector

23. _____ is the long dimension of any object. The _____ of a thing is the distance between its ends, its linear extent as measured from end to end. This may be distinguished from height, which is vertical extent, and width or breadth, which are the distance from side to side, measuring across the object at right angles to the _____.
   a. BDDC
   c. 15 theorem
   b. BIBO stability
   d. Length

24. In mathematics, the _____ of two monic polynomials P and Q over a field k is defined as the product

$$\operatorname{res}(P, Q) = \prod_{(x,y):\ P(x)=0,\ Q(y)=0} (x - y),$$

of the differences of their roots, where x and y take on values in the algebraic closure of k. For non-monic polynomials with leading coefficients p and q, respectively, the above product is multiplied by

$$p^{\deg Q} q^{\deg P}.$$

- The _____ is the determinant of the Sylvester matrix (and of the Bezout matrix.)

- When Q is separable, the above product can be rewritten to

$$\mathrm{res}(P,Q) = \prod_{P(x)=0} Q(x)$$

and this expression remains unchanged if Q is reduced modulo P. Note that, when non-monic, this includes the factor $q^{\deg P}$ but still needs the factor $p^{\deg Q}$.

- Let $P' = P \mod Q$. The above idea can be continued by swapping the roles of P' and Q. However, P' has a set of roots different from that of P. This can be resolved by writing $\prod_{Q(y)=0} P'(y)$ as a determinant again, where P' has leading zero coefficients. This determinant can now be simplified by iterative expansion with respect to the column, where only the leading coefficient q of Q appears.

$$\mathrm{res}(P,Q) = q^{\deg P - \deg P'} \cdot \mathrm{res}(P', Q)$$

Continuing this procedure ends up in a variant of the Euclidean algorithm. This procedure needs quadratic runtime.

a. Quadratic function
c. Difference polynomial
b. Resultant
d. Leading coefficient

25. In vector calculus, the _____ is an operator that measures the magnitude of a vector field's source or sink at a given point; the _____ of a vector field is a (signed) scalar. For example, consider air as it is heated or cooled. The relevant vector field for this example is the velocity of the moving air at a point.
    a. Green's theorem
    b. Gradient theorem
    c. Triple product
    d. Divergence

26. In vector calculus, the _____ Ostrogradskye;s theorem the _____ states that the outward flux of a vector field through a surface is equal to the triple integral of the divergence on the region inside the surface. Intuitively, it states that the sum of all sources minus the sum of all sinks gives the net flow out of a region.
    a. Green's theorem
    b. Divergence
    c. Del
    d. Divergence Theorem

27. In mathematics, the _____ is an operation which takes two vectors over the real numbers R and returns a real-valued scalar quantity. It is the standard inner product of the orthonormal Euclidean space. It contrasts with the cross product which produces a vector result.

a. Vector-valued function
b. Homogeneous function
c. Scalar multiplication
d. Dot product

28. In mathematics, _____ are a concept central to linear algebra and related fields of mathematics

Suppose that K is a field and V is a vector space over K. As usual, we call elements of V vectors and call elements of K scalars.

a. Linear combinations
b. 15 theorem
c. Fundamental theorem of algebra
d. Permutation

29. When a unit vector in space is expressed, with Cartesian notation, as a linear combination of i, j, k, its three scalar components can be referred to as '_____'. The value of each component is equal to the cosine of the angle formed by the unit vector with the respective basis vector. This is one of the methods used to describe the orientation (angular position) of a straight line, segment of straight line, oriented axis, or segment of oriented axis (vector.)

a. Scalar multiplication
b. Dot product
c. Vector-valued function
d. Direction cosines

30. In mathematics, two vectors are _____ if they are perpendicular, i.e., they form a right angle. For example, a subway and the street above, although they do not physically intersect, are _____ if they cross at a right angle.

a. ALGOR
b. AUSM
c. ACTRAN
d. Orthogonal

31. In algebra, a _____ is a function depending on n that associates a scalar, det(A), to an n×n square matrix A. The fundamental geometric meaning of a _____ is a scale factor for measure when A is regarded as a linear transformation. Determinants are important both in calculus, where they enter the substitution rule for several variables, and in multilinear algebra.

For a fixed nonnegative integer n, there is a unique _____ function for the n×n matrices over any commutative ring R. In particular, this function exists when R is the field of real or complex numbers.

a. BDDC
b. Determinant
c. 15 theorem
d. BIBO stability

32. In mathematics, the _____ is a binary operation on two vectors in a three-dimensional Euclidean space that results in another vector which is perpendicular to the plane containing the two input vectors. The algebra defined by the _____ is neither commutative nor associative. It contrasts with the dot product which produces a scalar result.

a. Permutation
b. Cross product
c. Fundamental theorem of algebra
d. 15 theorem

33. In mathematics and physics, the _____ is a common mnemonic for understanding notation conventions for vectors in 3 dimensions. It was invented for use in electromagnetism by British physicist Zachariah William Cole in the late 1800s.

When choosing three vectors that must be at right angles to each other, there are two distinct solutions, so when expressing this idea in mathematics, one must remove the ambiguity of which solution is meant.

a. BDDC
c. 15 theorem
b. BIBO stability
d. Right-hand rule

34. In vector calculus, there are two ways of multiplying three vectors together, to make a _____ of vectors. Three vectors defining a parallelepiped

The scalar _____ is defined as the dot product of one of the vectors with the cross product of the other two.

Geometrically, the scalar _____

$$\mathbf{a} \cdot (\mathbf{b} \times \mathbf{c})$$

is the (signed) volume of the parallelepiped defined by the three vectors given.

a. Gradient theorem
c. Divergence
b. Green's theorem
d. Triple product

35. The concept of _____ in mathematics evolved from the concept of _____ in physics. The nth _____ of a real-valued function f(x) of a real variable about a value c is

$$\mu'_n = \int_{-\infty}^{\infty} (x - c)^n f(x)\, dx.$$

It is possible to define moments for random variables in a more general fashion than moments for real values. See Moments in metric spaces.

a. Geometric mean
c. Median
b. Poisson distribution
d. Moment

36. _____ is the tendency of a force to rotate an object about an axis (or fulcrum or pivot.) Just as a force is a push or a pull, a _____ can be thought of as a twist. The symbol for _____ is τ, the Greek letter tau.

a. BIBO stability
c. 15 theorem
b. Torque
d. BDDC

37. In mathematics, a _____ is the graph of the system of parametric equations

$$x = A\sin(at + \delta), \quad y = B\sin(bt),$$

which describes complex harmonic motion. This family of curves was investigated by Nathaniel Bowditch in 1815, and later in more detail by Jules Antoine Lissajous in 1857.

The appearance of the figure is highly sensitive to the ratio a/b.

a. 15 theorem
c. BDDC
b. BIBO stability
d. Lissajous curve

38. In mathematics, a (topological) _____ is defined as follows: let I be an interval of real numbers (i.e. a non-empty connected subset of $\mathbb{R}$); then a _____ γ is a continuous mapping $\gamma : I \to X$, where X is a topological space. The _____ γ is said to be simple if it is injective, i.e. if for all x, y in I, we have $\gamma(x) = \gamma(y) \implies x = y$. If I is a closed bounded interval $[a, b]$, we also allow the possibility $\gamma(a) = \gamma(b)$ (this convention makes it possible to talk about closed simple _____.)

a. Curve
c. Prolate cycloid
b. Tractrix
d. Closed curve

39. In mathematics, _____ and minima, known collectively as extrema, are the largest value (maximum) or smallest value (minimum), that a function takes in a point either within a given neighbourhood (local extremum) or on the function domain in its entirety (global extremum.)

Throughout, a point refers to an input (x), while a value refers to an output (y): one distinguishing between the maximum value and the point (or points) at which it occurs.

A real-valued function f defined on the real line is said to have a local maximum point at the point x*, if there exists some ε > 0, such that f(x*) ≥ f(x) when $|x - x^*| < \varepsilon$.

a. Leibniz formula
c. Related rates
b. Racetrack principle
d. Maxima

40. A surface normal to a flat surface is a vector which is perpendicular to that surface. A normal to a non-flat surface at a point P on the surface is a vector perpendicular to the tangent plane to that surface at P. The word 'normal' is also used as an adjective: a line normal to a plane, the normal component of a force, the _____, etc. The concept of normality generalizes to orthogonality.

a. Normal line
c. Hyperbolic paraboloid
b. Paraboloid
d. Normal vector

41. A _____ officer is an officer of high military rank. The term or equivalent is used by nearly every country in the world. _____ can be used as a generic term for all grades of _____ officer, or it can specifically refer to a single rank that is just called _____.

a. BIBO stability
c. BDDC
b. 15 theorem
d. General

42. In mathematics, the _____ is the surface defined by the equation

$$z = x^3 - 3xy^2.$$

Chapter 12. THREE-DIMENSIONAL SPACE; VECTORS

It belongs to the class of saddle surfaces and its name derives from the observation that a saddle for a monkey requires three depressions: two for the legs, and one for the tail. The point (0,0,0) on the _____ corresponds to a degenerate critical point of the function z(x,y) at (0, 0.) The _____ has an isolated umbilic point with zero Gaussian curvature at the origin, while the curvature is strictly negative at all other points.

a. Second partial derivatives test
c. Contact
b. Shift theorem
d. Monkey saddle

43. In calculus, _____, was originally the use of expressions such as dx and dy and to represent 'infinitely small' (or infinitesimal) increments of quantities x and y, just as >Δx and >Δy represent finite increments of x and y respectively. So for y being a function of x, or

the derivative of y with respect to x, which later came to be viewed as

was, according to Leibniz, the quotient of an infinitesimal increment of y by an infinitesimal increment of x, or

where the right hand side is Lagrange's notation for the derivative of f at x.

Similarly, although mathematicians usually now view an integral

as a limit

where >Δx is an interval containing x_i, Leibniz viewed it as the sum (the integral sign denoting summation) of infinitely many infinitesimal quantities f(x) dx.

a. Smooth function
c. Time derivative
b. Stationary point
d. Leibniz's notation

44. In mathematics, the hyperbolic functions are analogs of the ordinary trigonometric functions. The basic hyperbolic functions are the hyperbolic sine 'sinh', and the _____ 'cosh', from which are derived the hyperbolic tangent 'tanh', etc., in analogy to the derived trigonometric functions. The inverse hyperbolic functions are the area hyperbolic sine 'arsinh' (also called 'asinh', or sometimes by the misnomer of 'arcsinh') and so on.

   a. Hyperbolic cosine
   b. Step function
   c. Hyperbolic tangent
   d. Square root function

45. An _____ is a type of quadric surface that is a higher dimensional analogue of an ellipse. The equation of a standard axis-aligned _____ body in an xyz-Cartesian coordinate system is

$$\frac{x^2}{a^2} + \frac{y^2}{b^2} + \frac{z^2}{c^2} = 1$$

where a and b are the equatorial radii (along the x and y axes) and c is the polar radius (along the z-axis), all of which are fixed positive real numbers determining the shape of the _____.

More generally, a not-necessarily-axis-aligned _____ is defined by the equation

$$\mathbf{x}^T A \mathbf{x} = 1$$

where A is a symmetric positive definite matrix and x is a vector.

   a. ACTRAN
   b. AUSM
   c. ALGOR
   d. Ellipsoid

46. The _____ is a doubly ruled surface shaped like a saddle. In a suitable coordinate system, it can be represented by the equation

$$z = \frac{x^2}{a^2} - \frac{y^2}{b^2}.$$

This is a _____ that opens up along the x-axis and down along the y-axis.

Paraboloid of revolution

With a = b an elliptic paraboloid is a paraboloid of revolution: a surface obtained by revolving a parabola around its axis.

   a. Paraboloid
   b. Parametric surface
   c. Torus
   d. Hyperbolic paraboloid

47. In mathematics, a hyperboloid is a quadric, a type of surface in three dimensions, described by the equation

$$\frac{x^2}{a^2} + \frac{y^2}{b^2} - \frac{z^2}{c^2} = 1$$ _____,

or

$$-\frac{x^2}{a^2} - \frac{y^2}{b^2} + \frac{z^2}{c^2} = 1$$ hyperboloid of two sheets.

These are also called elliptical hyperboloids. If, and only if, a = b, it is a hyperboloid of revolution, and is also called a circular hyperboloid.

a. Hyperboloid of one sheet
b. BIBO stability
c. 15 theorem
d. BDDC

48. In mathematics, a _____ is a quadric surface of special kind. There are two kinds of paraboloids: elliptic and hyperbolic. The elliptic _____ is shaped like an oval cup and can have a maximum or minimum point.
a. Torus
b. Paraboloid
c. Hyperbolic paraboloid
d. PDE surfaces

49. In mathematics, a _____ is a point in the domain of a function of two variables which is a stationary point but not a local extremum. At such a point, in general, the surface resembles a saddle that curves up in one direction, and curves down in a different direction (like a mountain pass.) In terms of contour lines, a _____ can be recognized, in general, by a contour that appears to intersect itself.
a. Saddle point
b. BDDC
c. BIBO stability
d. 15 theorem

50. In physics, _____ is movement that changes the position of an object, as opposed to rotation. For example, according to Whittaker:

A _____ is the operation changing the positions of all points (x, y, z) of an object according to the formula

$$(x, y, z) \to (x + \Delta x, y + \Delta y, z + \Delta z)$$

where $(\Delta x, \Delta y, \Delta z)$ is the same vector for each point of the object. The _____ vector $(\Delta x, \Delta y, \Delta z)$ common to all points of the object describes a particular type of displacement of the object, usually called a linear displacement to distinguish it from displacements involving rotation, called angular displacements.

a. BDDC
b. 15 theorem
c. Translation
d. BIBO stability

51. If a particular point on a sphere is (arbitrarily) designated as its _____, then the corresponding antipodal point is called the south pole and the equator is the great circle that is equidistant to them. Great circles through the two poles are called lines (or meridians) of longitude, and the line connecting the two poles is called the axis of rotation. Circles on the sphere that are parallel to the equator are lines of latitude.
   a. North pole
   b. Sphere
   c. Tangent line
   d. Minimal surface

52. _____ is a type of motion in which the velocity of an object changes equal amounts in equal time periods. An example of an object having _____ would be a ball rolling down a ramp. The object picks up velocity as it goes down the ramp with equal changes in time.
   a. Uniform Acceleration
   b. ACTRAN
   c. AUSM
   d. ALGOR

Chapter 13. VECTOR-VALUED FUNCTIONS

1. In calculus, a branch of mathematics, the _____ is a measurement of how a function changes when its input changes. Loosely speaking, a _____ can be thought of as how much a quantity is changing at some given point. For example, the _____ of the position (or distance) of a vehicle with respect to time is the instantaneous velocity (respectively, instantaneous speed) at which the vehicle is traveling.

The process of finding a _____ is called differentiation. The fundamental theorem of calculus states that differentiation is the reverse process to integration.

   a. Stationary phase approximation
   b. Bounded function
   c. Derivative
   d. Semi-differentiability

2. A _____ is a special kind of space curve, i.e. a smooth curve in three-space. As a mental image of a _____ one may take the spring (although the spring is not a curve, and so is technically not a _____, it does give a convenient mental picture.) A _____ is characterised by the fact that the tangent line at any point makes a constant angle with a fixed line.
   a. BIBO stability
   b. BDDC
   c. Helix
   d. 15 theorem

3. In mathematics, _____ are a method of defining a curve. A simple kinematical example is when one uses a time parameter to determine the position, velocity, and other information about a body in motion.

Abstractly, a relation is given in the form of an equation, and it is shown also to be the image of functions from items such as R^n.

   a. Partial derivative
   b. Critical point
   c. Shift theorem
   d. Parametric equations

4. In geometry, the _____ (or simply the tangent) to a curve at a given point is the straight line that 'just touches' the curve at that point (in the sense explained more precisely below.) As it passes through the point of tangency, the _____ is 'going in the same direction' as the curve, and in this sense it is the best straight-line approximation to the curve at that point. The same definition applies to space curves and curves in n-dimensional Euclidean space.
   a. Lie derivative
   b. Minimal surface
   c. North pole
   d. Tangent line

5. In geometry, a _____ (pl. tori) is a surface of revolution generated by revolving a circle in three dimensional space about an axis coplanar with the circle, which does not touch the circle. Examples of tori include the surfaces of doughnuts and inner tubes.
   a. Torus
   b. Hyperbolic paraboloid
   c. Prolate
   d. Paraboloid

6. In mathematics, a _____ is the graph of the system of parametric equations

$$x = A\sin(at + \delta), \quad y = B\sin(bt),$$

which describes complex harmonic motion. This family of curves was investigated by Nathaniel Bowditch in 1815, and later in more detail by Jules Antoine Lissajous in 1857.

The appearance of the figure is highly sensitive to the ratio a/b.

- a. Lissajous curve
- b. BIBO stability
- c. 15 theorem
- d. BDDC

7. In mathematics, a (topological) _____ is defined as follows: let I be an interval of real numbers (i.e. a non-empty connected subset of $\mathbb{R}$); then a _____ γ is a continuous mapping $\gamma : I \to X$, where X is a topological space. The _____ γ is said to be simple if it is injective, i.e. if for all x, y in I, we have $\gamma(x) = \gamma(y) \implies x = y$. If I is a closed bounded interval $[a, b]$, we also allow the possibility $\gamma(a) = \gamma(b)$ (this convention makes it possible to talk about closed simple _____.)

- a. Prolate cycloid
- b. Tractrix
- c. Closed curve
- d. Curve

8. A _____ is a mathematical function that maps real numbers to vectors. Vector-valued functions can be defined as:

- $\mathbf{r}(t) = f(t)\hat{\mathbf{i}} + g(t)\hat{\mathbf{j}}$ or
- $\mathbf{r}(t) = f(t)\hat{\mathbf{i}} + g(t)\hat{\mathbf{j}} + h(t)\hat{\mathbf{k}}$

where f(t), g(t) and h(t) are the coordinate functions of the parameter t, and $\hat{\mathbf{i}}$, $\hat{\mathbf{j}}$, and $\hat{\mathbf{k}}$ are unit vectors. r(t) is a vector which has its tail at the origin and its head at the coordinates evaluated by the function.

The vector shown in the graph to the right is the evaluation of the function near t=19.5 (between 6π and 6.5π; i.e., somewhat more than 3 rotations.)

- a. Scalar multiplication
- b. Direction cosines
- c. Direction vector
- d. Vector-valued function

9. In vector calculus, the _____ is an operator that measures the magnitude of a vector field's source or sink at a given point; the _____ of a vector field is a (signed) scalar. For example, consider air as it is heated or cooled. The relevant vector field for this example is the velocity of the moving air at a point.

- a. Green's theorem
- b. Triple product
- c. Gradient theorem
- d. Divergence

10. In vector calculus, the _____ Ostrogradskye;s theorem the _____ states that the outward flux of a vector field through a surface is equal to the triple integral of the divergence on the region inside the surface. Intuitively, it states that the sum of all sources minus the sum of all sinks gives the net flow out of a region.

- a. Del
- b. Green's theorem
- c. Divergence
- d. Divergence Theorem

Chapter 13. VECTOR-VALUED FUNCTIONS

11. In computer science and information science, _____ could also be a method or an algorithm. Again, an example will illustrate: There are systems of counting, as with Roman numerals, and various systems for filing papers, or catalogues, and various library systems, of which the Dewey Decimal _____ is an example. This still fits with the definition of components which are connected together (in this case in order to facilitate the flow of information.)

   a. BDDC
   b. BIBO stability
   c. 15 theorem
   d. System

12. In elementary mathematics, physics, and engineering, a _____ is a geometric object that has both a magnitude (or length), direction and sense, (i.e., orientation along the given direction.) A _____ is frequently represented by a line segment with a definite direction, or graphically as an arrow, connecting an initial point A with a terminal point B, and denoted by

   The magnitude of the _____ is the length of the segment and the direction characterizes the displacement of B relative to A: how much one should move the point A to 'carry' it to the point B.

   Many algebraic operations on real numbers have close analogues for vectors.

   a. BDDC
   b. Linear partial differential operator
   c. Vector
   d. 15 theorem

13. In mathematics, the _____ , is the curve defined as follows.

   Starting with a fixed circle, a point O on the circle is chosen. For any other point A on the circle, the secant line OA is drawn. The point M is diametrically opposite O. The line OA intersects the tangent at M at the point N. The line parallel to OM through N, and the line perpendicular to OM through A intersect at P. As the point A is varied, the path of P is the witch.

   a. Closed curve
   b. Witch of Agnesi
   c. Folium of Descartes
   d. Cochleoid

14. In mathematics, the concept of a '_____' is used to describe the behavior of a function as its argument or input either 'gets close' to some point, or as the argument becomes arbitrarily large; or the behavior of a sequence's elements as their index increases indefinitely. Limits are used in calculus and other branches of mathematical analysis to define derivatives and continuity.

   In formulas, _____ is usually abbreviated as lim

   a. 15 theorem
   b. BDDC
   c. Limit
   d. BIBO stability

15. The _____ of an angle is the ratio of the length of the adjacent side to the length of the hypotenuse. In our case

$$\cos A = \frac{\text{adjacent}}{\text{hypotenuse}} = \frac{b}{h}.$$

The tangent of an angle is the ratio of the length of the opposite side to the length of the adjacent side. In our case

$$\tan A = \frac{\text{opposite}}{\text{adjacent}} = \frac{a}{b}.$$

The remaining three functions are best defined using the above three functions.

    a. Trigonometric functions   b. Cosine
    c. Trigonometric   d. Sine integral

16. In mathematics, the _____ is a binary operation on two vectors in a three-dimensional Euclidean space that results in another vector which is perpendicular to the plane containing the two input vectors. The algebra defined by the _____ is neither commutative nor associative. It contrasts with the dot product which produces a scalar result.
    a. Cross product   b. Permutation
    c. 15 theorem   d. Fundamental theorem of algebra

17. The _____ of an angle is the ratio of the length of the opposite side to the length of the hypotenuse. In our case

$$\sin A = \frac{\text{opposite}}{\text{hypotenuse}} = \frac{a}{h}.$$

Note that this ratio does not depend on size of the particular right triangle chosen, as long as it contains the angle A, since all such triangles are similar.

The cosine of an angle is the ratio of the length of the adjacent side to the length of the hypotenuse.

    a. Sine   b. Sine integral
    c. Trigonometric   d. Trigonometric functions

18. Smooth functions with given closed support are used in the construction of smooth partitions of unity ; these are essential in the study of smooth manifolds, for example to show that Riemannian metrics can be defined globally starting from their local existence. A simple case is that of a bump function on the real line, that is, a _____ f that takes the value 0 outside an interval [a,b] and such that

    f(x) > 0 for a < x < b.

Given a number of overlapping intervals on the line, bump functions can be constructed on each of them, and on semi-infinite intervals (->∞, c] and [d,+>∞) to cover the whole line, such that the sum of the functions is always 1.

Chapter 13. VECTOR-VALUED FUNCTIONS

a. Symmetric derivative
c. Continuously differentiable
b. Gradient
d. Smooth function

19. _____ is the long dimension of any object. The _____ of a thing is the distance between its ends, its linear extent as measured from end to end. This may be distinguished from height, which is vertical extent, and width or breadth, which are the distance from side to side, measuring across the object at right angles to the _____.

a. 15 theorem
c. BIBO stability
b. Length
d. BDDC

20. For some curves there is a smallest number L that is an upper bound on the length of any polygonal approximation. If such a number exists, then the curve is said to be rectifiable and the curve is defined to have _____ L.

Let C be a curve in Euclidean (or, generally, a metric) space X = R^n, so C is the image of a continuous function f : [a, b] → X of the interval [a, b] into X.

a. Order of integration
c. Arc length
b. Integrand
d. Integration by parametric derivatives

21. In calculus, _____, was originally the use of expressions such as dx and dy and to represent 'infinitely small' (or infinitesimal) increments of quantities x and y, just as >Δx and >Δy represent finite increments of x and y respectively. So for y being a function of x, or

the derivative of y with respect to x, which later came to be viewed as

was, according to Leibniz, the quotient of an infinitesimal increment of y by an infinitesimal increment of x, or

where the right hand side is Lagrange's notation for the derivative of f at x.

Similarly, although mathematicians usually now view an integral

as a limit

where >Δx is an interval containing x_i, Leibniz viewed it as the sum (the integral sign denoting summation) of infinitely many infinitesimal quantities f(x) dx.

a. Leibniz's notation
c. Stationary point
b. Smooth function
d. Time derivative

22.   In geometry, a _____ is a special plane curve generated by the trace of a fixed point on a small circle that rolls within a larger circle. It is comparable to the cycloid but instead of the circle rolling along a line, it rolls within a circle. The red curve is a _____ traced as the smaller black circle rolls around inside the larger blue circle (parameters are R=3.0, r=1.0, and so k=3), giving a deltoid.

If the smaller circle has radius r, and the larger circle has radius R = kr, then the parametric equations for the curve can be given by either:

$$x(\theta) = (R - r)\cos\theta + r\cos\left(\frac{R-r}{r}\theta\right)$$
$$y(\theta) = (R - r)\sin\theta - r\sin\left(\frac{R-r}{r}\theta\right),$$

or:

$$x(\theta) = r(k-1)\cos\theta + r\cos\left((k-1)\theta\right)$$
$$y(\theta) = r(k-1)\sin\theta - r\sin\left((k-1)\theta\right).$$

If k is an integer, then the curve is closed, and has k cusps (i.e., sharp corners, where the curve is not differentiable.)

a. Hypocycloid
c. Bullet-nose curve
b. Kappa curve
d. Closed curve

23.   A surface normal to a flat surface is a vector which is perpendicular to that surface. A normal to a non-flat surface at a point P on the surface is a vector perpendicular to the tangent plane to that surface at P. The word 'normal' is also used as an adjective: a line normal to a plane, the normal component of a force, the _____, etc. The concept of normality generalizes to orthogonality.

a. Normal vector
c. Normal line
b. Hyperbolic paraboloid
d. Paraboloid

Chapter 13. VECTOR-VALUED FUNCTIONS

24. In mathematics, a _____ in a normed vector space is a vector (often a spatial vector) whose length is 1 (the unit length.) A _____ is often denoted by a lowercase letter with a superscribed caret or e;hate;, like this: $\hat{\imath}$.

In Euclidean space, the dot product of two unit vectors is simply the cosine of the angle between them.

a. ALGOR
b. ACTRAN
c. Overdetermined
d. Unit vector

25. The first Frenet vector $e_1(t)$ is the _____ in the same direction, defined at each regular point of γ:

$$\mathbf{e}_1(t) = \frac{\gamma'(t)}{\|\gamma'(t)\|}.$$

If t = s is the natural parameter then the tangent vector has unit length, so that the formula simplifies:

$$\mathbf{e}_1(s) = \gamma'(s).$$

The _____ determines the orientation of the curve, or the forward direction, corresponding to the increasing values of the parameter.

The normal vector, sometimes called the curvature vector, indicates the deviance of the curve from being a straight line.

It is defined as

$$\overline{\mathbf{e}_2}(t) = \gamma''(t) - \langle \gamma''(t), \mathbf{e}_1(t) \rangle \, \mathbf{e}_1(t).$$

Its normalized form, the unit normal vector, is the second Frenet vector $e_2(t)$ and defined as

$$\mathbf{e}_2(t) = \frac{\overline{\mathbf{e}_2}(t)}{\|\overline{\mathbf{e}_2}(t)\|}.$$

The tangent and the normal vector at point t define the osculating plane at point t.

a. Unit tangent vector
b. Isothermal coordinates
c. ACTRAN
d. Invariant differential operator

26. In mathematics, _____ refers to any of a number of loosely related concepts in different areas of geometry. Intuitively, _____ is the amount by which a geometric object deviates from being flat, or straight in the case of a line, but this is defined in different ways depending on the context. There is a key distinction between extrinsic _____, which is defined for objects embedded in another space (usually a Euclidean space) in a way that relates to the radius of _____ of circles that touch the object, and intrinsic _____, which is defined at each point in a differential manifold.

Chapter 13. VECTOR-VALUED FUNCTIONS

  a. Lie derivative
  b. Minimal surface
  c. Sphere
  d. Curvature

27. In geometry, _____ of a curve is found at a point that is at a distance equal to the radius of curvature lying on the normal vector. It is the point at infinity if the curvature is zero. The osculating circle to the curve is centered at the _____.
  a. Kampyle of Eudoxus
  b. Strophoid
  c. Center of curvature
  d. Dolbeault operator

28. In mathematics, a _____ is a method for approximating the total area underneath a curve on a graph, otherwise known as an integral. It may also be used to define the integration operation.

Consider a function $f: D \rightarrow \mathbf{R}$, where D is a subset of the real numbers $\mathbf{R}$, and let $I = [a, b]$ be a closed interval contained in D. A finite set of points $\{x_0, x_1, x_2, ... x_n\}$ such that $a = x_0 < x_1 < x_2 ... < x_n = b$ creates a partition

$$P = \{[x_0, x_1), [x_1, x_2), ... [x_{n-1}, x_n]\}$$

of I.

  a. Solid of revolution
  b. Signed measure
  c. Risch algorithm
  d. Riemann sum

29. A _____ is the path a moving object follows through space. The object might be a projectile or a satellite, for example. It thus includes the meaning of orbit - the path of a planet, an asteroid or a comet as it travels around a central mass.
  a. BDDC
  b. 15 theorem
  c. Trajectory
  d. BIBO stability

30. In physics, and more specifically kinematics, _____ is the change in velocity over time. Because velocity is a vector, it can change in two ways: a change in magnitude and/or a change in direction. In one dimension, _____ is the rate at which something speeds up or slows down.
  a. ALGOR
  b. AUSM
  c. ACTRAN
  d. Acceleration

31. In physics, _____ is defined as the rate of change of position. it is vector physical quantity; both speed and direction are required to define it. In the SI (metric) system, it is measured in meters per second: (m/s) or ms^{-1}.
  a. 15 theorem
  b. BIBO stability
  c. Velocity
  d. BDDC

32. In mathematics, a _____ that describes a line D is any vector

$$\overrightarrow{AB}$$

Chapter 13. VECTOR-VALUED FUNCTIONS

where A and B are two distinct points on the line D. If v is a _____ for D, so is kv for any nonzero scalar k; and these are in fact all of the direction vectors for the line D. Under some definitions, the _____ is required to be a unit vector, in which case each line has exactly two direction vectors, which are negatives of each other (equal in magnitude, opposite in direction.)

Any line in two-dimensional Euclidean space can be described as the set of solutions to an equation of the form

ax + by + c = 0

where a, b, c are real numbers. Then one _____ of (D) is (− b,a).

a. Direction cosines
b. Dot product
c. Direction vector
d. Vector-valued function

33. In mathematics, the _____ of a function is the set of all 'output' values produced by that function. Sometimes it is called the image, or more precisely, the image of the domain of the function. If a function is a surjection then its _____ is equal to its codomain.

a. Range
b. Surjective
c. Constant function
d. Piecewise-defined function

34. A _____, sometimes known as an energy shield, force shield typically made of energy or charged particles, that protects a person, area or object from attacks or intrusions.

A University of Washington in Seattle group has been experimenting with using a bubble of charged plasma to surround a spacecraft, contained by a fine mesh of superconducting wire. This would protect the spacecraft from interstellar radiation and some particles without needing physical shielding.

a. 15 theorem
b. BDDC
c. BIBO stability
d. Force field

35. _____ is a type of motion in which the velocity of an object changes equal amounts in equal time periods. An example of an object having _____ would be a ball rolling down a ramp. The object picks up velocity as it goes down the ramp with equal changes in time.

a. AUSM
b. Uniform Acceleration
c. ACTRAN
d. ALGOR

36. Integration is an important concept in mathematics, specifically in the field of calculus and, more broadly, mathematical analysis. Given a function f of a real variable x and an interval [a, b] of the real line, the _____

$$\int_a^b f(x)\,dx,$$

is defined informally to be the net signed area of the region in the xy-plane bounded by the graph of f, the x-axis, and the vertical lines x = a and x = b.

The term '_____' may also refer to the notion of antiderivative, a function F whose derivative is the given function f.

   a. Integral test for convergence
   b. Indefinite integral
   c. Integrand
   d. Integral

37. Derivative terms are used to identify the body being orbited. The most common are perigee and apogee, referring to orbits around the Earth , and perihelion and _____, referring to orbits around the Sun . During the Apollo program, the terms pericynthion and apocynthion were used when referring to the moon.
   a. ALGOR
   b. ACTRAN
   c. AUSM
   d. Aphelion

38. In mathematics, the hyperbolic functions are analogs of the ordinary trigonometric functions. The basic hyperbolic functions are the hyperbolic sine 'sinh', and the _____ 'cosh', from which are derived the hyperbolic tangent 'tanh', etc., in analogy to the derived trigonometric functions. The inverse hyperbolic functions are the area hyperbolic sine 'arsinh' (also called 'asinh', or sometimes by the misnomer of 'arcsinh') and so on.
   a. Hyperbolic cosine
   b. Hyperbolic tangent
   c. Step function
   d. Square root function

39. In physics, _____ is rotation along a circle: a circular path or a circular orbit. It can be uniform, that is, with constant angular rate of rotation, or non-uniform, that is, with a changing rate of rotation. The rotation around a fixed axis of a three-dimensional body involves _____ of its parts.
   a. BDDC
   b. BIBO stability
   c. 15 theorem
   d. Circular motion

40. A _____ is a set of standard clothing worn by members of an organization while participating in that organization's activity. Modern uniforms are worn by armed forces and paramilitary organisations such as police, emergency services, security guards, in some workplaces and schools and by inmates in prisons. In some countries, some other officials also wear uniforms in their duties; such is the case of the Commissioned Corps of the United States Public Health Service or the French prefects.
   a. ACTRAN
   b. AUSM
   c. ALGOR
   d. Uniform

Chapter 14. PARTIAL DERIVATIVES

1. In the mathematical subfield of numerical analysis, _____ is a method of constructing new data points within the range of a discrete set of known data points.

   In engineering and science one often has a number of data points, as obtained by sampling or experimentation, and tries to construct a function which closely fits those data points. This is called curve fitting or regression analysis.

   a. ALGOR
   b. AUSM
   c. ACTRAN
   d. Interpolation

2. In mathematics, an _____ space is a topological space whose dimension is n (where n is a fixed natural number.) The archetypical example is _____ Euclidean space, which describes Euclidean geometry in n dimensions.

   Many familiar geometric objects can be generalized to any number of dimensions.

   a. BIBO stability
   b. 15 theorem
   c. BDDC
   d. N-dimensional

3. The _____ of an angle is the ratio of the length of the opposite side to the length of the hypotenuse. In our case

$$\sin A = \frac{\text{opposite}}{\text{hypotenuse}} = \frac{a}{h}.$$

   Note that this ratio does not depend on size of the particular right triangle chosen, as long as it contains the angle A, since all such triangles are similar.

   The cosine of an angle is the ratio of the length of the adjacent side to the length of the hypotenuse.

   a. Trigonometric functions
   b. Trigonometric
   c. Sine
   d. Sine integral

4. In mathematics, a (topological) _____ is defined as follows: let I be an interval of real numbers (i.e. a non-empty connected subset of $\mathbb{R}$); then a _____ γ is a continuous mapping $\gamma : I \to X$, where X is a topological space. The _____ γ is said to be simple if it is injective, i.e. if for all x, y in I, we have $\gamma(x) = \gamma(y) \implies x = y$. If I is a closed bounded interval $[a, b]$, we also allow the possibility $\gamma(a) = \gamma(b)$ (this convention makes it possible to talk about closed simple _____.)

   a. Closed curve
   b. Curve
   c. Tractrix
   d. Prolate cycloid

5. When the number of variables is two, this is a _____, if it is three this is a level surface, and for higher values of n the level set is a level hypersurface.

   More specifically, a _____ is the set of all real-valued roots of an equation in two variables x_1 and x_2. A level surface is the set of all real-valued roots of an equation in three variables x_1, x_2 and x_3.

Chapter 14. PARTIAL DERIVATIVES

    a. Scalar field
    c. Level curve
    b. Partial derivative
    d. Multipole moment

6. A _____ is a type of map characterized by large-scale detail and quantitative representation of relief, usually using contour lines in modern mapping, but historically using a variety of methods. Traditional definitions require a _____ to show both natural and man-made features.

The Canadian Centre for Topographic Information provides this definition of a _____:

Other authors define topographic maps by contrasting them with another type of map; they are distinguished from smaller-scale 'chorographic maps' that cover large regions, 'planimetric maps' that do not show elevations, and 'thematic maps' that focus on specific topics.

    a. Topographic map
    c. 15 theorem
    b. BIBO stability
    d. BDDC

7. In computer science and information science, _____ could also be a method or an algorithm. Again, an example will illustrate: There are systems of counting, as with Roman numerals, and various systems for filing papers, or catalogues, and various library systems, of which the Dewey Decimal _____ is an example. This still fits with the definition of components which are connected together (in this case in order to facilitate the flow of information.)

    a. BDDC
    c. BIBO stability
    b. 15 theorem
    d. System

8. Integration is an important concept in mathematics, specifically in the field of calculus and, more broadly, mathematical analysis. Given a function f of a real variable x and an interval [a, b] of the real line, the _____

$$\int_a^b f(x)\,dx,$$

is defined informally to be the net signed area of the region in the xy-plane bounded by the graph of f, the x-axis, and the vertical lines x = a and x = b.

The term '_____' may also refer to the notion of antiderivative, a function F whose derivative is the given function f.

    a. Integral
    c. Indefinite integral
    b. Integral test for convergence
    d. Integrand

9. In mathematics, the concept of a '_____' is used to describe the behavior of a function as its argument or input either 'gets close' to some point, or as the argument becomes arbitrarily large; or the behavior of a sequence's elements as their index increases indefinitely. Limits are used in calculus and other branches of mathematical analysis to define derivatives and continuity.

In formulas, _____ is usually abbreviated as lim

a. 15 theorem
b. Limit
c. BIBO stability
d. BDDC

10. _____ or isopotential in mathematics and physics (especially electronics) refers to a region in space where every point in it is at the same potential. This usually refers to a scalar potential, although it can also be applied to vector potentials. Often, _____ surfaces are used to visualize an (n)-dimensional scalar potential function in (n-1) dimensional space.
   a. Implicit function theorem
   b. Inverse function theorem
   c. Upper convected time derivative
   d. Equipotential

11. An _____ process is a change in which the temperature of the system stays constant: ΔT = 0. This typically occurs when a system is in contact with an outside thermal reservoir (heat bath), and the change occurs slowly enough to allow the system to continually adjust to the temperature of the reservoir through heat exchange. An alternative special case in which a system exchanges no heat with its surroundings (Q = 0) is called an adiabatic process.
   a. ACTRAN
   b. ALGOR
   c. AUSM
   d. Isothermal

12. _____ is a type of motion in which the velocity of an object changes equal amounts in equal time periods. An example of an object having _____ would be a ball rolling down a ramp. The object picks up velocity as it goes down the ramp with equal changes in time.
   a. Uniform Acceleration
   b. ACTRAN
   c. AUSM
   d. ALGOR

13. In mathematics, a _____ is the graph of the system of parametric equations

$$x = A\sin(at + \delta), \quad y = B\sin(bt),$$

which describes complex harmonic motion. This family of curves was investigated by Nathaniel Bowditch in 1815, and later in more detail by Jules Antoine Lissajous in 1857.

The appearance of the figure is highly sensitive to the ratio a/b.

   a. BIBO stability
   b. Lissajous curve
   c. 15 theorem
   d. BDDC

14. In calculus, a branch of mathematics, the _____ is a measurement of how a function changes when its input changes. Loosely speaking, a _____ can be thought of as how much a quantity is changing at some given point. For example, the _____ of the position (or distance) of a vehicle with respect to time is the instantaneous velocity (respectively, instantaneous speed) at which the vehicle is traveling.

The process of finding a _____ is called differentiation. The fundamental theorem of calculus states that differentiation is the reverse process to integration.

   a. Derivative
   b. Semi-differentiability
   c. Stationary phase approximation
   d. Bounded function

Chapter 14. PARTIAL DERIVATIVES

15. The _____ is the equation of state of a hypothetical ideal gas, first stated by Benoît Paul Émile Clapeyron in 1834. The law is derived from the fact that in the ideal state of any gas a given number of its 'particles' occupy the same volume, and that volume changes are inverse to pressure changes and linear to temperature changes.

The state of an amount of gas is determined by its pressure, volume, and temperature according to the equation:

$$pV = nRT$$

where

> p is the absolute pressure of the gas,
> V is the volume of the gas,
> n is the number of moles of gas,
> R is the universal gas constant,
> T is the absolute temperature.

a. Ideal gas law
b. ACTRAN
c. AUSM
d. ALGOR

16. In mathematics, a _____ of a function of several variables is its derivative with respect to one of those variables with the others held constant (as opposed to the total derivative, in which all variables are allowed to vary.) Partial derivatives are useful in vector calculus and differential geometry.

The _____ of a function f with respect to the variable x is written as f'_x, $\partial_x f$, or $\partial f/\partial x$.

a. Differentiation operator
b. Jacobian
c. Partial derivative
d. Level curve

17. _____ is used to describe the steepness, incline, gradient, or grade of a straight line. A higher _____ value indicates a steeper incline. The _____ is defined as the ratio of the 'rise' divided by the 'run' between two points on a line, or in other words, the ratio of the altitude change to the horizontal distance between any two points on the line.

a. Y-intercept
b. Sequence
c. 15 theorem
d. Slope

18. In mathematics, a _____ is an ordered list of objects (or events). Like a set, it contains members (also called elements or terms), and the number of terms (possibly infinite) is called the length of the _____. Unlike a set, order matters, and the exact same elements can appear multiple times at different positions in the _____.

a. Slope
b. Y-intercept
c. 15 theorem
d. Sequence

19. The _____ is an important second-order linear partial differential equation that describes the propagation of a variety of waves, such as sound waves, light waves and water waves. It arises in fields such as acoustics, electromagnetics, and fluid dynamics. Historically, the problem of a vibrating string such as that of a musical instrument was studied by Jean le Rond d'Alembert, Leonhard Euler, Daniel Bernoulli, and Joseph-Louis Lagrange.

Chapter 14. PARTIAL DERIVATIVES

a. Lagrangian
c. Dirac equation

b. Volume
d. Wave equation

20. In infinitesimal calculus, a _____ is traditionally an infinitesimally small change in a variable. For example, if x is a variable, then a change in the value of x is often denoted Δx (or δx when this change is considered to be small.) The _____ dx represents such a change, but is infinitely small.

a. Local maximum
c. Dirichlet integral

b. The Method of Mechanical Theorems
d. Differential

21. A _____ is a mathematical equation for an unknown function of one or several variables that relates the values of the function itself and of its derivatives of various orders. they play a prominent role in engineering, physics, economics and other disciplines.

A simplified real world example of a _____ is modeling the acceleration of a ball falling through the air (considering only gravity and air resistance.)

a. Phase line
c. Differential equation

b. Structural stability
d. Caloric polynomial

22. Typically the pair u and v are taken to be the real and imaginary parts of a complex-valued function f(x + iy) = u(x,y) + iv (x,y.) Suppose that u and v are continuously differentiable on an open subset of C. Then f = u+iv is holomorphic if and only if the partial derivatives of u and v satisfy the _____ and (1b.)

The equations are one way of looking at the condition on a function to be differentiable (holomorphic) in the sense of complex analysis: in other words they encapsulate the notion of function of a complex variable by means of conventional differential calculus.

a. Spherical harmonics
c. Cauchy-Riemann equations

b. Viscosity solution
d. Solid harmonics

23. The _____ is an important partial differential equation which describes the distribution of heat (or variation in temperature) in a given region over time. For a function u(x,y,z,t) of three spatial variables (x,y,z) and the time variable t, the _____ is

$$\frac{\partial u}{\partial t} - k\left(\frac{\partial^2 u}{\partial x^2} + \frac{\partial^2 u}{\partial y^2} + \frac{\partial^2 u}{\partial z^2}\right) = 0$$

or equivalently

$$\frac{\partial u}{\partial t} = k\nabla^2 u$$

where k is a constant.

The _____ is of fundamental importance in diverse scientific fields.

a. Heat equation
b. BIBO stability
c. 15 theorem
d. BDDC

24. In mathematics, a _____ is an approximation of a general function using a linear function (more precisely, an affine function.)

Given a differentiable function f of one real variable, Taylor's theorem for n=1 states that

$$f(x) = f(a) + f\,'(a)(x-a) + R_2$$

where R_2 is the remainder term. The _____ is obtained by dropping the remainder:

$$f(x) \approx f(a) + f\,'(a)(x-a)$$

which is true for x close to a.

a. Lin-Tsien equation
b. Smooth function
c. Point of inflection
d. Linear approximation

25. f'(x) is twice the absolute value function, and it does not have a derivative at zero. Similar examples show that a function can have k derivatives for any non-negative integer k but no (k + 1)-order derivative. A function that has k successive derivatives is called _____.

a. Power series
b. Differential coefficient
c. Differential calculus
d. K times differentiable

26. _____ is a property of functions that says -- roughly -- that if you zoom in on a point on the graph of the function (with equal scaling horizontally and vertically), the graph will eventually look like a straight line. More precisely, a function is locally linear at a point if and only if a tangent line exists at said point.

Thus, _____ is the graphical manifestation of differentiability.

a. BIBO stability
b. BDDC
c. 15 theorem
d. Local linearity

27. In calculus, _____, was originally the use of expressions such as dx and dy and to represent 'infinitely small' (or infinitesimal) increments of quantities x and y, just as >Δx and >Δy represent finite increments of x and y respectively. So for y being a function of x, or

the derivative of y with respect to x, which later came to be viewed as

was, according to Leibniz, the quotient of an infinitesimal increment of y by an infinitesimal increment of x, or

where the right hand side is Lagrange's notation for the derivative of f at x.

Similarly, although mathematicians usually now view an integral

as a limit

where $>\Delta x$ is an interval containing x_i, Leibniz viewed it as the sum (the integral sign denoting summation) of infinitely many infinitesimal quantities f(x) dx.

a. Stationary point
c. Time derivative
b. Leibniz's notation
d. Smooth function

28. A _____ is a 2D geometric symbolic representation of information according to some visualization technique. Sometimes, the technique uses a 3D visualization which is then projected onto the 2D surface.

_____ has two meanings in common sense.

a. BIBO stability
c. BDDC
b. 15 theorem
d. Diagram

29. In calculus, a method called _____ can be applied to implicitly defined functions. This method is an application of the chain rule allowing one to calculate the derivative of a function given implicitly.

As explained in the introduction, y can be given as a function of x implicitly rather than explicitly. When we have an equation R (x,y) = 0, we may be able to solve it for y and then differentiate. However, sometimes it is simpler to differentiate R(x,y) with respect to x and then solve for dy / dx.

a. Ordinary differential equation
c. Implicit differentiation
b. Implicit function
d. Automatic differentiation

30. In a totally ordered set all elements are mutually comparable, so such a set can have at most one minimal element and at most one maximal element. Then, due to mutual comparability, the minimal element will also be the least element and the maximal element will also be the greatest element. Thus in a totally ordered set we can simply use the terms minimum and _____.

a. Racetrack principle
c. Nth term
b. Leibniz rule
d. Maximum

31. In calculus, the _____ is a formula for the derivative of the composite of two functions.

In intuitive terms, if a variable, y, depends on a second variable, u, which in turn depends on a third variable, x, then the rate of change of y with respect to x can be computed as the rate of change of y with respect to u multiplied by the rate of change of u with respect to x. Schematically,

$$\frac{dy}{dx} = \frac{dy}{du} \cdot \frac{du}{dx}.$$

a. Product rule
c. Reciprocal Rule
b. Differentiation rules
d. Chain rule

32.

In differential calculus, _____ problems involve finding a rate that a quantity changes by relating the population of the earth. The rate of change is usually with respect to people who have died.

a. Related rates
c. Standard part function
b. Visual Calculus
d. Mean Value Theorem

33. In mathematics, a _____ is a function with multiplicative scaling behaviour: if the argument is multiplied by a factor, then the result is multiplied by some power of this factor.

Suppose that $f : V \to W$ is a function between two vector spaces over a field F.

We say that f is homogeneous of degree k if

$$f(\alpha \mathbf{v}) = \alpha^k f(\mathbf{v})$$

for all nonzero $\alpha \in F$ and $\mathbf{v} \in V$.

a. Direction vector
b. Direction cosines
c. Homogeneous function
d. Dot product

34. In mathematics, the _____ of a multivariate differentiable function along a given vector V at a given point P intuitively represents the instantaneous rate of change of the function, moving through P, in the direction of V. It therefore generalizes the notion of a partial derivative, in which the direction is always taken parallel to one of the coordinate axes.

The _____ is a special case of the Gâteaux derivative.

The _____ of a scalar function $f(\vec{x}) = f(x_1, x_2, \ldots, x_n)$ along a vector $\vec{v} = (v_1, \ldots, v_n)$ is the function defined by the limit

<_____>
$$\nabla_{\vec{v}} f(\vec{x}) = \lim_{h \to 0} \frac{f(\vec{x} + h\vec{v}) - f(\vec{x})}{h}.$$

Sometimes authors write D_v instead of ∇_v.

a. Symmetrically continuous
b. Linearity of differentiation
c. Differentiation of trigonometric functions
d. Directional derivative

35. In vector calculus, the _____ of a scalar field is a vector field which points in the direction of the greatest rate of increase of the scalar field, and whose magnitude is the greatest rate of change.

A generalization of the _____ for functions on a Euclidean space which have values in another Euclidean space is the Jacobian. A further generalization for a function from one Banach space to another is the Fréchet derivative.

a. Gradient
b. Symmetric derivative
c. Smooth function
d. Lin-Tsien equation

36. In elementary mathematics, physics, and engineering, a _____ is a geometric object that has both a magnitude (or length), direction and sense, (i.e., orientation along the given direction.) A _____ is frequently represented by a line segment with a definite direction, or graphically as an arrow, connecting an initial point A with a terminal point B, and denoted by

$\boxed{x}_>$

The magnitude of the _____ is the length of the segment and the direction characterizes the displacement of B relative to A: how much one should move the point A to 'carry' it to the point B.

Many algebraic operations on real numbers have close analogues for vectors.

a. BDDC
b. Linear partial differential operator
c. 15 theorem
d. Vector

37. In geometry, the _____ (or simply the tangent) to a curve at a given point is the straight line that 'just touches' the curve at that point (in the sense explained more precisely below.) As it passes through the point of tangency, the _____ is 'going in the same direction' as the curve, and in this sense it is the best straight-line approximation to the curve at that point. The same definition applies to space curves and curves in n-dimensional Euclidean space.
   a. Lie derivative
   b. North pole
   c. Tangent line
   d. Minimal surface

38. In the two-dimensional case, a _____ perpendicularly intersects the tangent line to a curve at a given point.

The _____ is often used in computer graphics to determine a surface's orientation toward a light source for flat shading, or the orientation of each of the corners (vertices) to mimic a curved surface with Phong shading.

For a polygon (such as a triangle), a surface normal can be calculated as the vector cross product of two (non-parallel) edges of the polygon.

   a. Parametric surface
   b. Hyperbolic paraboloid
   c. PDE surfaces
   d. Normal line

39. A surface normal to a flat surface is a vector which is perpendicular to that surface. A normal to a non-flat surface at a point P on the surface is a vector perpendicular to the tangent plane to that surface at P. The word 'normal' is also used as an adjective: a line normal to a plane, the normal component of a force, the _____, etc. The concept of normality generalizes to orthogonality.
   a. Hyperbolic paraboloid
   b. Paraboloid
   c. Normal line
   d. Normal vector

40. In mathematics, _____ and minima, known collectively as extrema, are the largest value (maximum) or smallest value (minimum), that a function takes in a point either within a given neighbourhood (local extremum) or on the function domain in its entirety (global extremum.)

Throughout, a point refers to an input (x), while a value refers to an output (y): one distinguishing between the maximum value and the point (or points) at which it occurs.

A real-valued function f defined on the real line is said to have a local maximum point at the point x^*, if there exists some $\varepsilon > 0$, such that $f(x^*) \geq f(x)$ when $|x - x^*| < \varepsilon$.

   a. Maxima
   b. Related rates
   c. Racetrack principle
   d. Leibniz formula

41. In a totally ordered set all elements are mutually comparable, so such a set can have at most one minimal element and at most one maximal element. Then, due to mutual comparability, the minimal element will also be the least element and the maximal element will also be the greatest element. Thus in a totally ordered set we can simply use the terms _____ and maximum.

Chapter 14. PARTIAL DERIVATIVES

a. Minimum
c. Maximum
b. Ghosts of departed quantities
d. Nth term

42. In mathematics, two vectors are _____ if they are perpendicular, i.e., they form a right angle. For example, a subway and the street above, although they do not physically intersect, are _____ if they cross at a right angle.
   a. ACTRAN
   c. ALGOR
   b. Orthogonal
   d. AUSM

43. In topology, the boundary of a subset S of a topological space X is the set of points which can be approached both from S and from the outside of S. More formally, it is the set of points in the closure of S, not belonging to the interior of S. An element of the boundary of S is called a _____ of S. S is boundaryless when it contains no boundary, which is to say no _____ Notations used for boundary of a set S include bd(S), fr(S), and ∂S. Some authors (for example Willard, in General Topology) use the term 'frontier', instead of boundary in an attempt to avoid confusion with the concept of boundary used in algebraic topology.
   a. BIBO stability
   c. 15 theorem
   b. BDDC
   d. Boundary point

44. In mathematics, a function f defined on some set X with real or complex values is a _____ function, if the set of its values is _____. In other words, there exists a number M>0 such that

$$|f(x)| \leq M$$

for all x in X.

Sometimes, if $f(x) \leq A$ for all x in X, then the function is said to be _____ above by A.

   a. Stationary phase approximation
   c. Bounded
   b. Differential coefficient
   d. Concave upwards

45. In metric topology and related fields of mathematics, a set U is called _____ if, intuitively speaking, starting from any point x in U one can move by a small amount in any direction and still be in the set U. In other words, the distance between any point x in U and the edge of U is always greater than zero.

As an example, consider the _____ interval (0, 1) consisting of all real numbers x with 0 < x < 1. Here, the topology is the usual topology on the real line. We can look at this in two ways.

   a. ACTRAN
   c. AUSM
   b. ALGOR
   d. Open

Chapter 14. PARTIAL DERIVATIVES

46. In mathematics, a _____ (or critical number) is a point on the domain of a function where:

- one dimension: the derivative (or slope of the line when visualized) is equal to zero or a point where the function ceases to be differentiable.
- in general: there are two distinct concepts: either the derivative (Jacobian) vanishes, or it is not of full rank (or, in either case, the function is not differentiable); these agree in one dimension.

Note that in one dimension, a critical value or critical number x of function f is the domain element at which the derivative is zero or undefined, whereas the associated ordered pair (x, y) is the _____. In higher dimensions a critical value is in the range whereas a _____ is in the domain.

There are two situations in which a point becomes a _____ of a function of one variable. The first of which is that the value of the first derivative is equal to zero.

a. Multivariable calculus
b. Total derivative
c. Differentiation operator
d. Critical point

47. In mathematics, a _____ is a point in the domain of a function of two variables which is a stationary point but not a local extremum. At such a point, in general, the surface resembles a saddle that curves up in one direction, and curves down in a different direction (like a mountain pass.) In terms of contour lines, a _____ can be recognized, in general, by a contour that appears to intersect itself.

a. 15 theorem
b. BDDC
c. BIBO stability
d. Saddle point

48. The largest and the smallest element of a set are called extreme values, absolute extrema, or extreme records.

For a differentiable function f, if $f(x_0)$ is an _____ for the set of all values f(x), and if x_0 is in the interior of the domain of f, then x_0 is a critical point, by Fermat's theorem.

In the case of a general partial order one should not confuse a least element (smaller than all other) and a minimal element (nothing is smaller.)

a. Integration by substitution
b. Extreme value
c. Extreme Value Theorem
d. Infinitesimal

49. _____ is finding a curve which has the best fit to a series of data points and possibly other constraints. This section is an introduction to both interpolation (where an exact fit to constraints is expected) and regression analysis. Both are sometimes used for extrapolation.

a. Propagation of uncertainty
b. Curve fitting
c. Well-posed problem
d. Series acceleration

50. The method of _____ or ordinary _____ is used to solve overdetermined systems. _____ is often applied in statistical contexts, particularly regression analysis.

Chapter 14. PARTIAL DERIVATIVES

_____ can be interpreted as a method of fitting data. The best fit in the _____ sense is that instance of the model for which the sum of squared residuals has its least value, a residual being the difference between an observed value and the value given by the model.

a. Least squares
b. 15 theorem
c. BIBO stability
d. BDDC

51. In mathematical optimization, the method of Lagrange multipliers provides a strategy for finding the maximum/minimum of a function subject to constraints.

For example, consider the optimization problem

$$\text{maximize } f(x, y)$$
$$\text{subject to } g(x, y) = c.$$

We introduce a new variable (λ) called a _____, and study the Lagrange function defined by

$$\Lambda(x, y, \lambda) = f(x, y) - \lambda\big(g(x, y) - c\big).$$

If (x,y)′ is a maximum for the original constrained problem, then there exists a λ such that (x,y,λ)′ is a stationary point for the Lagrange function (stationary points are those points where the partial derivatives of Λ are zero.) However, not all stationary points yield a solution of the original problem.

a. 15 theorem
b. BDDC
c. BIBO stability
d. Lagrange multiplier

52. In economics, the _____ functional form of production functions is widely used to represent the relationship of an output to inputs. It was proposed by Knut Wicksell (1851-1926), and tested against statistical evidence by Charles Cobb and Paul Douglas in 1900-1928.

For production, the function is

$Y = AL^{\alpha}K^{\beta}$,

where:

- Y = total production (the monetary value of all goods produced in a year)
- L = labor input
- K = capital input
- A = total factor productivity
- α and β are the output elasticities of labor and capital, respectively. These values are constants determined by available technology.

Output elasticity measures the responsiveness of output to a change in levels of either labor or capital used in production, ceteris paribus. For example if α = 0.15, a 1% increase in labor would lead to approximately a 0.15% increase in output.

a. BIBO stability
c. BDDC
b. 15 theorem
d. Cobb-Douglas

Chapter 15. MULTIPLE INTEGRALS

1. The _____ is a type of definite integral extended to functions of more than one real variable, for example, f(x, y) or f(x, y, z.)

Introduction

Just as the definite integral of a positive function of one variable represents the area of the region between the graph of the function and the x-axis, the double integral of a positive function of two variables represents the volume of the region between the surface defined by the function (on the three dimensional Cartesian plane where z = f(x,y)) and the plane which contains its domain. (Note that the same volume can be obtained via the triple integral -- the integral of a function in three variables -- of the constant function f(x, y, z) = 1 over the above-mentioned region between the surface and the plane.)

   a. Multiple integral
   c. Quadratic integral
   b. Risch algorithm
   d. Surface of revolution

2. The _____ of an angle is the ratio of the length of the opposite side to the length of the hypotenuse. In our case

$$\sin A = \frac{\text{opposite}}{\text{hypotenuse}} = \frac{a}{h}.$$

Note that this ratio does not depend on size of the particular right triangle chosen, as long as it contains the angle A, since all such triangles are similar.

The cosine of an angle is the ratio of the length of the adjacent side to the length of the hypotenuse.

   a. Trigonometric functions
   c. Sine integral
   b. Trigonometric
   d. Sine

3. The _____ of any solid, liquid, plasma, vacuum or theoretical object is how much three-dimensional space it occupies, often quantified numerically. One-dimensional figures (such as lines) and two-dimensional shapes (such as squares) are assigned zero _____ in the three-dimensional space. _____ is commonly presented in units such as mL or cm^3 (milliliters or cubic centimeters.)
   a. Vector potential
   c. Volume
   b. Dirac equation
   d. Klein-Gordon equation

4. In vector calculus, the _____ is an operator that measures the magnitude of a vector field's source or sink at a given point; the _____ of a vector field is a (signed) scalar. For example, consider air as it is heated or cooled. The relevant vector field for this example is the velocity of the moving air at a point.
   a. Divergence
   c. Triple product
   b. Green's theorem
   d. Gradient theorem

5. In vector calculus, the _____ Ostrogradskye;s theorem the _____ states that the outward flux of a vector field through a surface is equal to the triple integral of the divergence on the region inside the surface. Intuitively, it states that the sum of all sources minus the sum of all sinks gives the net flow out of a region.

a. Del
b. Green's theorem
c. Divergence
d. Divergence Theorem

6. In mathematics, a _____ is a method for approximating the total area underneath a curve on a graph, otherwise known as an integral. It may also be used to define the integration operation.

Consider a function $f: D \longrightarrow \mathbf{R}$, where D is a subset of the real numbers $\mathbf{R}$, and let $I = [a, b]$ be a closed interval contained in D. A finite set of points $\{x_0, x_1, x_2, \ldots x_n\}$ such that $a = x_0 < x_1 < x_2 \ldots < x_n = b$ creates a partition

$$P = \{[x_0, x_1), [x_1, x_2), \ldots [x_{n-1}, x_n]\}$$

of I.

a. Signed measure
b. Risch algorithm
c. Solid of revolution
d. Riemann sum

7. In computer science and information science, _____ could also be a method or an algorithm. Again, an example will illustrate: There are systems of counting, as with Roman numerals, and various systems for filing papers, or catalogues, and various library systems, of which the Dewey Decimal _____ is an example. This still fits with the definition of components which are connected together (in this case in order to facilitate the flow of information.)

a. BDDC
b. 15 theorem
c. BIBO stability
d. System

8. Integration is an important concept in mathematics, specifically in the field of calculus and, more broadly, mathematical analysis. Given a function f of a real variable x and an interval [a, b] of the real line, the _____

$$\int_a^b f(x)\,dx,$$

is defined informally to be the net signed area of the region in the xy-plane bounded by the graph of f, the x-axis, and the vertical lines x = a and x = b.

The term '_____' may also refer to the notion of antiderivative, a function F whose derivative is the given function f.

a. Indefinite integral
b. Integral test for convergence
c. Integral
d. Integrand

9. Just as the definite integral of a positive function of one variable represents the area of the region between the graph of the function and the x-axis, the _____ of a positive function of two variables represents the volume of the region between the surface defined by the function (on the three dimensional Cartesian plane where z = f(x,y)) and the plane which contains its domain. (Note that the same volume can be obtained via the triple integral -- the integral of a function in three variables -- of the constant function f(x, y, z) = 1 over the above-mentioned region between the surface and the plane.) If there are more variables, a multiple integral will yield hypervolumes of multi-dimensional functions.

a. Double integral
c. Trigonometric substitution

b. Constant of integration
d. Risch algorithm

10. In mathematics, a _____ is the graph of the system of parametric equations

$$x = A\sin(at + \delta), \quad y = B\sin(bt),$$

which describes complex harmonic motion. This family of curves was investigated by Nathaniel Bowditch in 1815, and later in more detail by Jules Antoine Lissajous in 1857.

The appearance of the figure is highly sensitive to the ratio a/b.

a. BIBO stability
c. BDDC

b. 15 theorem
d. Lissajous curve

11. In mathematics, a (topological) _____ is defined as follows: let I be an interval of real numbers (i.e. a non-empty connected subset of $\mathbb{R}$); then a _____ γ is a continuous mapping $\gamma : I \to X$, where X is a topological space. The _____ γ is said to be simple if it is injective, i.e. if for all x, y in I, we have $\gamma(x) = \gamma(y) \implies x = y$. If I is a closed bounded interval $[a, b]$, we also allow the possibility $\gamma(a) = \gamma(b)$ (this convention makes it possible to talk about closed simple _____.)

a. Closed curve
c. Curve

b. Prolate cycloid
d. Tractrix

12. In calculus, an _____ is the limit of a definite integral as an endpoint of the interval of integration approaches either a specified real number or ∞ or −∞ or, in some cases, as both endpoints approach limits.

Specifically, an _____ is a limit of the form

$$\lim_{b \to \infty} \int_a^b f(x)\,dx, \qquad \lim_{a \to -\infty} \int_a^b f(x)\,dx,$$

or of the form

$$\lim_{c \to b^-} \int_a^c f(x)\,dx, \qquad \lim_{c \to a^+} \int_c^b f(x)\,dx,$$

in which one takes a limit in one or the other (or sometimes both) endpoints . Improper integrals may also occur at an interior point of the domain of integration, or at multiple such points.

a. ACTRAN
c. AUSM

b. Improper integral
d. ALGOR

13. In calculus, an antiderivative, primitive or _____ of a function f is a function F whose derivative is equal to f, i.e., F ' = f. The process of solving for antiderivatives is antidifferentiation (or indefinite integration.) Antiderivatives are related to definite integrals through the fundamental theorem of calculus: the definite integral of a function over an interval is equal to the difference between the values of an antiderivative evaluated at the endpoints of the interval.

    a. Integral test for convergence
    c. Arc length
    b. Integration by parts operator
    d. Indefinite integral

14. In probability theory and statistics, the _____ (or expectation value or mean and for continuous random variables with a density function it is the probability density -weighted integral of the possible values.

The term '_____' can be misleading.

    a. ACTRAN
    c. ALGOR
    b. AUSM
    d. Expected value

15. In mathematics, the concept of a '_____' is used to describe the behavior of a function as its argument or input either 'gets close' to some point, or as the argument becomes arbitrarily large; or the behavior of a sequence's elements as their index increases indefinitely. Limits are used in calculus and other branches of mathematical analysis to define derivatives and continuity.

In formulas, _____ is usually abbreviated as lim

    a. Limit
    c. BIBO stability
    b. BDDC
    d. 15 theorem

16. In calculus and mathematical analysis the _____ of the integral

$$\int_a^b f(x)\,dx$$

of a Riemann integrable function f defined on a closed and bounded interval [a, b] are the real numbers a and b.

_____ can also be defined for improper integrals, with the _____ of both

$$\lim_{z \to a^+} \int_z^b f(x)\,dx$$

and

$$\lim_{z \to b^-} \int_a^z f(x)\,dx$$

Chapter 15. MULTIPLE INTEGRALS

again being a and b. For an improper integral

$$\int_a^\infty f(x)\,dx$$

or

$$\int_{-\infty}^b f(x)\,dx$$

the _____ are a and ∞, or −∞ and b, respectively.

a. Maxima
b. Limits of integration
c. Test for Divergence
d. Differential

17. _____ is the magnitude of change in the oscillating variable, with each oscillation, within an oscillating system. For instance, sound waves are oscillations in atmospheric pressure and their amplitudes are proportional to the change in pressure during one oscillation. If the variable undergoes regular oscillations, and a graph of the system is drawn with the oscillating variable as the vertical axis and time as the horizontal axis, the _____ is visually represented by the vertical distance between the extrema of the curve.

a. ACTRAN
b. ALGOR
c. Amplitude
d. AUSM

18. In calculus, interchange of the _____ is a methodology that transforms multiple integrations of functions into other, hopefully simpler, integrals by changing the order in which the integrations are performed.

The problem for examination is evaluation of an integral of the form:

$$\iint_D dx\,dy\ f(x,y),$$

where D is some two-dimensional area in the xy-plane. For some functions f straightforward integration is feasible, but where that is not true, the integral can sometimes be reduced to simpler form by changing the _____.

a. Order of integration
b. Arc length
c. Integration by parts
d. Indefinite integral

19. In mathematics and its applications, a _____ system is a system for assigning an n-tuple of numbers or scalars to each point in an n-dimensional space. This concept is part of the theory of manifolds. 'Scalars' in many cases means real numbers, but, depending on context, can mean complex numbers or elements of some other commutative ring.

a. Cylindrical coordinate system
b. 15 theorem
c. Spherical coordinate system
d. Coordinate

20.   In mathematics, the _____ is a two-dimensional coordinate system in which each point on a plane is determined by an angle and a distance. The _____ is especially useful in situations where the relationship between two points is most easily expressed in terms of angles and distance; in the more familiar Cartesian or rectangular coordinate system, such a relationship can only be found through trigonometric formulation.

As the coordinate system is two-dimensional, each point is determined by two polar coordinates: the radial coordinate and the angular coordinate.

a. Polar coordinate system
b. BDDC
c. 15 theorem
d. BIBO stability

21.   _____ is a type of motion in which the velocity of an object changes equal amounts in equal time periods. An example of an object having _____ would be a ball rolling down a ramp. The object picks up velocity as it goes down the ramp with equal changes in time.
a. AUSM
b. ACTRAN
c. ALGOR
d. Uniform Acceleration

22.   A _____ is a surface in the Euclidean space R^3 which is defined by a parametric equation with two parameters. Parametric representation is the most general way to specify a surface. Surfaces that occur in two of the main theorems of vector calculus, Stokes' theorem and divergence theorem, are frequently given in a parametric form.
a. Parametric surface
b. Prolate
c. Torus
d. Paraboloid

23.   In calculus, a branch of mathematics, the _____ is a measurement of how a function changes when its input changes. Loosely speaking, a _____ can be thought of as how much a quantity is changing at some given point. For example, the _____ of the position (or distance) of a vehicle with respect to time is the instantaneous velocity (respectively, instantaneous speed) at which the vehicle is traveling.

The process of finding a _____ is called differentiation. The fundamental theorem of calculus states that differentiation is the reverse process to integration.

a. Stationary phase approximation
b. Bounded function
c. Semi-differentiability
d. Derivative

24.   In mathematics, a _____ of a function of several variables is its derivative with respect to one of those variables with the others held constant (as opposed to the total derivative, in which all variables are allowed to vary.) Partial derivatives are useful in vector calculus and differential geometry.

The _____ of a function f with respect to the variable x is written as f'_x, $\partial_x f$, or $\partial f/\partial x$.

a. Level curve
b. Jacobian
c. Differentiation operator
d. Partial derivative

Chapter 15. MULTIPLE INTEGRALS

25. In elementary mathematics, physics, and engineering, a _____ is a geometric object that has both a magnitude (or length), direction and sense, (i.e., orientation along the given direction.) A _____ is frequently represented by a line segment with a definite direction, or graphically as an arrow, connecting an initial point A with a terminal point B, and denoted by

The magnitude of the _____ is the length of the segment and the direction characterizes the displacement of B relative to A: how much one should move the point A to 'carry' it to the point B.

Many algebraic operations on real numbers have close analogues for vectors.

- a. Linear partial differential operator
- b. BDDC
- c. 15 theorem
- d. Vector

26. A _____ is a mathematical function that maps real numbers to vectors. Vector-valued functions can be defined as:

- $\mathbf{r}(t) = f(t)\hat{\mathbf{i}} + g(t)\hat{\mathbf{j}}$ or
- $\mathbf{r}(t) = f(t)\hat{\mathbf{i}} + g(t)\hat{\mathbf{j}} + h(t)\hat{\mathbf{k}}$

where f(t), g(t) and h(t) are the coordinate functions of the parameter t, and $\hat{\mathbf{i}}$, $\hat{\mathbf{j}}$, and $\hat{\mathbf{k}}$ are unit vectors. r(t) is a vector which has its tail at the origin and its head at the coordinates evaluated by the function.

The vector shown in the graph to the right is the evaluation of the function near t=19.5 (between 6π and 6.5π; i.e., somewhat more than 3 rotations.)

- a. Direction cosines
- b. Direction vector
- c. Vector-valued function
- d. Scalar multiplication

27. In geometry, the _____ (or simply the tangent) to a curve at a given point is the straight line that 'just touches' the curve at that point (in the sense explained more precisely below.) As it passes through the point of tangency, the _____ is 'going in the same direction' as the curve, and in this sense it is the best straight-line approximation to the curve at that point. The same definition applies to space curves and curves in n-dimensional Euclidean space.

- a. Minimal surface
- b. North pole
- c. Lie derivative
- d. Tangent line

28. A surface normal to a flat surface is a vector which is perpendicular to that surface. A normal to a non-flat surface at a point P on the surface is a vector perpendicular to the tangent plane to that surface at P. The word 'normal' is also used as an adjective: a line normal to a plane, the normal component of a force, the _____, etc. The concept of normality generalizes to orthogonality.

Chapter 15. MULTIPLE INTEGRALS

    a. Paraboloid
    b. Normal vector
    c. Hyperbolic paraboloid
    d. Normal line

29. In mathematics, a _____ in a normed vector space is a vector (often a spatial vector) whose length is 1 (the unit length.) A _____ is often denoted by a lowercase letter with a superscribed caret or e;hate;, like this: $\hat{\imath}$.

In Euclidean space, the dot product of two unit vectors is simply the cosine of the angle between them.

    a. Unit vector
    b. Overdetermined
    c. ALGOR
    d. ACTRAN

30. _____ is how much exposed area an object has. It is expressed in square units. If an object has flat faces, its _____ can be calculated by adding together the areas of its faces.

    a. Lipschitz domain
    b. Plane curve
    c. Vector area
    d. Surface area

31. The _____, after the plane and the catenoid, is the third minimal surface to be known. It was first discovered by Jean Baptiste Meusnier in 1776. Its name derives from its similarity to the helix: for every point on the _____ there is a helix contained in the _____ which passes through that point.

    a. 15 theorem
    b. BDDC
    c. Scherk surface
    d. Helicoid

32. In geometry, a _____ (pl. tori) is a surface of revolution generated by revolving a circle in three dimensional space about an axis coplanar with the circle, which does not touch the circle. Examples of tori include the surfaces of doughnuts and inner tubes.

    a. Hyperbolic paraboloid
    b. Paraboloid
    c. Torus
    d. Prolate

33. In mathematics, a _____ is an ordered list of objects (or events). Like a set, it contains members (also called elements or terms), and the number of terms (possibly infinite) is called the length of the _____. Unlike a set, order matters, and the exact same elements can appear multiple times at different positions in the _____.

    a. Y-intercept
    b. 15 theorem
    c. Sequence
    d. Slope

34. The _____ of a material is defined as its mass per unit volume. The symbol of _____ is ρ '>rho.)

Mathematically:

$$d = \frac{m}{V}$$

where:

    d is the _____,
    m is the mass,
    V is the volume.

a. 15 theorem
c. BIBO stability
b. BDDC
d. Density

35. In mathematics, a probability _____ is a function that represents a probability distribution in terms of integrals.

Formally, a probability distribution has density f, if f is a non-negative Lebesgue-integrable function $\mathbb{R} \rightarrow \mathbb{R}$ such that the probability of the interval [a, b] is given by

$$\int_a^b f(x)\,dx$$

for any two numbers a and b. This implies that the total integral of f must be 1.

a. Density function
c. Factorial moment generating function
b. BDDC
d. 15 theorem

36. In mathematics and elsewhere, the adjective _____ means 'fourth order', such as the function x^4. A _____ number is a number which equals the fourth power of an integer.
a. Quartic
c. BDDC
b. Reduction
d. 15 theorem

37. The concept of _____ in mathematics evolved from the concept of _____ in physics. The nth _____ of a real-valued function f(x) of a real variable about a value c is

$$\mu'_n = \int_{-\infty}^{\infty} (x-c)^n f(x)\,dx.$$

It is possible to define moments for random variables in a more general fashion than moments for real values. See Moments in metric spaces.

a. Moment
c. Median
b. Geometric mean
d. Poisson distribution

38. In geometry, the _____, geometric center, or barycenter of a plane figure X is the intersection of all straight lines that divide X into two parts of equal moment about the line. Informally, it is the 'average' of all points of X. The definition extends to any object X in n-dimensional space: its _____ is the intersection of all hyperplanes that divide X into two parts of equal moment.
a. Centroid
c. BDDC
b. 15 theorem
d. BIBO stability

39. A _____ is one of the most curvilinear basic geometric shapes:It has two faces, zero vertices, and zero edges. The surface formed by the points at a fixed distance from a given straight line, the axis of the _____. The solid enclosed by this surface and by two planes perpendicular to the axis is also called a _____.

Chapter 15. MULTIPLE INTEGRALS

    a. BDDC
    c. Right circular cylinder
    b. 15 theorem
    d. Cylinder

40. _____, also called mass _____ or the angular mass, (SI units kg m^2) is a measure of an object's resistance to changes in its rotation rate. It is the rotational analog of mass. That is, it is the inertia of a rigid rotating body with respect to its rotation.
    a. Dirac equation
    c. Klein-Gordon equation
    b. Wave equation
    d. Moment of inertia

41. If a particular point on a sphere is (arbitrarily) designated as its _____, then the corresponding antipodal point is called the south pole and the equator is the great circle that is equidistant to them. Great circles through the two poles are called lines (or meridians) of longitude, and the line connecting the two poles is called the axis of rotation. Circles on the sphere that are parallel to the equator are lines of latitude.
    a. Tangent line
    c. Minimal surface
    b. North pole
    d. Sphere

42. In calculus, _____, was originally the use of expressions such as dx and dy and to represent 'infinitely small' (or infinitesimal) increments of quantities x and y, just as >Δx and >Δy represent finite increments of x and y respectively. So for y being a function of x, or

$$\boxed{\times}_>$$

the derivative of y with respect to x, which later came to be viewed as

$$\boxed{\times}_>$$

was, according to Leibniz, the quotient of an infinitesimal increment of y by an infinitesimal increment of x, or

$$\boxed{\times}_>$$

where the right hand side is Lagrange's notation for the derivative of f at x.

Similarly, although mathematicians usually now view an integral

$$\boxed{\times}_>$$

as a limit

$$\boxed{\times}_>$$

where >Δx is an interval containing x_i, Leibniz viewed it as the sum (the integral sign denoting summation) of infinitely many infinitesimal quantities f(x) dx.

    a. Time derivative
    b. Leibniz's notation
    c. Stationary point
    d. Smooth function

43. Trigonometry is a branch of mathematics that deals with triangles, particularly those plane triangles in which one angle has 90 degrees (right triangles.) Trigonometry deals with relationships between the sides and the angles of triangles and with the _____ functions, which describe those relationships.

Trigonometry has applications in both pure mathematics and in applied mathematics, where it is essential in many branches of science and technology.

    a. Sine
    b. Trigonometric functions
    c. Trigonometric integrals
    d. Trigonometric

44. In mathematics, the _____ are functions of an angle. They are important in the study of triangles and modeling periodic phenomena, among many other applications. _____ are commonly defined as ratios of two sides of a right triangle containing the angle, and can equivalently be defined as the lengths of various line segments from a unit circle.
    a. Sine integral
    b. Trigonometric
    c. Trigonometric integrals
    d. Trigonometric functions

45. In vector calculus, the _____ is shorthand for either the _____ matrix or its determinant, the _____ determinant.

In algebraic geometry the _____ of a curve means the _____ variety: a group variety associated to the curve, in which the curve can be embedded.

These concepts are all named after the mathematician Carl Gustav Jacob Jacobi.

    a. Saddle surface
    b. Vector Laplacian
    c. Critical point
    d. Jacobian

46. In mathematics, the _____ of a function y = f(x) is a function that, in some fashion, 'undoes' the effect of f The _____ of f is denoted f^{-1}. The statements y=f(x) and $x=f^{-1}(y)$ are equivalent.
    a. ALGOR
    b. AUSM
    c. ACTRAN
    d. Inverse

47. An injective function is called an injection, and is also said to be a _____ function (not to be confused with _____ correspondence, i.e. a bijective function.)

A function f that is not injective is sometimes called many-to-one. (However, this terminology is also sometimes used to mean 'single-valued', i.e. each argument is mapped to at most one value.)

a. Onto
c. One-to-one function
b. Injective function
d. One-to-one

48. In mathematics, a _____ is a basic technique used to simplify problems in which the original variables are replaced with new ones; the new and old variables being related in some specified way. The intent is that the problem expressed in new variables may be simpler, or else equivalent to a better understood problem.

A very simple example of a useful variable change can be seen in the problem of finding the roots of the eighth order polynomial:

$$x^8 + 3x^4 + 2 = 0$$

Eighth order polynomial equations are generally impossible to solve in terms of elementary functions.

a. Cubic function
c. Linear equation
b. Change of variables
d. Quadratic formula

49. A _____ is perfectly round geometrical object in three-dimensional space, such as the shape of a round ball. Like a circle in two dimensions, a perfect _____ is completely symmetrical around its center, with all points on the surface lying the same distance r from the center point. This distance r is known as the radius of the _____.

a. North pole
c. Minimal surface
b. Sphere
d. Tangent line

Chapter 16. TOPICS IN VECTOR CALCULUS

1. A _____ is a model used within physics to explain how gravity exists in the universe. In its original concept, gravity was a force between point masses. Following Newton, Laplace attempted to model gravity as some kind of radiation field or fluid, and since the 19th century explanations for gravity have usually been sought in terms of a field model, rather than a point attraction.

   a. BDDC
   b. BIBO stability
   c. 15 theorem
   d. Gravitational field

2. In mathematics, a _____ is an ordered list of objects (or events). Like a set, it contains members (also called elements or terms), and the number of terms (possibly infinite) is called the length of the _____. Unlike a set, order matters, and the exact same elements can appear multiple times at different positions in the _____.

   a. Y-intercept
   b. 15 theorem
   c. Slope
   d. Sequence

3. A _____ is the path a moving object follows through space. The object might be a projectile or a satellite, for example. It thus includes the meaning of orbit - the path of a planet, an asteroid or a comet as it travels around a central mass.

   a. 15 theorem
   b. BDDC
   c. BIBO stability
   d. Trajectory

4. In elementary mathematics, physics, and engineering, a _____ is a geometric object that has both a magnitude (or length), direction and sense, (i.e., orientation along the given direction.) A _____ is frequently represented by a line segment with a definite direction, or graphically as an arrow, connecting an initial point A with a terminal point B, and denoted by

The magnitude of the _____ is the length of the segment and the direction characterizes the displacement of B relative to A: how much one should move the point A to 'carry' it to the point B.

Many algebraic operations on real numbers have close analogues for vectors.

   a. 15 theorem
   b. Vector
   c. BDDC
   d. Linear partial differential operator

5. In mathematics a _____ is a construction in vector calculus which associates a vector to every point in a (locally) Euclidean space.

Vector fields are often used in physics to model, for example, the speed and direction of a moving fluid throughout space, or the strength and direction of some force, such as the magnetic or gravitational force, as it changes from point to point.

In the rigorous mathematical treatment, (tangent) vector fields are defined on manifolds as sections of a manifold's tangent bundle.

a. 15 theorem
b. BDDC
c. BIBO stability
d. Vector field

6. In physics, _____ is defined as the rate of change of position. it is vector physical quantity; both speed and direction are required to define it. In the SI (metric) system, it is measured in meters per second: (m/s) or ms⁻¹.
   a. Velocity
   b. BDDC
   c. BIBO stability
   d. 15 theorem

7. In computer science and information science, _____ could also be a method or an algorithm. Again, an example will illustrate: There are systems of counting, as with Roman numerals, and various systems for filing papers, or catalogues, and various library systems, of which the Dewey Decimal _____ is an example. This still fits with the definition of components which are connected together (in this case in order to facilitate the flow of information.)
   a. 15 theorem
   b. BIBO stability
   c. System
   d. BDDC

8. _____ is a type of motion in which the velocity of an object changes equal amounts in equal time periods. An example of an object having _____ would be a ball rolling down a ramp. The object picks up velocity as it goes down the ramp with equal changes in time.
   a. ALGOR
   b. AUSM
   c. ACTRAN
   d. Uniform Acceleration

9. In mathematics, a (topological) _____ is defined as follows: let I be an interval of real numbers (i.e. a non-empty connected subset of $\mathbb{R}$); then a _____ γ is a continuous mapping $\gamma : I \to X$, where X is a topological space. The _____ γ is said to be simple if it is injective, i.e. if for all x, y in I, we have $\gamma(x) = \gamma(y) \implies x = y$. If I is a closed bounded interval $[a, b]$, we also allow the possibility $\gamma(a) = \gamma(b)$ (this convention makes it possible to talk about closed simple _____.)
   a. Closed curve
   b. Prolate cycloid
   c. Tractrix
   d. Curve

10. In vector calculus, the _____ of a scalar field is a vector field which points in the direction of the greatest rate of increase of the scalar field, and whose magnitude is the greatest rate of change.

A generalization of the _____ for functions on a Euclidean space which have values in another Euclidean space is the Jacobian. A further generalization for a function from one Banach space to another is the Fréchet derivative.

   a. Symmetric derivative
   b. Gradient
   c. Smooth function
   d. Lin-Tsien equation

11. A vector field V defined on a set S is called a _____ or a conservative field if there exists a real valued function (a scalar field) f on S such that

$$V = \nabla f.$$

The associated flow is called the gradient flow, and is used in the method of gradient descent.

The path integral along any closed curve γ (γ(0) = γ(1)) in a _____ is zero:

$$\int_\gamma \langle V(x), dx \rangle = \int_\gamma \langle \nabla f(x), dx \rangle = f(\gamma(1)) - f(\gamma(0))$$

a. BDDC
b. 15 theorem
c. BIBO stability
d. Gradient field

12. In vector calculus, the _____ is an operator that measures the magnitude of a vector field's source or sink at a given point; the _____ of a vector field is a (signed) scalar. For example, consider air as it is heated or cooled. The relevant vector field for this example is the velocity of the moving air at a point.
  a. Green's theorem
  b. Gradient theorem
  c. Triple product
  d. Divergence

13. Integration is an important concept in mathematics, specifically in the field of calculus and, more broadly, mathematical analysis. Given a function f of a real variable x and an interval [a, b] of the real line, the _____

$$\int_a^b f(x)\, dx,$$

is defined informally to be the net signed area of the region in the xy-plane bounded by the graph of f, the x-axis, and the vertical lines x = a and x = b.

The term '_____' may also refer to the notion of antiderivative, a function F whose derivative is the given function f.

  a. Integral test for convergence
  b. Integrand
  c. Indefinite integral
  d. Integral

14. _____ is the long dimension of any object. The _____ of a thing is the distance between its ends, its linear extent as measured from end to end. This may be distinguished from height, which is vertical extent, and width or breadth, which are the distance from side to side, measuring across the object at right angles to the _____.
  a. BIBO stability
  b. BDDC
  c. 15 theorem
  d. Length

15. In mathematics, a _____ is an integral where the function to be integrated is evaluated along a curve. Various different line integrals are in use. A specific case of an integration along a closed curve in two dimensions or the complex plane is the contour integral.
  a. Picard theorem
  b. Radius of convergence
  c. Line integral
  d. Mittag-Leffler star

16. The _____ of a material is defined as its mass per unit volume. The symbol of _____ is ρ '>rho.)

Mathematically:

$$d = \frac{m}{V}$$

where:

        d is the _____,
        m is the mass,
        V is the volume.

a. Density
c. BIBO stability
b. 15 theorem
d. BDDC

17. In mathematics, a probability _____ is a function that represents a probability distribution in terms of integrals.

Formally, a probability distribution has density f, if f is a non-negative Lebesgue-integrable function $\mathbb{R} \to \mathbb{R}$ such that the probability of the interval [a, b] is given by

$$\int_a^b f(x)\,dx$$

for any two numbers a and b. This implies that the total integral of f must be 1.

a. Factorial moment generating function
c. 15 theorem
b. BDDC
d. Density function

18. _____, linear mass density or linear mass is a measure of mass per unit of length, and it is a characteristic of strings or other one-dimensional objects. The SI unit of _____ is the kilogram per metre (kg/m.) The _____, μ (sometimes denoted by λ), of an object is defined as:

$$\mu = \frac{\partial m}{\partial x}$$

where m is the mass, and x is a coordinate along the (one dimensional) object.

a. 15 theorem
c. BDDC
b. BIBO stability
d. Linear density

19. For some curves there is a smallest number L that is an upper bound on the length of any polygonal approximation. If such a number exists, then the curve is said to be rectifiable and the curve is defined to have _____ L.

Chapter 16. TOPICS IN VECTOR CALCULUS

Let C be a curve in Euclidean (or, generally, a metric) space $X = R^n$, so C is the image of a continuous function $f : [a, b] \to X$ of the interval [a, b] into X.

a. Integrand
b. Order of integration
c. Integration by parametric derivatives
d. Arc length

20. In mathematics, a _____ is a function whose definition is dependent on the value of the independent variable. Mathematically, a real-valued function f of a real variable x is a relationship whose definition is given differently on disjoint subsets of its domain

The word piecewise is also used to describe any property of a _____ that holds for each piece but may not hold for the whole domain of the function.

a. Piecewise-defined function
b. Range
c. Constant function
d. Surjective

21. A _____ is a type of manifold that is locally similar enough to Euclidean space to allow one to do calculus Any manifold can be described by a collection of charts, also known as an atlas.
a. Tangent line
b. Differentiable manifold
c. Sphere
d. Minimal surface

22. Smooth functions with given closed support are used in the construction of smooth partitions of unity ; these are essential in the study of smooth manifolds, for example to show that Riemannian metrics can be defined globally starting from their local existence. A simple case is that of a bump function on the real line, that is, a _____ f that takes the value 0 outside an interval [a,b] and such that

$f(x) > 0$ for $a < x < b$.

Given a number of overlapping intervals on the line, bump functions can be constructed on each of them, and on semi-infinite intervals $(-\infty, c]$ and $[d,+\infty)$ to cover the whole line, such that the sum of the functions is always 1.

a. Continuously differentiable
b. Symmetric derivative
c. Smooth function
d. Gradient

23. In mathematics, the concept of a '_____' is used to describe the behavior of a function as its argument or input either 'gets close' to some point, or as the argument becomes arbitrarily large; or the behavior of a sequence's elements as their index increases indefinitely. Limits are used in calculus and other branches of mathematical analysis to define derivatives and continuity.

In formulas, _____ is usually abbreviated as lim

a. BIBO stability
b. Limit
c. 15 theorem
d. BDDC

Chapter 16. TOPICS IN VECTOR CALCULUS

24. A _____, sometimes known as an energy shield, force shield typically made of energy or charged particles, that protects a person, area or object from attacks or intrusions.

A University of Washington in Seattle group has been experimenting with using a bubble of charged plasma to surround a spacecraft, contained by a fine mesh of superconducting wire. This would protect the spacecraft from interstellar radiation and some particles without needing physical shielding.

   a. 15 theorem
   c. Force field
   b. BDDC
   d. BIBO stability

25. In mathematics, an _____ on a real vector space is a choice of which ordered bases are 'positively' oriented and which are 'negatively' oriented. In the three-dimensional Euclidean space, the two possible basis orientations are called right-handed and left-handed (or right-chiral and left-chiral), respectively. However, the choice of _____ is independent of the handedness or chirality of the bases (although right-handed bases are typically declared to be positively oriented, they may also be assigned a negative _____.)
   a. ACTRAN
   c. Orientation
   b. ALGOR
   d. Unit vector

26. In vector calculus a _____ is a vector field which is the gradient of a scalar potential. There are two closely related concepts: path independence and irrotational vector fields. Every _____ has zero curl (and is thus irrotational), and every _____ has the path independence property.
   a. Conservative vector field
   c. Del
   b. Green's theorem
   d. Divergence Theorem

27. In calculus, _____, was originally the use of expressions such as dx and dy and to represent 'infinitely small' (or infinitesimal) increments of quantities x and y, just as >Δx and >Δy represent finite increments of x and y respectively. So for y being a function of x, or

> ×

the derivative of y with respect to x, which later came to be viewed as

> ×

was, according to Leibniz, the quotient of an infinitesimal increment of y by an infinitesimal increment of x, or

> ×

where the right hand side is Lagrange's notation for the derivative of f at x.

Chapter 16. TOPICS IN VECTOR CALCULUS

Similarly, although mathematicians usually now view an integral

as a limit

where >Δx is an interval containing x_i, Leibniz viewed it as the sum (the integral sign denoting summation) of infinitely many infinitesimal quantities f(x) dx.

a. Leibniz's notation
b. Stationary point
c. Time derivative
d. Smooth function

28. In mathematics, the _____ (or replacement set) of a given function is the set of 'input' values for which the function is defined. For instance, the _____ of cosine would be all real numbers, while the _____ of the square root would be only numbers greater than or equal to 0 (ignoring complex numbers in both cases.) In a representation of a function in a xy Cartesian coordinate system, the _____ is represented on the x axis (or abscissa.)

a. BIBO stability
b. BDDC
c. 15 theorem
d. Domain

29. In mathematics, _____ are a method of defining a curve. A simple kinematical example is when one uses a time parameter to determine the position, velocity, and other information about a body in motion.

Abstractly, a relation is given in the form of an equation, and it is shown also to be the image of functions from items such as R^n.

a. Shift theorem
b. Partial derivative
c. Critical point
d. Parametric equations

30. In mathematics, a _____ is the graph of the system of parametric equations

$$x = A\sin(at + \delta), \quad y = B\sin(bt),$$

which describes complex harmonic motion. This family of curves was investigated by Nathaniel Bowditch in 1815, and later in more detail by Jules Antoine Lissajous in 1857.

The appearance of the figure is highly sensitive to the ratio a/b.

a. 15 theorem
b. BDDC
c. BIBO stability
d. Lissajous curve

Chapter 16. TOPICS IN VECTOR CALCULUS

31. _____ can be thought of as energy stored within a physical system. It is called _____ because it has the potential to be converted into other forms of energy, such as kinetic energy, and to do work in the process. The standard (SI) unit of measure for _____ is the joule, the same as for work or energy in general.
   a. 15 theorem
   b. Potential energy
   c. BDDC
   d. Law of Conservation of Energy

32. A curve γ is said to be closed or a loop if $I = [a, b]$ and if $\gamma(a) = \gamma(b)$. A _____ is thus a continuous mapping of the circle S^1; a simple _____ is also called a Jordan curve or a Jordan arc. The Jordan curve theorem states that such curves divide the plane into an 'interior' and an 'exterior'.
   a. Curve
   b. Kappa curve
   c. Bullet-nose curve
   d. Closed curve

33. In mathematics, particularly in complex analysis, a _____, first studied by and named after Bernhard Riemann, is a one-dimensional complex manifold. Riemann surfaces can be thought of as 'deformed versions' of the complex plane: locally near every point they look like patches of the complex plane, but the global topology can be quite different. For example, they can look like a sphere or a torus or a couple of sheets glued together.
   a. Lacunary value
   b. Pole
   c. Radius of convergence
   d. Riemann surface

34. In mathematics and elsewhere, the adjective _____ means 'fourth order', such as the function x^4. A _____ number is a number which equals the fourth power of an integer.
   a. Quartic
   b. Reduction
   c. 15 theorem
   d. BDDC

35. _____ is how much exposed area an object has. It is expressed in square units. If an object has flat faces, its _____ can be calculated by adding together the areas of its faces.
   a. Vector area
   b. Lipschitz domain
   c. Plane curve
   d. Surface area

36. In mathematics, a _____ is a definite integral taken over a surface (which may be a curved set in space); it can be thought of as the double integral analog of the line integral. Given a surface, one may integrate over it scalar fields (that is, functions which return numbers as values), and vector fields (that is, functions which return vectors as values.)

Surface integrals have applications in physics, particularly with the classical theory of electromagnetism.

   a. Surface integral
   b. Contact
   c. Symmetry of second derivatives
   d. Differential operator

37. For an orientable surface, a consistent choice of 'clockwise' (as opposed to counter-clockwise) is called an orientation, and the surface is called _____. An orientable surface admits exactly 2 orientations, and the distinction between an _____ surface and an orientable surface is subtle and frequently blurred. An orientable surface is an abstract surface that admits an orientation, while an _____ surface is a surface that is abstractly orientable, and has the additional datum of a choice of one of the 2 possible orientations.
   a. ALGOR
   b. Oriented
   c. ACTRAN
   d. AUSM

Chapter 16. TOPICS IN VECTOR CALCULUS

38. A _____ is a surface in the Euclidean space R^3 which is defined by a parametric equation with two parameters. Parametric representation is the most general way to specify a surface. Surfaces that occur in two of the main theorems of vector calculus, Stokes' theorem and divergence theorem, are frequently given in a parametric form.
   a. Parametric surface
   b. Paraboloid
   c. Prolate
   d. Torus

39. In vector calculus, the _____ Ostrogradskye;s theorem the _____ states that the outward flux of a vector field through a surface is equal to the triple integral of the divergence on the region inside the surface. Intuitively, it states that the sum of all sources minus the sum of all sinks gives the net flow out of a region.
   a. Del
   b. Divergence
   c. Green's theorem
   d. Divergence Theorem

40. In the various subfields of physics, there exist two common usages of the term _____, both with rigorous mathematical frameworks.

   - In the study of transport phenomena (heat transfer, mass transfer and fluid dynamics), _____ is defined as the amount that flows through a unit area per unit time. _____ in this definition is a vector.
   - In the field of electromagnetism and mathematics, _____ is usually the integral of a vector quantity over a finite surface. The result of this integration is a scalar quantity. The magnetic _____ is thus the integral of the magnetic vector field B over a surface, and the electric _____ is defined similarly. Using this definition, the _____ of the Poynting vector over a specified surface is the rate at which electromagnetic energy flows through that surface. Confusingly, the Poynting vector is sometimes called the power _____, which is an example of the first usage of _____, above. It has units of watts per square metre (WÂ·m^{-2})

One could argue, based on the work of James Clerk Maxwell, that the transport definition precedes the more recent way the term is used in electromagnetism. The specific quote from Maxwell is 'In the case of fluxes, we have to take the integral, over a surface, of the _____ through every element of the surface. The result of this operation is called the surface integral of the _____.

   a. 15 theorem
   b. BIBO stability
   c. BDDC
   d. Flux

41. A _____ is a differential equation that describes the conservative transport of some kind of quantity. Since mass, energy, momentum, and other natural quantities are conserved, a vast variety of physics may be described with continuity equations.

All the examples of continuity equations below express the same idea.

   a. BIBO stability
   b. Continuity equation
   c. 15 theorem
   d. BDDC

42. In vector calculus a conservative vector field is a vector field which is the gradient of a scalar potential. There are two closely related concepts: path independence and _____ vector fields. Every conservative vector field has zero curl (and is thus _____), and every conservative vector field has the path independence property.

Chapter 16. TOPICS IN VECTOR CALCULUS

    a. ALGOR
    c. ACTRAN
    b. AUSM
    d. Irrotational

43. The largest and the smallest element of a set are called extreme values, absolute extrema, or extreme records.

For a differentiable function f, if $f(x_0)$ is an _____ for the set of all values f(x), and if x_0 is in the interior of the domain of f, then x_0 is a critical point, by Fermat's theorem.

In the case of a general partial order one should not confuse a least element (smaller than all other) and a minimal element (nothing is smaller.)

    a. Extreme value
    c. Integration by substitution
    b. Extreme Value Theorem
    d. Infinitesimal

44. In physics (specifically mechanics and electrical engineering), _____ ω (also referred to by the terms angular speed, radial frequency, circular frequency, orbital frequency, and radian frequency) is a scalar measure of rotation rate. _____ is the magnitude of the vector quantity angular velocity. The term _____ vector $\vec{\omega}$ is sometimes used as a synonym for the vector quantity angular velocity .

    a. ALGOR
    c. ACTRAN
    b. AUSM
    d. Angular frequency

45. A _____ is a set of standard clothing worn by members of an organization while participating in that organization's activity. Modern uniforms are worn by armed forces and paramilitary organisations such as police, emergency services, security guards, in some workplaces and schools and by inmates in prisons. In some countries, some other officials also wear uniforms in their duties; such is the case of the Commissioned Corps of the United States Public Health Service or the French prefects.

    a. Uniform
    c. AUSM
    b. ACTRAN
    d. ALGOR

46. In mathematics, a _____ in a normed vector space is a vector (often a spatial vector) whose length is 1 (the unit length.) A _____ is often denoted by a lowercase letter with a superscribed caret or e;hate;, like this: $\hat{\imath}$.

In Euclidean space, the dot product of two unit vectors is simply the cosine of the angle between them.

    a. ALGOR
    c. Overdetermined
    b. ACTRAN
    d. Unit vector

ANSWER KEY

Chapter 1

1. c	2. d	3. d	4. c	5. a	6. a	7. a	8. d	9. a	10. a
11. d	12. c	13. d	14. d	15. a	16. c	17. d	18. d	19. a	20. d
21. a	22. c	23. d	24. a	25. a	26. b	27. b	28. d	29. a	30. d
31. d	32. b	33. d	34. b	35. d	36. b	37. d	38. c	39. b	40. b
41. d	42. c	43. a	44. d	45. d	46. d	47. a	48. d	49. d	50. b
51. b	52. c	53. b	54. a	55. a	56. d	57. a	58. c	59. d	60. d
61. d	62. b	63. d	64. c	65. b	66. d	67. d	68. a	69. d	70. d
71. d	72. d	73. d	74. c	75. c	76. b	77. b			

Chapter 2

1. b	2. d	3. d	4. b	5. a	6. d	7. b	8. a	9. c	10. a
11. c	12. c	13. d	14. b	15. a	16. d	17. d	18. b	19. c	20. b
21. d	22. a	23. d	24. a	25. d	26. b	27. d	28. d	29. d	30. d
31. d									

Chapter 3

1. a	2. b	3. b	4. d	5. d	6. a	7. d	8. d	9. d	10. d
11. d	12. d	13. d	14. d	15. a	16. d	17. d	18. d	19. c	20. d
21. a	22. d	23. d	24. a	25. d	26. d	27. d	28. d	29. d	30. a
31. d	32. b	33. d	34. d	35. d	36. c	37. d	38. d	39. b	40. c
41. c	42. d	43. b	44. d	45. d	46. c				

Chapter 4

1. d	2. d	3. d	4. d	5. b	6. c	7. a	8. d	9. a	10. a
11. a	12. c	13. b	14. b	15. a	16. d	17. b	18. d	19. d	20. b
21. d	22. d	23. d	24. a	25. b	26. b	27. c	28. a	29. b	30. b
31. b	32. c	33. d	34. c	35. d					

Chapter 5

1. d	2. b	3. d	4. b	5. d	6. d	7. d	8. a	9. d	10. b
11. b	12. d	13. d	14. a	15. d	16. a	17. d	18. c	19. a	20. a
21. d	22. d	23. d	24. a	25. d	26. d	27. d	28. d	29. c	30. d
31. d	32. d	33. d	34. b	35. d	36. d				

Chapter 6

1. a	2. b	3. b	4. a	5. d	6. c	7. d	8. d	9. a	10. a
11. d	12. d	13. d	14. c	15. d	16. c	17. a	18. d	19. b	20. a
21. b	22. c	23. c	24. a	25. d	26. c	27. c	28. d	29. d	30. d
31. b	32. d	33. d	34. d	35. d	36. b	37. a	38. d	39. d	40. d
41. b	42. c	43. c	44. b	45. d	46. d	47. b	48. d	49. a	50. d
51. a	52. d	53. a	54. a	55. c	56. a	57. b	58. d	59. a	60. c
61. c	62. c	63. c	64. d						

Chapter 7

1. d	2. d	3. b	4. d	5. d	6. d	7. d	8. c	9. d	10. d
11. c	12. d	13. a	14. a	15. d	16. d	17. a	18. b	19. d	20. c
21. d	22. d	23. c	24. d	25. b	26. c	27. c	28. a	29. a	30. c
31. d	32. d	33. d	34. a	35. b	36. d	37. c	38. b	39. d	40. b
41. d	42. a	43. a	44. d	45. d	46. d				

Chapter 8

1. d	2. d	3. a	4. d	5. d	6. d	7. d	8. d	9. b	10. d
11. a	12. c	13. d	14. a	15. c	16. b	17. c	18. d	19. d	20. d
21. d	22. a	23. d	24. b	25. d	26. d	27. d	28. d	29. d	30. d
31. d	32. d								

Chapter 9

1. d	2. b	3. b	4. c	5. b	6. d	7. b	8. a	9. c	10. d
11. a	12. d	13. a	14. d	15. a	16. a	17. c	18. b	19. c	20. d
21. a	22. b	23. d	24. d	25. a	26. d	27. d	28. d	29. d	30. d
31. a	32. a	33. c	34. d	35. d					

Chapter 10

1. d	2. c	3. a	4. d	5. d	6. a	7. d	8. b	9. c	10. a
11. a	12. b	13. a	14. c	15. a	16. c	17. d	18. d	19. d	20. d
21. a	22. d	23. c	24. d	25. a	26. a	27. a	28. a	29. d	30. c
31. d	32. a	33. d	34. d	35. c	36. c	37. d	38. c	39. d	40. b
41. d	42. d	43. c	44. d	45. c	46. b	47. c	48. d	49. c	50. d
51. d	52. c								

Chapter 11

1. d	2. d	3. a	4. b	5. c	6. d	7. d	8. c	9. d	10. a
11. b	12. d	13. d	14. d	15. d	16. d	17. d	18. a	19. a	20. d
21. c	22. c	23. c	24. a	25. d	26. d	27. d	28. a	29. d	30. b
31. a	32. b	33. d	34. d	35. c	36. d	37. c	38. c	39. b	40. a
41. b	42. b	43. d	44. c	45. d	46. b				

Chapter 12

1. d	2. d	3. c	4. c	5. d	6. d	7. c	8. d	9. b	10. d
11. c	12. d	13. d	14. c	15. d	16. b	17. d	18. b	19. c	20. d
21. d	22. d	23. d	24. b	25. d	26. d	27. d	28. a	29. d	30. d
31. b	32. b	33. d	34. d	35. d	36. b	37. d	38. a	39. d	40. d
41. d	42. d	43. d	44. a	45. d	46. d	47. a	48. b	49. a	50. c
51. a	52. a								

ANSWER KEY

Chapter 13
1. c	2. c	3. d	4. d	5. a	6. a	7. d	8. d	9. d	10. d
11. d	12. c	13. b	14. c	15. b	16. a	17. a	18. d	19. b	20. c
21. a	22. a	23. a	24. d	25. a	26. d	27. c	28. d	29. c	30. d
31. c	32. c	33. a	34. d	35. b	36. d	37. d	38. a	39. d	40. d

Chapter 14
1. d	2. d	3. c	4. b	5. c	6. a	7. d	8. a	9. b	10. d
11. d	12. a	13. b	14. a	15. a	16. c	17. d	18. d	19. d	20. d
21. c	22. c	23. a	24. d	25. d	26. d	27. b	28. d	29. c	30. d
31. d	32. a	33. c	34. d	35. a	36. d	37. c	38. d	39. d	40. a
41. a	42. b	43. d	44. c	45. d	46. d	47. d	48. b	49. b	50. a
51. d	52. d								

Chapter 15
1. a	2. d	3. c	4. a	5. d	6. d	7. d	8. c	9. a	10. d
11. c	12. b	13. d	14. d	15. a	16. b	17. c	18. a	19. d	20. a
21. d	22. a	23. d	24. d	25. d	26. c	27. d	28. b	29. a	30. d
31. d	32. c	33. c	34. d	35. a	36. a	37. a	38. a	39. d	40. d
41. b	42. b	43. d	44. d	45. d	46. d	47. d	48. b	49. b	

Chapter 16
1. d	2. d	3. d	4. b	5. d	6. a	7. c	8. d	9. d	10. b
11. d	12. d	13. d	14. d	15. c	16. a	17. d	18. d	19. d	20. a
21. b	22. c	23. b	24. c	25. c	26. a	27. a	28. d	29. d	30. d
31. b	32. d	33. d	34. a	35. d	36. a	37. b	38. a	39. d	40. d
41. b	42. d	43. a	44. d	45. a	46. d				

www.ingramcontent.com/pod-product-compliance
Lightning Source LLC
Chambersburg PA
CBHW082147230426
43672CB00015B/2860